AN

INQUIRY

INTO

THE SYMBOLICAL LANGUAGE

OF

ANCIENT ART AND MYTHOLOGY.

⚬⚬⚬⚬⚬⚬⚬⚬⚬⚬⚬⚬⚬⚬

BY R. P. KNIGHT.

⚬⚬⚬⚬⚬⚬⚬⚬⚬⚬⚬⚬⚬⚬

Intended to be prefixed to the Second Volume of the Select Specimens of Ancient Sculpture, published by the Society of Dilettanti; but the necessarily slow progress of that work, in the exhausted state of the funds to be applied to it, affording the Author little probability of seeing its completion, he has been induced to print a few copies of this proposed Part of it, that any information which he may have been able to collect, upon a subject so interesting to all lovers of elegant art, may not be lost to his successors in such pursuits, but receive any additions and corrections which may render it more worthy to appear in the splendid form, and with the beautiful illustrations of the preceding Volume.

1818.

CAMBRIDGE LIBRARY COLLECTION

Books of enduring scholarly value

Spiritualism and Esoteric Knowledge

Magic, superstition, the occult sciences and esoteric knowledge appear regularly in the history of ideas alongside more established academic disciplines such as philosophy, natural history and theology. Particularly fascinating are periods of rapid scientific advances such as the Renaissance or the nineteenth century which also see a burgeoning of interest in the paranormal among the educated elite. This series provides primary texts and secondary sources for social historians and cultural anthropologists working in these areas, and all who wish for a wider understanding of the diverse intellectual and spiritual movements that formed a backdrop to the academic and political achievements of their day. It ranges from works on Babylonian and Jewish magic in the ancient world, through studies of sixteenth-century topics such as Cornelius Agrippa and the rapid spread of Rosicrucianism, to nineteenth-century publications by Sir Walter Scott and Sir Arthur Conan Doyle. Subjects include astrology, mesmerism, spiritualism, theosophy, clairvoyance, and ghost-seeing, as described both by their adherents and by sceptics.

An Inquiry into the Symbolical Language of Ancient Art and Mythology

This influential work of 1818 by dilettante and critic Richard Payne Knight (1751–1824) has stood the test of time. The study investigates the sexual symbolism of the art of different religions, providing a key to the mythology of the ancients and fostering a clear understanding of the canons and principles of art. An eminent art historian, collector and textual critic, Knight led the way in convincing British taste that Roman art was inferior to Greek, arguing that Greek art was the more authentic and original. Here, he calls for more correct versions of Homer, Plato and other Hellenic writers, to obtain accurate perceptions of Grecian ideas. Demonstrating his in-depth knowledge of classical architecture and literature, and drawing upon his considerable resources as a collector, Knight analyses the genetic character of symbols, and the patterns of their occurrence in different cultures.

Cambridge University Press has long been a pioneer in the reissuing of out-of-print titles from its own backlist, producing digital reprints of books that are still sought after by scholars and students but could not be reprinted economically using traditional technology. The Cambridge Library Collection extends this activity to a wider range of books which are still of importance to researchers and professionals, either for the source material they contain, or as landmarks in the history of their academic discipline.

Drawing from the world-renowned collections in the Cambridge University Library, and guided by the advice of experts in each subject area, Cambridge University Press is using state-of-the-art scanning machines in its own Printing House to capture the content of each book selected for inclusion. The files are processed to give a consistently clear, crisp image, and the books finished to the high quality standard for which the Press is recognised around the world. The latest print-on-demand technology ensures that the books will remain available indefinitely, and that orders for single or multiple copies can quickly be supplied.

The Cambridge Library Collection will bring back to life books of enduring scholarly value (including out-of-copyright works originally issued by other publishers) across a wide range of disciplines in the humanities and social sciences and in science and technology.

An Inquiry into the Symbolical Language of Ancient Art and Mythology

Richard Payne Knight

CAMBRIDGE
UNIVERSITY PRESS

CAMBRIDGE UNIVERSITY PRESS

Cambridge, New York, Melbourne, Madrid, Cape Town,
Singapore, São Paolo, Delhi, Tokyo, Mexico City

Published in the United States of America by Cambridge University Press, New York

www.cambridge.org
Information on this title: www.cambridge.org/9781108028103

This edition first published 1818
This digitally printed version 2011

ISBN 978-1-108-02810-3 Paperback

AN INQUIRY,

&c. &c.

LONDON:

PRINTED BY A. J. VALPY,
TOOKE'S COURT, CHANCERY LANE.

1818.

AN INQUIRY,

&c. &c.

––––•––––

1. As all the most interesting and important subjects of ancient art are taken from the religious or poetical mythology of the times; a general analysis of the principles and progress of that mythology will afford a more complete, as well as more concise, explanation of particular monuments, than can be conveyed in separate dissertations annexed to each.

2. The primitive religion of the Greeks, like that of all other nations not enlightened by Revelation, appears to have been elementary; and to have consisted in an indistinct worship of the sun, the moon, the stars, the earth, and the waters,[1] or rather to the spirits supposed to preside over those bodies, and to direct their motions and regulate their modes of existence. Every river, spring, or mountain, had its local genius or peculiar deity; and as men naturally endeavour to obtain the favor of their gods, by such means as they feel best adapted to win their own, the first worship consisted in offering to them certain portions

[1] Φαινονται μοι οι πρωτοι των ανθρωπων των περι την Ἑλλαδα τουτους μονους θεους ἡγεισθαι, οὑσπερ νυν πολλοι των βαρβαρων, ἡλιον, και σεληνην, και γην, και αστρα, και ουρανον. Platon. in Cratyl.

A

of whatever they held to be most valuable. At the same time that the regular motions of the heavenly bodies, the stated returns of summer and winter, of day and night, with all the admirable order of the universe, taught them to believe in the existence and agency of such superior powers; the irregular and destructive efforts of nature, such as lightning and tempests, inundations and earthquakes, persuaded them that these mighty beings had passions and affections similar to their own, and only differed in possessing greater strength, power, and intelligence.

3. In every stage of society men naturally love the marvellous; but in the early stages, a certain portion of it is absolutely necessary to make any narration sufficiently interesting to attract attention, or obtain an audience: whence the actions of gods are intermixed with those of men in the earliest traditions or histories of all nations; and poetical fable occupied the place of historical truth in their accounts of the transactions of war and policy, as well as in those of the revolutions of nature and origin of things. Each had produced some renowned warriors, whose mighty achievements had been assisted by the favor, or obstructed by the anger of the gods; and each had some popular tales concerning the means by which those gods had constructed the universe, and the principles upon which they continued to govern it: whence the Greeks and Romans found a Hercules in every country which they visited, as well as in their own; and the adventures of some such hero supply the first materials for history, as a cosmogony or theogony exhibits the first system of philosophy, in every nation.

4. As the maintenance of order and subordination among men required the authority of a supreme magistrate, the continuation and general predominance of order and regularity in the universe would naturally suggest the idea of a supreme God, to whose sovereign control all the rest were subject; and this ineffable personage the primitive Greeks appear to have called by a name expressive of the sentiment, which the contemplation of his great characteristic attribute naturally inspired, Ζευς, Δσευς, or *Deus*, signifying, according to the most probable etymology, reverential

fear or awe. Their poets, however, soon debased his dignity, and made him the subject of as many wild and extravagant fables, as any of his subject progeny; which fables became a part of their religion, though never seriously believed by any but the lowest of the vulgar.

5. Such appear to be the general principles and outlines of the popular faith, not only among the Greeks, but among all other primitive nations, not favored by the lights of Revelation: for though the superiority and subsequent universality of the Greek language, and the more exalted genius and refined taste of the early Greek poets, have preserved the knowledge of their sacred mythology more entire; we find traces of the same simple principles and fanciful superstructures, from the shores of the Baltic to the banks of the Ganges : and there can be little doubt, that the voluminous poetical cosmogonies still extant among the Hindoos, and the fragments preserved of those of the Scandinavians, may afford us very competent ideas of the style and subjects of those ponderous compilations in verse, which constituted the mystic lore of the ancient priests of Persia,[2] Germany,[3] Spain,[4] Gaul, and Britain ; and which in the two latter countries were so extensive, that the edu-

---

[1] Παρα τισι δε και Δευς λεγεται (ὁ Ζευς).   Phurnut. de Nat. Deor. c. 2.

The letter Z was, as is well known, no other than ΔΣ, or ΣΔ, expressed by one character ; and in the refinement of the language, and variation of dialects, the Σ was frequently dropped, as appears from the very ancient medals of Zanclè in Sicily, inscribed ΔΑΝΚΛΕ.

In the genuine parts of the Iliad and Odyssey, there is no instance of a vowel continuing short before ΔΕΟΣ, ΔΕΙΝΟΣ, ΔΕΙΔΩ, &c. ; so that the initial was originally a double consonant, probably ΔΣ ; which at first became ΔΔ, and afterwards Δ, though the metre of the old bards has preserved the double time in the utterance.

[2] Vicies centum millia versuum a Zoroastre condita.   Hermippus apud Plin. lib. xxx. c. 1.

[3] Celebrant (Germani) carminibus antiquis, quod unum apud illos memoriæ et annalium genus, Tuistonem deum terra editum, et filium Mannum originem gentis conditoresque.   Tacit. de M. G.

[4] Της παλαιας μνημης εχουσι (τουρδουλοι) τα συγγραμματα και ποιηματα, και νομους εμμετρους εξακισχιλιων ετων, ὡς φασι.   Strab. lib. iii. p. 139.

cation of a Druid sometimes required twenty years.[1] From the specimens above mentioned, we may, nevertheless, easily console ourselves for the loss of all of them, as poetical compositions; whatever might have been their value in other respects.

6. But besides this vulgar religion, or popular mythology, there existed, in the more civilized countries of Greece, Asia, and Egypt, a secret or mystic system, preserved, generally by an hereditary priesthood, in temples of long-established sanctity; and only revealed, under the most solemn vows of secresy, to persons who had previously proved themselves to be worthy of the important trust. Such were the mysteries of Eleusis, in Attica; which being so near to the most polished, powerful, and learned city of Greece, became more celebrated and more known than any others; and are, therefore, the most proper for a particular investigation, which may lead to a general knowledge of all.

7. These mysteries were under the guardianship of Ceres and Proserpine; and were called τελεται, *endings* or *finishes;* because no person could be perfect that had not been initiated, either into them, or some others. They were divided into two stages or degrees; the first or lesser of which was a kind of holy purification, to prepare the mind for the divine truths, which were to be revealed to it in the second or greater.[2] From one to five years of probation were required between them; and at the end of it, the initiate, on being found worthy, was admitted into the inmost recesses of the temple, and made acquainted with the first principles of religion;[3] the *knowledge of the God of nature; the first, the supreme, the intellectual;*[4] *by which men had been reclaimed from rudeness and*

---

[1] Magnum ibi numerum versuum ediscere dicuntur: itaque nonnulli annos vicenos in disciplina permanent; neque fas esse existimant ea litteris mandare. Cæs. de B. G. lib. vi.

[2] Μυστηρια δε δυο τελειται του ενιαυτου, Δημητρι και Κορῃ, τα μικρα και τα μεγαλα. και εστι τα μικρα ὡσπερ προκαθαρσις και προαγνευσις των μεγάλων. Scholiast. in Aristoph.

[3] Salmas. not. in El. Spartan. Hist. p. 116. Meurs. Eleusin. c. viii. &c.

[4] ὡν τελος εστιν ἡ του πρωτου, και κυριου, και νοητου γνωσις. Plutarch de Is. et Osir.

barbarism, to elegance and refinement ; and been taught not only to live with more comfort, but to die with better hopes.

8. When Greece lost her liberty, the periods of probation were dispensed with in favor of her acknowledged sovereigns :[2] but, nevertheless, so sacred and awful was this subject, that even in the lowest stage of her servitude and depression, the Emperor Nero did not dare to compel the priests to initiate him, on account of the murder of his mother.[3] To divulge any thing thus learnt was everywhere considered as the extreme of wickedness and impiety ; and at Athens was punished with death ;[4] on which account Alcibiades was condemned, together with many other illustrious citizens, whose loss contributed greatly to the ruin of that republic, and the subversion of its empire.[5]

9. Hence it is extremely difficult to obtain any accurate information concerning any of the mystic doctrines : all the early writers turning away from the mention of them with a sort of religious horror ;[6] and those of later times, who have pretended to explain them, being to be read with much caution; as their assertions are

---

[1] Mihi cum multa eximia divinaque videntur Athenæ tuæ peperisse— tum nihil melius illis mysteriis, quibus ex agresti immanique vita exculti, ad humanitatem mitigati sumus: initiaque, ut appellantur, ita revera principia vitæ cognovimus: neque solum cum lætitia vivendi rationem accepimus, sed etiam cum spe meliori moriendi. Ciceron. de Leg. l. i. c. 24.

και μην ά των αλλων ακουεις, οι πειθουσι πολλους, λεγοντες ώς ουδεν ουδαμη τῳ διαλυθεντι κακον, ουδε λυπηρον εστιν, οιδα ότι κωλυει σε πιστευειν ὁ πατριος λογος, και τα μυστικα συμβολα των περι τον Διονυσον οργιασμων, ά συνισμεν αλληλοις οι κοινωνουντες. Plutarch. de Consol. L x.

[2] Plutarch. in Demetr.

[3] Sueton. in Neron. c. 34.

[4] Andocid. orat. de myst. Sam. Petit. in leg. Attic. p. 33.

[5] Thucyd. lib. iv. c. 45, &c.

[6] Τ' αλλα μεν ευστομα κεισθω, καθ' Ηροδοτον, εστι γαρ μυστικωτερα. Plutarch. Symp. l. ii. q. 3.

Æschylus narrowly escaped being torn to pieces on the stage for bringing out something supposed to be mystic ; and saved himself by proving that he had never been initiated. Clem. Alex. Strom. ii. Aristot. Nicom. Eth. l. iii. c. 1.

generally founded in conjecture, and oftentimes warped by prejudices in favor of their own particular systems and opinions in religion and philosophy. Little more direct information is, indeed, to be obtained from ancient writers, than that contained in the above cited passages; from which we only learn that more pure, exalted, and philosophical doctrines concerning the nature of the Deity, and the future state of man, were taught, than those which were derived from the popular religion.

10. From other passages, however, we learn that these doctrines were conveyed under allegories and symbols;[1] and that the completely initiated were called *inspectors:*[2] whence we may reasonably infer that the last stage of initiation consisted in an explanation and exposition of those allegorical tales and symbolical forms, under which they were veiled. " All that can be said concerning the gods," says Strabo, " must be by the exposition of old opinions and fables; it being the custom of the ancients to wrap up in enigma and fable their thoughts and discourses concerning nature; which are not therefore easily explained."[3] " In all initiations and mysteries," says Proclus, " the gods exhibit themselves under many forms, and with a frequent change of shape; sometimes as light, defined to no particular figure; sometimes in a human form; and sometimes in that of some other creature."[4] The wars of the Giants and Titans; the battle of the Python against Apollo; the

---

Ορφικοι δια συμβολων, Πυθαγορειοι δια εικονων τα θεια μηνυειν εφιεμενοι. Procl. in Theol. Plat. l. i, c. 4.

————— διο και τα μυστηρια εν αλληγοριαις λεγεται προς εκπληξιν και φρικην, ωσπερ εν σκοτω και νυκτι. Demetr. Phaler. de Eloc. s. 100.

[2] Εποπται. All that is left in ancient authors concerning the ceremonies of initiation, &c., has been diligently collected and arranged by Meursius in his Eleusinia.

[3] Πας δ' ὁ περι των θεων λογος αρχαιας εξεταζει δοξας και μυθους, αινιττομενων των παλαιων, ἁς ειχον εννοιας φυσικας περι των πραγματων, και προστιθεντων αει τοις λογοις τον μυθον· ἁπαντα μεν ουν τα αινιγματα λυειν ακριβως ου ρᾳδιον. lib. x. p. 474.

[4] Εν ἁπασι γαρ τουτοις οἱ θεοι πολλας μεν ἑαυτων προτεινουσι μορφας, πολλα δε σχηματα διαλλαττοντες φαινονται· και τοτε μεν ατυπωτον αυτων προβεβληται φως, τοτε δε εις ανθρωπου μορφην εσχηματισμενον, τοτε δε εις αλλοιον τυπον προεληλυθος. εις την πολιτ. Πλατ. p. 380.

fiight of Bacchus, and wandering of Ceres, are ranked, by Plutarch, with the Ægyptian tales concerning Osiris and Typhon, as having the same meaning as the other modes of concealment employed in the mystic religion.[1]

11. The remote antiquity of this mode of conveying knowledge by symbols, and its long-established appropriation to religious subjects, had given it a character of sanctity unknown to any other mode of writing; and it seems to have been a very generally received opinion, among the more discreet Heathens, that divine truth was better adapted to the weakness of human intellect, when veiled under symbols, and wrapt in fable and enigma, than when exhibited in the undisguised simplicity of genuine wisdom, or pure philosophy.[2]

12. The art of conveying ideas to the sight, has passed through four different stages in its progress to perfection. In the first, the objects and events meant to be signified, were simply represented: in the second, some particular characteristic quality of the individual was employed to express a general quality or abstract idea; as a horse for swiftness, a dog for vigilance, or a hare for fecundity: in the third, signs of convention were contrived to represent ideas; as is now practised by the Chinese: and, in the fourth, similar signs of convention were adopted to represent the different modifications of tone in the voice; and its various divisions, by articulation, into distinct portions or syllables. This is what we call alphabetic writing; which is much more clear and simple than any other; the modifications of tone by the organs of the mouth, being much less various, and more distinct, than the modifications of ideas by the operations of the mind. The second, however, which, from its use among the Ægyptians, has been denominated

---

[1] Τα γαρ Γιγαντικα και Τιτανικα παρ' Ελλησιν αδομενα, και Κρονου τινος αθεσμοι πραξεις, και Πυθωνος αντιταξεις προς Απολλωνα, φυγαι τε Διονυσου και πλαναι Δημητρος, ουδεν απολειπουσι των Οσιριακων και Τυφωνικων, αλλων τε, ων πασιν εξεστιν ανεδην μυθολογουμενων ακουειν· όσα τε μυστικοις ιεροις περικαλυπτομενα και τελεταις, αρρητα διασωζεται και αθεατα προς τους πολλους, όμοιον εχει λογον. Plutarch. de Is, et Osir.

[2] Maxim. Tyr. Dissert. x. s. 4.

the hieroglyphical mode of writing, was every where employed to convey or conceal the dogmas of religion ; and we shall find that the same symbols were employed to express the same ideas in almost every country of the northern hemisphere.

13. In examining these symbols in the remains of ancient art, which have escaped the barbarism and bigotry of the middle ages, we may sometimes find it difficult to distinguish between those compositions which are mere efforts of taste and fancy, and those which were emblems of what were thought divine truths : but, nevertheless, this difficulty is not so great, as it, at first view, appears to be : for there is such an obvious analogy and connection between the different emblematical monuments, not only of the same, but of different and remote countries, that, when properly arranged, and brought under one point of view, they, in a great degree, explain themselves by mutually explaining each other. There is one class, too, the most numerous and important of all, which must have been designed and executed under the sanction of public authority; and therefore whatever meaning they contain, must have been the meaning of nations, and not the caprice of individuals.

14. This is the class of coins, the devices upon which were always held so strictly sacred, that the most proud and powerful monarchs never ventured to put their portraits upon them until the practice of deifying sovereigns had enrolled them among the gods. Neither the kings of Persia, Macedonia, or Epirus, nor even the tyrants of Sicily ever took this liberty ; the first portraits, that we find upon money, being those of the Ægyptian and Syrian dynasties of Macedonian princes, whom the flattery of their subjects had raised to divine honors. The artists had indeed before found a way of gratifying the vanity of their patrons without offending their piety, which was by mixing their features with those of the deity, whose image was to be impressed ; an artifice which seems to have been practised in the coins of several of the Macedonian kings, previous to the custom of putting their portraits upon them.[1]

---

[1] See those of Archelaus, Amyntas, Alexander II. Perdiccas, Philip, Alexander the Great, Philip Aridæus, and Seleucus I. in all which the dif-

15. It is, in a great degree, owing to the sanctity of the devices that such numbers of very ancient coins have been preserved fresh and entire : for it was owing to this that they were put into tombs, with vases and other sacred symbols, and not, as Lucian has ludicrously supposed, that the dead might have the means of paying for their passage over the Styx : the whole fiction of Charon and his boat being of late date, and posterior to many tombs, in which coins have been found.

16. The first species of money that was circulated by tale, and not by weight, of which we have any account, consisted of spikes, or small obelisks of brass or iron ; which were, as we shall show, symbols of great sanctity and high antiquity. Six of them being as many as the hand could conveniently grasp, the words *obolus* and *drachma*, signifying *spike* and *handful*, continued, after the invention of coining, to be employed in expressing the respective value of two pieces of money, the one of which was worth six of the other.[1] In Greece and Macedonia ; and, probably, wherever the Macedonians extended their conquests, the numerary division seems to have regulated the scale of coinage; but, in Sicily and Italy, the mode of reckoning by weight, or according to the lesser talent and its subdivisions,[2] universally prevailed. Which mode was in use among the Asiatic colonies, prior to their subjection to the Athenians or Macedonians, or which is the most ancient, we have not been able to discover. Probably, however, it was that by weight, the only one which appears to have been known to the Homeric Greeks ; the other may have been introduced by the Dorians.

17. By opening the tombs, which the ancients held sacred, and

---

ferent characters and features, respectively given to the different heads of Hercules, seem meant to express those of the respective princes. For the frequency of this practice in private families among the Romans, see Statii Sylv. l. V. i. 231—4.

[1] Το μεντοι των οβελων ονομα, οἱ μεν ὅτι παλαι βουπορois οβελois εχρωντο προς τας αμοιβας, ὧν το ὑπο τη δρακι πληθος εδοκει καλεισθαι δραχμη. τα δε ονοματα, και του νομισματος καταπεσοντος, εις την νυν χρειαν ενεμεινεν εκ της χρειας της παλαιας. Poll. lib. ix. c. vi. s. 77. see also Eustath. in Il. p. 136. Ed. Rom.

[2] See Bentley on the Epistles of Phalaris, &c.

exploring the foundations of ruined cities, where money was concealed, modern cabinets have been enriched with more complete
serieses of coins than could have been collected in any period of
antiquity.   We can thus bring under one point of view the whole
progress of the art from its infancy to its decline, and compare the
various religious symbols which have been employed in ages and
countries remote from each other.   These symbols have the great
advantage over those preserved in other branches of sculpture, that
they have never been mutilated or restored ; and also that they exhibit two compositions together, one on each side of the coin,
which mutually serve to explain each other, and thus enable us to
read the symbolical or mystical writing with more certainty than
we are enabled to do in any other monuments.   It is principally,
therefore, under their guidance that we shall endeavour to explore
the vast and confused labyrinths of poetical and allegorical fable ;
and to separate as accurately as we can, the theology from the mythology of the ancients : by which means alone we can obtain a competent knowledge of the mystic, or, as it was otherwise called,
the Orphic faith,[1] and explain the general style and language of
symbolical art in which it was conveyed.

18. Ceres and Bacchus,[2] called, in Ægypt, Isis and Osiris;
and, in Syria, Venus and Adonis, were the deities, in whose
names, and under whose protection, persons were most commonly instructed in this faith.[3]   The word Bacchus or Iacchus is a

---

[1] Pausan. l. i. c. 39.

[2] Πλησιον ναος εστι Δημητρος· αγαλματα δε αυτητε και ἡ παις, και δαδα εχων Ιακχος.
Pausan. in Att. c. ii. s. 4.

[3] Την μεν γαρ Οσιριδος τελετην τῃ Διονυσου την αυτην ειναι, την Ισιδος τῃ της Δημη-
τρης ὁμοιοτατην ὑπαρχειν, των ονοματων μονον ενηλλαγμενων. Diodor. Sic. lib. i. p.
104. Ed. Wessel.

Οσιριν Διονυσον ειναι λεγουσιν (Αιγυπτιοι). Herodot. lib. ii. c. 42.

Ω μακαρ, οστις ευδαιμων
τελετας θεων ειδως
βιοταν ἁγιστευει·
τατε Ματρος μεγαλας
οργια Κυβελας θεμιστευων,
ανα θυρσον τε τινασσων,
κισσῳ τε στεφανωθεις,
Διωννσον θεραπευει.   Eurip. Bacch. v. 73.

title derived from the exclamations uttered in the festivals of this god ;¹ whose other Latin name Liber is also a title signifying the same attribute as the Greek epithet *ΛΥΣΙΟΣ* or *ΛΥΣΩΝ*, which will be hereafter explained. But, from whence the more common Greek name *ΔΙΟΝΥΣΟΣ* is derived, or what it signifies, is not so easy to determine, or even to conjecture with any reasonable probability. The first part of it appears to be from *ΔΕΥΣ*, *ΔΙΟΣ*, or *ΔΙΣ*, the ancient name of the supreme universal god; but whether the remainder is significant of the place, from which this deity came into Greece, or of some attribute belonging to him, we cannot pretend to say; and the conjectures of etymologists, both ancient and modern, concerning it are not worthy of notice.² An ingenious writer in the Asiatic Researches derives the whole name from a Sanscrit title of an Oriental demi-god ;³ and as Ausonius says it was Indian,⁴ this derivation appears more probable than most others of the kind.

19. At Sicyon, in the Peloponnesus, he was worshipped under another title, which we shall not venture to explain, any further than that it implies his having the peculiar superintendance and direction of the characteristics of the female sex.⁵ At Lampsacus too, on the Hellespont, he was venerated under a symbolical form adapted to a similar office; though with a title of a different signification, Priapus, which will be hereafter explained.⁶

---

¹ They are in fact the same name in different dialects, the ancient verb ΓΑΧΩ, in Laconian ΒΑΧΩ, having become by the accession of the augment ΓΙΓΑΧΩ, v. ιαχω.

² See Macrob. l. i. c. 18. Bryant on Ancient Mythology.

³ Vol. iii. p. 304.

⁴   Ogygia me Bacchum vocat,
    Osirin Ægyptus putat;
    Mystæ Phanaum nominant;
    Dionysum Indi existimant, &c.

⁵ Διονυσον δε ηδη σιωπω τον ΧΟΙΡΟΨΑΛΗΝ· Σικυωνιοι τουτον προσκυνουσιν, επι των γυναικειων ταξαντες τον Διονυσον μοριων. Clem. Alex. Cohort. p. 33.

⁶ Τιμαται δε παρα Λαμψακηνοις ὁ Πριαπος, ὁ αυτος ων τῳ Διονυσῳ εξ επιθετου καλουμενος ούτως, ὡς Θριαμβος και Διθυραμβος. Athenæ. Deipnor. lib. i. c. 23.

20. According to Herodotus, the name Dionysus or Bacchus, with the various obscene and extravagant rites that distinguished his worship, was communicated to the Greeks by Melampus;[1] who appears to have florished about four generations before the Trojan war;[2] and who is said to have received his knowledge of the subject from Cadmus and the Phœnicians, who settled in Bœotia.[3] The whole history, however, of this Phœnician colony is extremely questionable; and we shall show in the sequel that the name Cadmus was probably a corruption of a mystic title of the deity. The Cadmeii, a people occupying Thebes, are mentioned in the Iliad,[4] and Ino or Leucothoe, a daughter of Cadmus, is mentioned as a sea-goddess in the Odyssey;[5] but no notice is taken in either poem of his being a Phœnician; nor is it distinctly explained whether the poet understood him to have been a man or a god; though the former is most probable, as his daughter is said to have been born mortal.

21. General tradition has attributed the introduction of the mystic religion into Greece, to Orpheus, a Thracian;[6] who, if he ever lived at all, lived probably about the same time with Melampus, or a little earlier.[7] The traditions concerning him are, how-

---

[1] Ἑλλησι γαρ δη Μελαμπους εστι ὁ εξηγησαμενος του Διονυσου το τε ουνομα, και την θυσιην, και την πομπην του φαλλου. lib. ii. c. 49.

[2] Odyss. O. 226. et seqq.

[3] Πυθεσθαι δε μοι δοκεει Μελαμπους τα περι τον Διονυσον παρα Καδμου τε του Τυριου, και των συν αυτῳ εκ Φοινικης απικομενων ες την νυν βοιωτιην καλεομενην χωρην. Herodot. ii. 49.

[4] E. 807.   [5] E. 334.

[6] Φασι πρωτον Ορφεα, τον Ἱαγρου, μεταστησαμενον τα παρ' Αιγυπτιοις, Ἑλλησι μεταδουναι μυστηρια. Euseb. Præp. Evang. lib. i. c. 6.
Ορφευς μεν γαρ τελετας θ' ἡμιν κατεδειξε,
φονων τ'απεχεσθαι.   Aristoph. Βατραχ. v. 1032.
Ἁπασα γαρ ἡ παρ' Ἑλλησι θεολογια της Ορφικης εστι μυσταγωγιας εκγονος. Proclus in Theol. Plat. lib. i. c. 5.
Τελετην αγουσιν (Αιγινηται) ανα παν ετος Ἑκατης, Ορφεα τον Θρᾳκα καταστησασθαι την τελετην λεγοντες. Pausan. in Cor. c. xxx. l. 2.

[7] According to the Parian or Arundelian marble, the Eleusinian mysteries were introduced 175 years before the Trojan war; but Plutarch attributes their introduction to Eumolpus. de Exil.

ever, extremely vague and uncertain; and the most learned and sagacious of the Greeks is said to have denied that such a person had ever existed:[1] but, nevertheless, we learn from the very high authority of Strabo that the Greek music was all Thracian or Asiatic;[2] and, from the unquestionable testimony of the Iliad, that the very ancient poet Thamyris was of that country;[3] to which tradition has also attributed the other old sacerdotal bards, Musæus and Eumolpus.[4]

22. As there is no mention, however, of any of the mystic deities; nor of any of the rites with which they were worshipped, in any of the genuine parts either of the Iliad or Odyssey, nor any trace of the symbolical style in any of the works of art described in them ; nor of allegory or enigma in the fables, which adorn them ; we may fairly presume that both the rites of initiation and the worship of Bacchus, are of a later period, and were not generally known to the Greeks till after the composition of those poems. The Orphic hymns, too, which appear to have been invocations or litanies used in the mysteries,[5] are proved, both by the language and the matter, to be of a date long subsequent to the Homeric times; there being in all of them abbreviations and modes of speech not then known; and the form of worshipping or glorifying the deity by repeating adulatory titles not being then in use, though afterwards common.[6]

23. In Ægypt, nevertheless, and all over Asia, the mystic and symbolical worship appears to have been of immemorial antiquity. The women of the former country carried images of Osiris, in

---

[1] Orpheum poetam docet Aristoteles nunquam fuisse. Cic. de N. D. lib. i. c. 28. The passage is not in the works of Aristotle now extant.

[2] Lib. x. p. 471.

[3] Il. B. 595.

[4] Plutarch. de Exil.

[5] Ὁστις δε ηδη τελετην Ελευσινι ειδεν, η τα καλουμενα Ορφικα επελεξατο, οιδεν ὁ λεγω. Pausan. in Attic. c. xxxvii. s. 3.

[6] ——στεφανος σπουδη απ' αυτου (του κισσου) ποιεισθαι, ὡς και στεφανωσασθαι ειχον, εφυμνουντας και τας επωνυμιας του θεου ανακαλουντας. Arrian. lib. v.

their sacred processions, with a moveable phallus of disproportionate magnitude, the reason for which Herodotus does not think proper to relate, because it belonged to the mystic religion.[1] Diodorus Siculus, however, who lived in a more communicative age, informs us that it signified the generative attribute,[2] and Plutarch that the Ægyptian statues of Osiris had the phallus to signify his procreative and prolific power;[3] the extension of which through the three elements of air, earth, and water, they expressed by another kind of statue, which was occasionally carried in procession, having a triple symbol of the same attribute.[4] The Greeks usually represented the phallus alone, as a distinct symbol, the meaning of which seems to have been among the last discoveries revealed to the initiated.[5] It was the same, in emblematical writing, as the Orphic epithet *ΠΑΓΓΕΝΕΤΩΡ, universal generator;* in which sense it is still employed by the Hindoos.[6] It has also been observed among the idols of the native Americans,[7] and ancient Scandinavians;[8] nor do we think the conjecture of an ingenious writer improbable, who supposes that the may-pole was a symbol of the same meaning; and the first of May a great phallic festival both among the ancient Britons and Hindoos; it being still celebrated with nearly the same rites in both countries.[9] The Greeks changed, as usual, the personified attribute into a distinct deity called Priapus, whose universality was, however, acknowledged to the latest periods of heathenism.[10]

---

[1] Διοτι δε μειζον τε εχει το αιδοιον, και κινεει μουνον του σωματος, εστι λογος περι αυτου ιερος λεγομενος. lib. ii. c. 88.

[2] Lib. i. c. 88.

[3] Πανταχου δε και ανθρωπομορφον Οσιριδος αγαλμα δεικνυουσιν, εξορθιαζον τῳ αιδοιῳ, δια το γονιμον και τροφιμον. de Is. et Osir.

[4] Αγαλμα προτιθενται, και περιφερουσιν, ου το αιδοιον τριπλασιον εστιν. Ibid. p. 365.

[5] Post tot suspiria epoptarum, totum signaculum linguæ, simulachrum membri virilis revelatur. Tertull. adv. Valentinianas.

[6] Sonnerat Voyage aux Indes.

[7] Lafitan Mœurs des Sauvages. vol. i. p. 150.

[8] Ol. Rudbeck. Atlant. p. ii. c. v. p. 165, 192, 194, and 305.

[9] Maurice's Indian Antiquities, vol. vi. p. 87—94.

[10] PRIEΓO PANTHEO. Titul. ant. in Gruter. vol. i. p. 195. No. 1.

24. In this universal character, he is celebrated by the Greek poets under the title of Love or Attraction, the first principle of animation; the father of gods and men; and the regulator and disposer of all things.[1] *He is said to pervade the universe with the motion of his wings, bringing pure light: and thence to be called the splendid, the self-illumined, the ruling Priapus;*[2] light being considered, in this primitive philosophy, as the great nutritive principle of all things.[3] Wings are attributed to him as the emblems of spontaneous motion; and he is said to have sprung from the egg of night, because the egg was the ancient symbol of organic matter in its inert state; or, as Plutarch calls it, the material of generation,[4] containing the seeds and germs of life and motion without being actually possessed of either. It was, therefore, carried in procession at the celebration of the mysteries, for which reason, Plutarch, in the passage above cited, declines entering into a more particular disquisition concerning its nature; the Platonic Interlocutor, in the Dialogue, observing, that though *a small question, it comprehended a very great one, concerning the generation of the world itself, known to those who understood the Orphic and sacred language; the egg being consecrated, in the Bacchic mysteries, as the image of that, which generated and contained all things in itself.*[5]

---

[1] See Aristoph. Ορνιθ. 693. ed. Brunk. Hesiod. Theogon. 116. Parmenid. apud Stobæ. c. xii. Orph. Hymn. v. xxix. et lvii.

————————————παμφαες ερνος,
δσσων ὁς σκοτοεσσαν απημαυρωσας ὁμιχλην,
παντη δινηεις πτερυγων ριπαις κατα κοσμον,
λαμπρον αγων φαος αγνον· αφ᾽ ού σε φανητα κικλησκον,
ηδη Πριηπον ανακτα, και αυταυγη ἑλικωπον.
                                        Orph. Hymn. V. v. 5.
ει τα θνητων μη καταισχυνεσθ᾽ ετι
γενεθλα, την γουν παντα βοσκουσαν φλογα
αιδεισθ᾽ ανακτος ηλιου.   Sophocl. Œd. Tyr. 1457.

[4] Ῥλη της γενεσεως. Sympos. lib. ii. q. 3.

[5] Ες μεσον εἱλκε προβλημα περι του ωου και της ορνιθος, ὁποτερον γενοιτο προτερον αυτων. και Συλλας ὁ ἑταιρος, ειπων, ὁτι μικρῳ προβληματι, καθαπερ οργανῳ, μεγα και βαρυ σαλευομεν το περι του κοσμου της γενεσεως, απηγορευσε.——— αεισω ξυνετοισι τον Ορφικον και ἱερον λογον, ὁς ουκ ορνιθος μονον το ωον αποφαινει πρεσβυτερον, αλλα και συλλαβων ἁπασαν αυτῳ την ἁπαντων ὁμου πρεσβυγενειαν αγατιθησι· και τ᾽ αλλα μεν

25. As organic substance was represented by the symbol of the egg; so the principle of life, by which it was called into action, was represented by that of the serpent; which having the property of casting its skin, and apparently renewing its youth, was naturally adopted for that purpose. We sometimes find it coiled round the egg, to express the incubation of the vital spirit; and it is not only the constant attendant upon the guardian deities of health,[1] but occasionally employed as an accessary symbol to almost every other god,[2] to signify the general attribute of immortality. For this reason it served as a general sign of consecration;[3] and not only the deified heroes of the Greeks, such as Cecrops and Erichthonius, but the virgin Mother of the Scythians, and the consecrated Founder of the Japanese, were represented terminating in serpents.[4] Both the Scythians and Parthians, too, carried the image of a serpent or dragon, upon the point of a spear, for their military standard;[5] as the Tartar princes of China still continue to do; whence we find this figure perpetually represented on their stuffs and porcelaine, as well as upon those of the Japanese. The inhabitants of Norway and Sweden continued to pay divine honors to serpents down to the sixteenth century;[6] and almost all the

---

ευστομα κεισθω (καθ' 'Ηροδοτον), εστι γαρ μυστικωτερα.——— όθεν ουκ απο τροπου τοις περι τον Διονυσον οργιασμοις, ώς μιμημα του τα παντα γεννωντος και περιεχοντος εν εαυτψ, συγκαθωσιωται.—ενεχεσθαι δογμασιν Ορφικοις η Πυθαγορικοις, και το ωον,——— αρχην ηγουμενοις γενεσεως, αφοσιουσθαι. Plutarch. Sympos. l. ii. q. iii. s. 1.

[1] Δρακοντα αυτψ (τψ Ασκληπιψ) παριστωσι, ότι όμοιον τι τουτψ πασχουσιν οί χρωμενοι τη ιατρικη, κατα το οίονει ανανεαζειν εκ των νοσων, και αποδυεσθαι το γηρας. Phurnut. de Nat. Deor. c. xxxiii.

[2] Παρ παντι των νομιζομενων παρ' ύμιν θεων οφις συμβολον μεγα και μυστηριον αναγραφεται. Justin Martyr. Apol. ii. p. 70.

[3] Pinge duos angues, pueri, sacer est locus. Pers. Sat. i.

[4] Μυθολογουσι Σκυθαι γηγενη παρ' αυτοις γενεσθαι παρθενον· ταυτην δ' εχειν τα μεν ανω μερη του σωματος μεχρι της ζωνης γυναικεια, τα δε κατωτερα εχιδνης· ταυτη δε Δια μιγεντα γεννησαι παιδα Σκυθην ονομα. Diodor. Sic. ii. 43. Kæmpfer, Hist. of Japan, b. ii. p. 145.

[5] Arrian. in Præf. p. 80. Lucian. de Hist. conscrib. p. 39.

[6] Serpentes ut sacros colebant;—ædium servatores atque penates existimantes;—reliquiæ tamen hujus superstitione culturæ—in nonnullis secretis solitudinum ædibusquæ perseverant; sicuti in septentrionalibus regnis Norvegia ac Vermelandiæ. Ol. Magn. de Gent. Septent. Hist. Epit. l. iii.

Runic inscriptions, found upon tombs, are engraved upon the sculptured forms of them ;[1] the emblems of that immortality, to which the deceased were thus consecrated. Macha Alla, the god of life and death among the Tartars, has serpents entwined round his limbs and body to express the first attribute, and human skulls and scalps on his head, and at his girdle, to express the second.[2] The jugglers and divines also, of North America, make themselves girdles and chaplets of serpents, which they have the art to tame and familiarise ;[3] and, in the great temple of Mexico, the captives taken in war, and sacrificed to the sun, had each a wooden collar in the shape of a serpent put round his neck while the priest performed the horrid rites.[4] In the kingdom of Juida, about the fourth degree of latitude, on the western coast of Africa, one of these reptiles was lately, and perhaps is still, worshipped as the symbol of the Deity ;[5] and when Alexander entered India, Taxilus, a powerful prince of the country, showed him a serpent of enormous size, which he nourished with great care, and revered as the image of the god, whom the Greek writers, from the similitude of his attributes, call Dionysus or Bacchus.[6] The Epidaurians kept one in the same manner to represent Æsculapius ;[7] as did likewise the Athenians, in their celebrated temple of Minerva, to signify the guardian or preserving deity of the Acropolis.[8] The Hindoo women still carry the lingam, or consecrated symbol of the generative attribute of the Deity, in solemn procession between two serpents ;[9] and, in the sacred casket, which held the egg and

[1] Ol. Varelii Hunagr. Ol. Rudbeck. Atlant. No. iii. c. 1.

[2] Voyage en Sibérie par l'Abbé Chappe d'Auteroche, pl. xviii. The figure in brass is in the collection of Mr. Knight.

[3] Lafitan Mœurs des Sauvages, t. i. p. 253.

[4] Acosta's History of the Indies, p. 382.

[5] Hist. gén. des Voyages, t. iv. p. 305.

[6] Max. Tyr. Dissert. viii. c. 6.

[7] Liv. Hist. lib. xi. epitom.

[8] Herodot. lib. viii. 41.

[9] Sonnerat Voyage aux Indes, t. i. p. 253.

B

phallus in the mystic processions of the Greeks, was also a serpent.[1] Over the porticoes of all the ancient Ægyptian temples, the winged disc of the sun is placed between two hooded snakes, signifying that luminary placed between its two great attributes of motion and life. The same combination of symbols, to express the same attributes, is observable upon the coins of the Phœnicians and Carthaginians;[2] and appears to have been anciently employed by the Druids of Britain and Gaul, as it still is by the idolaters of China.[3] The Scandinavian goddess Isa or Disa was sometimes represented between two serpents;[4] and a similar mode of canonization is employed in the apotheosis of Cleopatra, as expressed on her coins. Water-snakes, too, are held sacred among the inhabitants of the Friendly Islands;[5] and, in the mysteries of Jupiter Sebazius, the initiated were consecrated by having a snake put down their bosoms.[6]

26. The sort of serpent most commonly employed, both by the Ægyptians, Phœnicians, and Hindoos, is the hooded snake : but the Greeks frequently use a composite or ideal figure ; sometimes with a radiated head, and sometimes with the crest or comb of a cock ;[7] accessary symbols, which will be hereafter further

---

[1] See the cistæ mysticæ on the nummi cistaphori of the Greek cities of Asia, which are extremely common, and to be found in all cabinets and books of ancient coins.

[2] Médailles de Dutens, p. 1. Mus. Hunter. tab. 15. fig. v. and viii.

[3] See Stukeley's Abury ; the original name of which temple, he observes, was the snake's head : and it is remarkable the remains of a similar circle of stones in Bœotia had the same name in the time of Pausanias.
Κατα δε την ες Γλισαντα ευθειαν εκ Θηβων λιθοις χωριον περιεχομενον λογασιν Οφεως καλουσιν οἱ Θηβαιοι κεφαλην. Pausan. Bœot. c. xix. s. 2.

[4] Ol. Rudbeck. Atlant. pt. iii. c. 1. p. 25., and pt. ii. p. 343. fig. A., and p. 510.

[5] Missionaries' first Voyage, p. 238.

[6] Arnob. lib. v. p. 171. Clem. Alex. Cohort. ad Gentes, p. 14. Jul. Firmic. c. 27.

[7] See La Chausse Mus. Rom. vol. ii. tab. xiii. and xiv. The radiated serpent is common on gems.

noticed. The mystical serpent of the Hindoos, too, is generally represented with five heads, to signify, perhaps, the five senses: but still it is the hooded snake, which we believe to be a native of India, and consequently to have been originally employed as a religious symbol in that country; from whence the Ægyptians and Phœnicians probably borrowed it, and transmitted it to the Greeks and Romans; upon whose bracelets, and other symbolical ornaments, we frequently find it.

27. Not only the property of casting the skin, and acquiring a periodical renovation of youth, but also that of pertinaciously retaining life even in amputated parts, may have recommended animals of the serpent kind as symbols of health and immortality, though noxious and deadly in themselves. Among plants, the olive seems to have been thought to possess the same property in a similar degree;[1] and therefore was probably adopted to express the same attribute. At Athens it was particularly consecrated to Minerva; but the statue of Jupiter at Olympia was crowned with it;[2] and it is also observable on the heads of Apollo, Hercules, Cybelè, and other deities;[3] the preserving power, or attribute of immortality, being, in some mode or other, common to every personification of the divine nature. The victors in the Olympic games were also crowned with branches of the oleaster or wild olive;[4] the trunk of which, hung round with the arms of the vanquished in war, was the trophy of victory consecrated to the immortal glory of the conquerors :[5] for as it was a religious, as well as mili-

---

[1] Virgil Georgic. ii. v. 30. and 181.

Εκβλαστανει δε μαλιστα τα ελαινα, και αργα κειμενα· και ʼεργασμενα πολλακις εαν ικμαδα λαμβανη, και εχη τοπον νοτερον, ὡσπερ ηδη τις στροφευς της θυρας εβλαστησε, και ἡ κυλιου πλινθινου κωπη τιθεισα εις πηλον. Theophrast. Hist. Plant. lib. v. c. ix.

[2] Στεφανος δε επικειται οἱ τη κεφαλη μεμιμημενος ελαιας κλωνας. Pausan. in Eliac. 1. c. xi. s. 1.

[3] See coins of Rhegium, Macedonia, Aradus, Tyre, &c.

[4] Κοτινου στεφανῳ. Aristoph. Plut. 586.

[5] Ibid. 943.

tary symbol, it was contrary to the laws of war, acknowledged among the Greeks, to take it down, when it had been once duly erected.

28. Among the sacred animals of the Ægyptians, the bull, worshipped under the titles of Mnevis and Apis, is one of the most distinguished. The Greeks called him Epaphus,[1] and we find his image, in various actions and attitudes, upon an immense number of their coins, as well as upon some of those of the Phœnicians, and also upon other religious monuments of almost all nations. The species of bull most commonly employed is the urus or wild bull, the strongest animal known in those climates, which are too cold for the propagation of the elephant;[2] a creature not known in Europe, nor even in the northern or western parts of Asia, till Alexander's expedition into India, though ivory was familiarly known even in the Homeric times.[3] To express the attribute strength, in symbolical writing, the figure of the strongest animal would naturally be adopted: wherefore this emblem, generally considered, explains itself, though, like all others of the kind, it was modified and applied in various ways. The mystic Bacchus, or generative power, was represented under this form, not only upon the coins but in the temples of the Greeks:[4] sometimes simply as a bull; at others, with a human face; and, at others, entirely

---

[1] Ὁ δε Απις κατα την Ἑλληνων γλωσσαν εστι Επαφος. Herodot. l. ii. c. 153.

Ιους ποτ᾽ εκγονον
Επαφον, ω Διος γενεθλον,
εκαλεσ᾽ εκαλεσα. Eurip. Phœnis. 688.

[2] Cæsar. de B. B. lib. vi.

[3] Pausan. lib. i. c. 12. This proves that the coins with an elephant's skin on the head, are of Alexander II., king of Epirus, son of Pyrrhus.

[4] Ταυρῳ, i. e. Διονυσῳ. Lycophr. 209.

Ταυρομορφον Διονυσον ποιουσιν αγαλματα πολλοι των Ἑλληνων· αἱ δ᾽ Ηλειων γυναικες και παρακαλουσιν ευχομεναι, ποδι βοειῳ τον θεον ελθειν προς αυτας. Αργειοις δε Βουγενης Διονυσος επικλην εστι. Plutarch. de Is. et Osir.

Εν δε Κυζικῳ και ταυρομορφος ἱδρυται (ὁ Διονυσος.) Athen. Deipnos. lib. xi. p. 476.

human except the horns or ears.¹ The age, too, is varied; the bull being in some instances quite old, and in others quite young; and the humanised head being sometimes bearded, and sometimes not.²

29. The Mnevis of the Ægyptians was held by some to be the mystic father of Apis;³ and as the one has the disc upon his head, and was kept in the City of the Sun, while the other is distinguished by the crescent,⁴ it is probable that the one was the emblem of the divine power acting through the sun; and the other, of it acting through the moon, or (what was the same) through the sun by night. Apis, however, held the highest rank, he being exalted by the superstition of that superstitious people into something more than a mere symbol, and supposed to be a sort of incarnation of the Deity in a particular animal, revealed to them at his birth by certain external marks, which announced his having been miraculously conceived by means of a ray from Heaven.⁵ Hence, when found, he was received by the whole nation with every possible testimony of joy and gratulation, and treated in a manner worthy of the exalted character bestowed on him;⁶ which was that of the terrestrial image or representative of Osiris;⁷ in whose statues the remains of the animal symbol may be traced.⁸

Bronzi d'Ercolano, t. i. tav. 1. Coins of Camerina, and plate ii. of the 1st volume of "the Select Specimens."

² Coins of Lampsacus, Naxus, and plates xvi. and xxxix. of vol. i.

³ Ὁ δε εν Ἡλιοπολει τρεφομενος βους, ὁν Μνευιν καλουσιν, (Οσιριδος δε ἱερον, ενιοι δε και του Απιος πατερα νομιζουσι) μελας εστι, και δευτερας εχει τιμας μετα τον Απιν. Plutarch. de Is. et Osir.

⁴ See Tab. Isiac. &c.

⁵ Ὁ δε Απις ουτος ὁ Επαφος γινεται μοσχος εκ βοος, ἡτις ουκετι οἱη τε γινεται ες γαστερα αλλον βαλλεσθαι γονον. Αιγυπτιοι δε λεγουσι σελας επι την βουν εκ του ουρανου κατισχειν και μιν εκ τουτου τικτειν τον Απιν. Herodot. lib. iii. c. 28.

⁶ Ib. c. 27.

⁷ Εν δε Μεμφει τρεφεσθαι τον Απιν, ειδωλον οντα της εκεινου (του Οσιριδος) ψυχης Plutarch. de Is. et Osir.

⁸ See plate ii. vol. i. of the Select Specimens, where the horns of the bull are signified in the disposition of the hair.—του Απιδος, ὁς εστιν ὁ αυτος και Οσιρις. Strab. l. xvii.

Their neighbours the Arabs appear to have worshipped their god under the same image, though their religion was more simple and pure than that of any Heathen nation of antiquity, except the Persians, and perhaps the Scythians. They acknowledged only the male and female, or active and passive powers of creation ; the former of whom they called Urotalt ;[1] a name, which evidently alludes to the urus. Herodotus calls him Bacchus, as he does the female deity, *celestial Venus;* by which he means no more than that they were personifications of the attributes, which the Greeks worshipped under those titles.

31. The Chinese have still a temple called the Palace of the horned Bull ;[2] and the same symbol is worshipped in Japan, and all over Hindostan.[3] In the extremity of the West it was, also, once treated with equal honour ; the Cimbrians having carried a brazen bull with them, as the image of their god, when they overran Spain and Gaul ;[4] and the name of the god 'Thor, the Jupiter of the ancient Scandinavians, signifying in their language a bull ; as it does likewise in the Chaldee.[5] In the great metropolitan temple of the ancient northern hierachy at Upsal, in Sweden, this god was represented with the head of a bull upon his breast ;[6] and on an ancient Phœnician coin, we find a figure exactly resembling the Jupiter of the Greeks, with the same head on his chair, and the words Baal Thurz, in Phœnician characters, on the exergue.[7] In many Greek, and in some Ægyptian monuments, the bull is represented in an attitude of attack, as if striking at some-

---

[1] Διονυσον δε θεων μουνον και την Ουρανιην ἡγεονται ειναι.——ονομαζουσι δε τον μεν Διονυσον Ουροταλτ. Herodot. lib. iii. c. 8.

[2] Hist. gen. des Voyages, t. vi. p. 452.

[3] Recherches sur les Arts de la Grece, &c.

[4] Plutarch. in Mario.

[5] In the Phœnician it signified a cow.
ΘΩΡ γαρ οἱ Φοινικες την βουν καλουσιν. Plutarch. in Sylla, c. 17.

[6] Ol. Rudbeck. Atlantic. pt. ii. c. 5. p. 300. fig. 28., and p. 321, 338 and 9.

[7] Médailles de Dutens, p. 1. The coin, still better preserved, is in the cabinet of Mr. Knight.

thing with his horns ;[1] and at Meaco in Japan, the creation of the world, or organization of matter, is represented by the Deity under the image or symbol of a bull breaking the shell of an egg with his horns, and animating the contents of it with his breath ;[2] which probably explains the meaning of this attribute in the Greek and Ægyptian monuments ; the practice of putting part of a composition for the whole being common in symbolical writing.[3]

32. In most of the Greek and Roman statues of the bull, that we have seen, whether in the character of Mnevis or Apis, of both which many are extant of a small size in bronze, there is a hole upon the top of the head between the horns, where the disc or crescent, probably of some other material, was fixed :[4] for as the mystical or symbolical was engrafted upon the old elementary worship, there is always a link of connexion remaining between them. The Bacchus of the Greeks, as well as the Osiris of the Ægyptians, comprehended the whole creative or generative power, and is therefore represented in a great variety of forms, and under a great variety of symbols, signifying his subordinate attributes.

33. Of these the goat is one that most frequently occurs ; and as this animal has always been distinguished for its lubricity, it probably represents the attribute directed to the propagation of organized being in general.[5] The choral odes sung in honour of Bacchus were called ΤΡΑΓΩΙΔΙΑΙ, or goat-songs ; and a goat was the symbolical prize given on the occasion ; it being one of the

---

[1] See coins of Thurium, Syracuse, Tauromenium, Attabyrium, Magnesia, &c., and Denon Ægypte, pl. cxxxii. No. 1.

[2] Memorable Embassy to the Emperor of Japan, p. 283.

[3] See coins of Acanthus, Maronea, Eretria, &c.

[4] Five are in the cabinet of Mr. Payne Knight, one of which has the disc remaining.
Μεταξυ δε τών κερεων ὁ του ἡλιου κυκλος μεμιμημενος επεστι χρυσεος. εστι δε ἡ βους ουκ ορθη, αλλ' εν γουνασι κειμενη. Herodot. ii. 132.

[5] See Diodor. Sic. l. i. c. 88.

forms under which the god himself had appeared. The fauns and satyrs, the attendants and ministers of Bacchus, were the same symbol more or less humanised ; and appear to have been peculiar to the Greeks, Romans, and Etruscans : for though the goat was among the sacred animals of the Ægyptians, and honored with singular rites of worship at Mendes, we do not find any traces of these mixed beings in the remains of their art, nor in those of any other ancient nations of the East; though the Mendesian rites were admirably adapted to produce them in nature, had it been possible for them to exist;[2] and the god Pan was there represented under such a form.[3]

34. But notwithstanding that this first-begotten Love, or mystic Bacchus, was called the Father of gods and men, and the Creator of all things, he was not the primary personification of the divine nature ; *Κρονος* or *Ζευς*, the unknown Father, being every where reverenced as the supreme and almighty. In the poetical mythology, these titles are applied to distinct personages, the one called the Father, and the other the Son : but in the mystic theology, they seem to have signified only one being—the being that fills eternity and infinity.[4] The ancient theologists appear to have known that we can form no distinct or positive idea of infinity, whether of power, space, or time; it being fleeting and fugitive, and eluding

---

[1] Apollodor. Biblioth. l. iii. c. 4. s. 3.

[2] Γυναικι τραγος εμισγετο αναφανδον. Herodot. ii. 46.

[3] Γραφουσι τε δη και γλυφουσι οἱ ζωγραφοι του Πανος τωγαλμα, καταπερ Ἑλληνες, αιγοπροσωπον και τραγοσκελεα. Ibid.

[4] Ὁρας τον ὑψου τονδ᾽ απειρον αιθερα
και γην περιξ εχοντ᾽ ὑγραις εν αγκαλαις ;
τουτον νομιζε Ζην, τον δ᾽ ἡγου Θεον.
Eurip. apud Heraclid. Pontic. p. 441. ed. Gale.
Κρονου δε και Χρονου λεγεται (ὁ Ζευς) διηκων εξ αιωνος ατερμονος εις ἑτερον αιωνα. Pseudo-Aristot. de Mundo, c. 7. This treatise is the work of some professed rhetorician of later times, who has given the common opinions of his age in the common language of a common declaimer; and by a strange inconsistency, attributed them to the deep, abstruse, condensed Stagirite.

the understanding by a continued and boundless progression. The only notion that we have of it, arises from the multiplication or division of finite things ; which suggest the vague abstract notion, expressed by the word infinity, merely from a power, which we feel in ourselves, of still multiplying and dividing without end. Hence they adored the Infinite Being through personified attributes, signifying the various modes of exerting his almighty power; the most general, beneficial, and energetic of which being that universal principle of desire, or mutual attraction, which leads to universal harmony, and mutual co-operation, it naturally held the first rank among them. " The self-created mind of the eternal Father," says the Orphic poet, " spread the heavy bond of Love through all things, that they might endure for ever;"¹ which heavy bond of love is no other than the *ΕΡΩΣ ΠΡΩΤΟΓΟΝΟΣ* or mystic Bacchus ; to whom the celebration of the mysteries was therefore dedicated.

35. But the mysteries were also dedicated to the female or passive powers of production supposed to be inherent in matter.² Those of Eleusis were under the protection of Ceres, called by the Greeks *ΔΗΜΗΤΗΡ;* that is, Mother Earth ;³ and, though the

---

¹ Εργα νοησας γαρ πατρικος νοος αυτογενεθλος
Πασιν ενεσπειρεν δεσμον περιβριθη ερωτος
Οφρα τα παντα μενει χρονον εις απεραντον ερωτα.
           Fragm. Orphic. No. xxxviii. ed. Gesn.

A fragment of Empedocles preserved by Athenagoras may serve as a comment upon these Orphic verses. Speaking of the eléments which compose the world, he enumerates,

Πυρ και ύδωρ και γαια, και ηερος ηπιον ύψος,
Και φ ι λ ι η μετα τοισιν.

² Ή γαρ ύλη λογον εχει προς τα γινομενα μ η τ ρ o s (ώs φησι Πλατων) και τ ι θ η ν η s·
ύλη δε παν εξ ού συστασιν εχει γεννωμενον. Plutarch. Symposiac. lib. ii. qu. 3.

³ —Ταυτην παραπλησιως Δημητρα καλειν, βραχυ μετατεθεισης, δια τον χρονον, της λεξεως· το γαρ παλαιον ονομαζεσθαι γ η ν μ η τ ε ρ α. Diodor. Sic. lib. i. s. 12.

Μητηρ μεγιστη δαιμονων Ολυμπιων
αριστα, Γη μελαίνα. Solon. in Brunck. Analect. vol. i. xxiv.

Δημητηρ παρα το γ η και το μ η τ η ρ, γ η μ η τ η ρ. Etymol. Magn. See also Lucret. lib. V. v. 796.

meaning of her Latin name be not quite so obvious, it is in reality the same; the Roman C being originally the same letter, both in figure and power, as the Greek Γ;[1] which was often employed as a mere guttural aspirate, especially in the old Æolic dialect, from which the Latin is principally derived. The hissing termination, too, in the S belonged to the same: wherefore the word, which the Attics and Ionians wrote ΕΡΑ, ΕΡΕ, or 'ΗΡΗ, would naturally be written ΓΕΡΕΣ by the old Æolics; the Greeks always accommodating their orthography to their pronunciation; and not, like the English and French, encumbering their words with a number of useless letters.

36. Ceres, however, was not a personification of the brute matter which composed the earth, but of the passive productive principle supposed to pervade it;[2] which, joined to the active, was held to be the cause of the organization and animation of its substance; from whence arose her other Greek name ΔΗΩ, *the Inventress.* She is mentioned by Virgil, as the Wife of the omnipotent Father, Æther or Jupiter;[3] and therefore the same with Juno; who is usually honored with that title; and whose Greek name 'ΗΡΗ signifies, as before observed, precisely the same.[4] The Latin name IUNO is derived from the Greek name ΔΙΩΝΗ, the female ΖΕΥΣ or ΔΙΣ; the Etruscan, through which the Latin received much of its orthography, having no D nor O in its alphabet. The ancient Germans worshipped the same goddess under the name of Hertha;[5] the form and meaning of which still remain in

---

[1] See Senatus-consultum Marcianum, and the coins of Gela, Agrigentum, and Rhegium.

[2] Officium commune Ceres et Terra tuentur;
Hæc præbet causam frugibus, illa locum.
Ovid. Fast. lib. i. v. 673.

[3] Tum pater omnipotens, fecundis imbribus Æther
Conjugis in gremium lætæ descendit, et omnes
Magnus alit, magno conmixtus corpore, fetus.
Georg. ii. 324.

[4] Γη μεν εστιν ἡ 'Ηρα. Plutarch. apud Euseb. Præp. Evang. lib. iii. c. 1.

[5] Tacit. de Mor. Germanor.

our word Earth. Her fecundation by the descent of the active
spirit, as described in the passage of Virgil before cited, is most
distinctly represented in an ancient bronze at Strawberry Hill.
As the personified principle of the productive power of the Earth,
she naturally became the patroness of agriculture ; and thus the
inventress and tutelar deity of legislation and social order, which
firstiarose out of the division, appropriation, and cultivation of the
soil.

37. The Greek title seems originally to have had a more general
signification : for without the aspirate (which was anciently added
and omitted almost arbitrarily) it becomes *EPE* ; and, by an abbre-
viation very common in the Greek tongue, *PE* or *PEE* ; which,
pronounced with the broad termination of some dialects, become
PEA ; and with the hissing one of others, *PEΣ* or RES ; a word
retained in the Latin, signifying properly matter, and figuratively,
every quality and modification that can belong to it. The Greek
has no word of such comprehensive meaning ; the old general term
being, in the refinement of their language, rendered more specific,
and appropriated to that principal mass of matter, which forms the
terraqueous globe ; and which the Latins also expressed by the same
word united to the Greek article τη ερα—TERRA.

38. The ancient word, with its original meaning, was however
retained by the Greeks in the personification of it : Rhea, the first
of the goddesses, signifying universal matter, and being thence
said, in the figurative language of the poets, to be the mother of
Jupiter, who was begotten upon her by Time. In the same figurative language, Time is said to be the son of Ουρανος, or Heaven;
that is, of the supreme termination and boundary, which appears to
have been originally called κοιλον, the hollow or vault ; which the
Latins retained in their word CŒLUM, sometimes employed to
signify the pervading Spirit, that fills and animates it. Hence
Varro says that Cœlum and Terra ; that is, *universal mind and
productive body;* were the great gods of the Samothracian mysteries;
and the same as the Serapis and Isis of the later Egyptians ; the
Taautes and Astartè of the Phœnicians ; and the Saturn and Ops

of the Latians.[1] The licentious imaginations of the poets gave
a progenitor even to the personification of the supreme boundary
ουρανος; which progenitor they called *AKMΩN*, the *indefatiga-
ble ;*[2] a title by which they seem to have meant perpetual motion,
the primary attribute of the primary Being.[3]

39. The allegory of *Κρονος* or Saturn devouring his own children
seems to allude to the rapid succession of creation and destruction
before the world had acquired a permanent constitution; after
which Time only swallowed the stone : that is, exerted its destroying influence upon brute matter; the generative spirit, or vital
principle of order and renovation, being beyond its reach. In conjunction with the Earth, he is said to have cut off the genitals of his
father, Heaven ;[4] an allegory, which evidently signifies that Time,
in operating upon Matter, exhausted the generative powers of
Heaven; so that no new beings were created.

40. The notion of the supreme Being having parents, though
employed by the poets to embellish their wild theogonies, seems
to have arisen from the excessive refinement of metaphysical theology : a Being purely mental and absolutely immaterial, having no
sensible quality, such as form, consistence, or extension, can only
exist, according to our limited notions of existence, in the modes
of his own action, or as a mere abstract principle of motion. These
modes of action, being turned into eternal attributes, and personified into distinct personages, Time and Matter, the means of
their existing, might, upon the same principle of personification,
be turned into the parents of the Being to which they belong.
Such refinement may, perhaps, seem inconsistent with the simplicity of the early ages : but we shall find, by tracing them to
their source, that many of the gross fictions, which exercised the

---

[1] De Lingua Latina, lib. iv. s. 10.

[2] Ακαματος, ακαμων, ακμων, &c.

[3] See Phurnut. de Nat. Deor. c. 1.

[4] Hesiod. Theog. 160.

credulity of the vulgar Heathens, sprang from abstruse philosophy conveyed in figurative and mysterious expressions.

41. The elements Fire and Water were supposed to be those, in which the active and passive productive powers of the universe respectively existed;[1] since nothing appeared to be produced without them ; and wherever they were joined there was production of some sort, either vegetable or animal. Hence they were employed as the primary symbols of these powers on numberless occasions. Among the Romans, a part of the ceremony of marriage consisted in the bride's touching them, as a form of consecration to the duties of that state of life, upon which she was entering. [2] Their sentence of banishment, too, was an interdiction from fire and water; which implied an exclusion from any participation in those elements, to which all organised and animated beings owed their existence. Numa is said to have consecrated the perpetual fire, as the first of all things, and the soul of matter ; which, without it, is motionless and dead.[3] Fires of the same kind were, for the same reasons, preserved in most of the principal temples both Greek and Barba-

---

[1] Quippe ubi temperiem sumpsere humorque calorque,
Concipiunt: et ab his oriuntur cuncta duobus.
Ovid. Met. i. 430.

Ξυνισταται μεν ουν τα ζωα, τα τε αλλα παντα, και ὁ ανθρωπος, απο δυοιν· διαφοροιν μεν την δυναμιν, συμφοροιν δε την χρησιν· πυρος λεγω και ὑδατος. Hippocrat. Διαιτ. i. 4.

Το μεν γαρ πυρ δυναται παντα δια παντος κινησαι, το δε ὑδωρ παντα δια παντος θρεψαι, —το μεν ουν πυρ και το ὑδωρ αυταρκεα εστι πασι δια παντος ες το μηκιστον και το ελακιστον ὡσαυτως. Hippocrat. Diæt. i. 4.

Εσερπει δ' ες ανθρωπον ψυχη, πυρος και ὑδατος συγκρησιν εχουσα, μοιραν σωματος ανθρωπου. Ib. s. 8.

Τουτο παντα δια παντος κυβερνᾳ, και ταδε και εκεινα, ουδεποτε ατρεμιζον (το πυρ). Ib. s. 11.

Πυρι και ὑδατι παντα ξυνισταται, και ζωα και φυτα, και ὑπο τουτεων αυξεται, και ες ταυτα διακρινεται. Ib. l. ii. s. 31.

[2] Δια τι την γαμουμενην ἁπτεσθαι πυρος και ὑδατος κελευουσι ; ποτερον τουτων, ὡς εν στοιχειοις και αρχαις, το αρρεν εστι, το δε θηλυ· και το μεν αρχας κινησεως ενιησι, το δε ὑποκειμενου και ὑλης δυναμιν. Plutarch. Qu. Rom. sub. init.

[3] Ὡς αρχην ἁπαντων——τα δ' αλλα της ὑλης μορια, θερμοτητος επιλειπουσης, αργα κειμενα και εκροις εοικοτα, ποθει την πυρος δυναμιν ὡς· ψυχην. Plutarch. in Numa.

rian; there being scarcely a country in the world, where some traces of the adoration paid to it are not to be found.[1] The pry-taneia of the Greek cities, in which the supreme councils were usually held, and the public treasures kept, were so called from the sacred fires always preserved in them. Even common fires were reputed holy by them; and therefore carefully preserved from all contagion of impiety. After the battle of Platæa, they extinguished all that remained in the countries which had been occupied by the Persians, and rekindled them, according to the direction of the Oracle, with consecrated fire from the altar at Delphi.[2] A similar prejudice still prevails among the native Irish; who annually extinguish their fires, and rekindle them from a sacred bonfire.[3] Perpetual lamps are kept burning in the inmost recesses of all the great pagodas in India; the Hindoos holding fire to be the essence of all active power in nature. At Sais in Ægypt, there was an annual religious festival called the Burning of Lamps;[4] and lamps were frequently employed as symbols upon coins by the Greeks;[5] who also kept them burning in tombs, and sometimes swore by them, as by known emblems of the Deity.[6] The torch held erect, as it was by the statue of Bacchus at Eleusis,[7] and as it is by other figures of him still extant, means life; while its being reversed, as it frequently is upon sepulchral urns and other monuments of the kind, invariably signifies death or extinction. [8]

---

[1] Huet. Demonstr. Evang. Præp. iv. c. 5.   Lafitan Mœurs des Sauvages, t. i. p. 153.

[2] Plutarch. in Aristid.

[3] Collect. Hibern. No. v. p. 64.

[4] Λυχνοκαιη.   Herodot. lib. ii. 62.

[5] See coins of Amphipolis, Alexander the Great, &c.

[6] Λυχνε, σε γαρ παρεουσα τρις ωμοσεν
'Ηρακλεια————ηξειν.
                    Asclepiad. Epigr. xxv. in Brunck. Analect. vol. i. p. 216.

[7] Pausan. in l. c.

[8] See Portland vase, &c.   Polynices infers his own approaching death from seeing in a vision,
          Conjugis Argeiæ lacera cum lampade mœstam
          Effigiem.   Stat. Theb. xi. 142.

42. Though water was thought to be the principle of the passive, as fire was of the active power; yet, both being esteemed unproductive when separate,[1] both were occasionally considered as united in each. Hence Vesta, whose symbol was fire, was held to be, equally with Ceres, a personification of the Earth ;[2] or rather of the genial heat, which pervades it, to which its productive powers were supposed to be owing; wherefore her temple at Rome was of a circular form, having the sacred fire in the centre, but no statue.[3] She was celebrated by the poets, as the daughter of Rhea, the sister of Jupiter and Juno, and the first of the goddesses.[4] As the principle of universal order, she presided over the prytaneia or magisterial seats ; and was therefore the same as Themis, the direct personification of that attribute, and the guardian of all assemblies, both public and private, both of men and gods :[5] whence all legislation was derived from Ceres, a more general personification including the same powers. The universal mother of the Phrygians and Syrians, called by the Greeks Cybelè, because

---

[1] Το πυρ χωρις ὑγροτητος ατροφον εστι και ξηρον, το δε ὑδωρ ανευ θερμοτητος αγονον και αργον. Plutarch. Qu. Rom. sub init.

[2] Εκατερα δ' (ἡ Δημητηρ και ἡ Ἑστια) εοικεν ουχ' ετερα της γης ειναι. Phurnut. de Nat. Deor. c. 28.

Vesta eadem est quæ Terra, subest vigil ignis utrique.
Ovid. Fast. lib. vi. v. 267.

Nec tu aliud Vestam quam vivam intellige flammam.
Ibid. v. 291.

[3] Ovid. ibid. The temple is still extant, converted into a church ; and the ruins of another more elegant one, called the Sibyl's temple, at Tivoli.

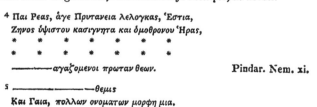

[4] Παι Ρεας, ἀγε Πρυτανεια λελογκας, Ἑστια,
Ζηνος ὑψιστου κασιγνητα και ὁμοθρονου Ἡρας,
* * * * * * *
* * * * * * *
————αγαζομενοι πρωταν θεων.   Pindar. Nem. xi.

[5] —————————θεμις
Και Γαια, πολλων ονοματων μορφη μια.
Æschyl. Prom. Vinct. 209.

represented under a globular or square form,[1] was the same more general personification worshipped with different rites, and exhibited under different symbols, according to the different dispositions and ideas of different nations. She was afterwards represented under the form of a large handsome woman, with her head crowned with turrets; and very generally adopted as the local tutelar deity of particular cities : but we have never seen any figure of this kind, which was not proved, by the style of composition and workmanship, to be either posterior, or very little anterior, to the Macedonian conquest.[2]

43. The characteristic attribute of the passive generative power was expressed in symbolical writing, by different enigmatical representations of the most distinctive characteristic of the sex ; such as the shell, called the Concha Veneris,[3] the Fig-leaf,[4] Barley Corn,[5] or the letter Delta ;[6] all which occur very frequently, upon coins, and other ancient monuments, in this sense. The same attribute, personified as the goddess of love or desire, is usually represented under the voluptuous form of a beautiful woman, frequently distinguished by one of these symbols, and called Venus, Cypris, or Aphroditè, names of rather uncertain etymology.[7] She is said to

---

[1] Ἡ Δημητηρ πολεως εστι καταρκτικη, οιονει ἡ γη. ὁθεν και πυργοφορον αυτην γραφουσιν. λεγεται δε και Κυβελη απο του κυβικου σχηματος κατα γεωμετριαν ἡ γη. Lex. Antiq. Frag. in Herm. Gramm.

[2] It is most frequent on the coins of the Asiatic colonies; but all that we have seen with it are of late date.

[3] August. de Civ. Dei lib. vi. c. 9.
Κτεις γυναικειος· ὁ εστιν, ευφημως και μυστικως ειπειν, μοριον γυναικειον. Clem. Alexand. Cohort. p. 19.

[4] Plutarch. de Is. et Osir. p. 365.

[5] Κριθη, αιδοιος γυναικειος κατα τους κωμικους. Eustath. in Homer. p. 134.
Των οστρεων γενος————Σεληνη συμπασχει. Clem. Alex. Cohort. s. iii.
Shell-fish in general were also thought to sympathise with the Moon.

[6] Δελτα. το τεταρτον στοιχειον· σημαινει δε και το γυναικειον αιδοιον. Suidas.

[7] The first may be from the verb BEINEIN; Suidas explaining BEINOΣ or BINOΣ to be the name of a goddess; and the name VENUS only differs from it in a well-known variation of dialect.

be the daughter of Jupiter and Dione; that is, of the male and female personifications of the all-pervading spirit of the universe; *Dione* being, as before explained, the female *ΔΙΣ* or *ΖΕΥΣ*, and therefore associated with him in the most ancient oracular temple of Greece at Dodona.[1] No other genealogy appears to have been known in the Homeric times; though a different one is employed to account for the name of Aphroditè in the theogony attributed to Hesiod.

44. The *Γενετυλλιδες* or *Γεναιδαι* were the original and appropriate ministers and companions of Venus;[2] who was however afterwards attended by the Graces, the proper and original attendants of Juno:[3] but as both these goddesses were occasionally united and represented in one image,[4] the personifications of their respective subordinate attributes might naturally be changed. Other attributes were on other occasions added; whence the symbolical statue of Venus at Paphos had a beard, and other appearances of virility;[5] which seems to have been the most ancient mode of representing the celestial, as distinguished from the popular goddess of that name; the one being a personification of a general procreative power, and the other only of animal desire or concupiscence.

The second may be from κυοπορις, i. e. κυειν πορισκουσα, though the theogonists derive it from the island of Cyprus. Schol. Ven. in Il. E. 458. Hesiod. Theogon.

The third is commonly derived from αφρος the foam of the sea, from which she is fabled to have sprung: but the name appears to be older than the fable, and may have been received from some other language.

[1] Συνναος τῳ Διι προσεδειχθη και ἡ Διωνη. Strabo Lib. viii. p. 506.

[2] Pausan. Lib. 1. c. i. s. 4.

[3] Il. Ξ. 267.

Το δε αγαλμα της ‘Ηρας επι θρονου καθηται μεγεθει μεγα, χρυσου μεν και ελεφαντος· Πολυκλειτου δε εργον· επεστι δε οἱ στεφανος χαριτας εχων και ‘Ωρας επειργασμενας, και των χειρων, τῃ μεν καρπον φερει ροιας, τῃ δε σκηπτρον. Τα μεν ουν ες την ροιαν (αποσηιοτερος γαρ εστιν ὁ λογος) αφεισθω μοι. Pausan. in Cor. c. 17. s. 4.

[4] Ξοανον δε αρχαιον καλουσιν Αφροδιτης ‘Ηρας. Pausan. in Lacon. c. 13. s. 6.

[5] Signum et hujus Veneris est Cypri barbatum corpore, sed veste muliebri, cum sceptro et statura viri. Macrob. lib. iii. p. 74.

C

The refinement of Grecian art, however, when advanced to maturity, contrived more elegant modes of distinguishing them; and, in a celebrated work of Phidias, we find the former represented with her foot upon a tortoise, and in a no less celebrated one of Scopas, the latter sitting upon a goat.' The tortoise, being an androgynous animal, was aptly chosen as a symbol of the double power; and the goat was equally appropriate to what was meant to be expressed in the other.

45. The same attribute was on other occasions signified by the dove or pigeon,² by the sparrow,³ and perhaps by the polypus; which often appears upon coins with the head of the goddess, and which was accounted an aphrodisiac;⁴ though it is likewise of the androgynous class. The fig was a still more common symbol; the statues of Priapus being made of the tree,⁵ and the fruit being carried with the phallus in the ancient processions in honor of Bacchus;⁶ and still continuing, among the common people of Italy, to be an emblem of what it anciently meant: whence we often see portraits of persons of that country painted with it in one hand, to signify their orthodox devotion to the fair sex.⁷ Hence, also,

---

¹ Την μεν εν τω ναω καλουσιν ουρανιαν· ελεφαντος δε εστι και χρυσου, τεχνη Φειδιου, τω δε ετερω ποδι επι χελωνης βεβηκε———και—αγαλμα Αφροδιτης χαλκουν επι τραγω καθηται χαλκω. Σκοπα τουτο εργον, Αφροδιτην δε Πανδημιον ονομαζουσι· τα δε επι χελωνη τε και ες το τραγον παριημι τοις θελουσιν εικαζειν. Pausan. Eliac. ii. c. 25. s. 2.

² Ελληνες——νομιζουσιν ιερον Αφροδιτης ζωον ειναι την περιστεραν, και τον δρακοντα της Αθηνας, και τον κορακα του Απολλωνος, και τον κυνα της Αρτεμιδος. Plutarch. de Is. et Osir.

³ Η δε στρουθος ανακειται μεν τη Αφροδιτη δια το πολυγονον, ετι δε και θερμον ες μιξιν· ω δη λογω και η περιστερα οικειουται τη του μυθου Αφροδιτη. Eustath. in Homer. p. 226. στρουθους·———η πολλη μεν ειδησις οχευτικους οιδε· Τερψικλης δε τις και τους εμφαγοντας αυτων, καταφορους λεγει προς τα 'εις Αφροδιτην γινεσθαι. Id. in Od. A. p. 1411. l. 10.

⁴ Athenæ. Deipnos. lib. ii. c. 23.

⁵ Horat. Sat. l. i. Sat. viii. v. 1.

⁶ Η πατριος των Διονυσιων εορτη το παλαιον επεμπετο δημοτικως και ιλαρως, αμφορευς οινου και κληματις, ειτα τραγον τις ειλκεν, αλλος ισχαδων αρρικον ηκολουθει κομιζων, επι πασι δε ο φαλλος. Plutarch. περι Φιλοπλ. η'.

⁷ See portrait of Tassoni prefixed to the 4to. edition of the Secchia Rapita, &c.

arose the Italian expression *far la fica;* which was done by putting the thumb between the middle and fore fingers, as it appears in many priapic ornaments now extant ; or by putting the finger or the thumb into the corner of the mouth, and drawing it down ; of which there is a representation in a small priapic figure of exquisite sculpture engraved among the antiquities of Herculaneum.[1]

46. The key, which is still worn, with the priapic hand, as an amulet, by the women of Italy, appears to have been an emblem of similar meaning, as the equivocal use of the name of it, in the language of that country, implies. Of the same kind, too, appears to have been the cross in the form of the letter τ, attached to a circle, which many of the figures of Ægyptian deities both male and female carry in the left hand, and by which the Syrians, Phœnicians, and other inhabitants of Asia, represented the planet Venus, worshipped by them as the natural emblem or image of that goddess.[2] The cross in this form is sometimes observable on coins ; and several of them were found in a temple of Serapis, demolished at the general destruction of those edifices by the emperor Theodosius ; and were said, by the Christian antiquaries of that time, to signify the future life.[3] In solemn sacrifices all the Lapland idols were marked with it from the blood of the victims ;[4] and it occurs on many Runic monuments found in Sweden and Denmark, which are of an age long anterior to the approach of Christianity to those countries ; and, probably, to its

---

[1] Bronzi, tab. xciv.

It is to these obscene gestures that the expressions of *figging* and *biting the thumb,* which Shakspeare probably took from translations of Italian novels, seem to allude; see 1 Henry IV. act v. sc. 3.; and Romeo and Juliet, act i. sc. 1. Another old writer, who probably understood Italian, calls thy latter *giving the fico;* and, according to its ancient meaning, it might very naturally be employed as a silent reproach of effeminacy.

[2] Procli Paraphr. Ptolem. lib. ii. p. 97. See also Mich. Ang. De la Chausse, Part ii. No. xxxvi. fol. 62. and Jablonski Panth. Ægypt. lib. ii. c. vii. s. 6.

[3] Suidas in v. ταυρος.

[4] Sheffer. Lapponic. c. x. p. 112.

appearance in the world.¹ On some of the early coins of the Phœnicians, we find it attached to a chaplet of beads placed in a circle; so as to form a complete rosary; such as the lamas of Thibet and China, the Hindoos, and the Roman Catholics, now tell over while they pray.²

47. Beads were anciently used to reckon time; and a circle, being a line without termination, was the natural emblem of its perpetual continuity; whence we often find circles of beads upon the heads of deities, and enclosing the sacred symbols, upon coins, and other monuments.³ Perforated beads are also frequently found in tombs, both in the northern and southern parts of Europe and Asia, which are fragments of the chaplets of consecration buried with the deceased. The simple diadem or fillet, worn round the head as a mark of sovereignty, had a similar meaning; and was originally confined to the statues of deities and deified personages, as we find it upon the most ancient coins. Chryses, the priest of Apollo, in the Iliad, brings the diadem or sacred fillet of the god upon his sceptre, as the most imposing and inviolable emblem of sanctity: but no mention is made of its being worn by kings in either of the Homeric poems; nor of any other ensign of temporal power and command, except the royal staff or sceptre.

48. The myrtle was a symbol both of Venus and Neptune, the male and female personifications of the productive powers of the waters, which appears to have been occasionally employed in the same sense as the fig and fig-leaf;⁴ but upon what account, it is not easy to guess. Grains of barley may have been adopted

---

¹ Ol. Rudbeck. Atlant. p. 11. c. xi. p. 662. and p. 111. c. i. s. 111. Ol. Varelii Scandagr. Runic. Borlase Hist. of Cornwall, p. 106.

² Pellerin. Villes. T. iii. pl. cxxii. fig. 4. Archæol. Vol. xiv. pl. 2. Nichoff s. ix. Maurice Indian Antiquities, Vol. v.

³ See Coins of Syracuse. Lydia.

⁴ See Coins of Syracuse, Marseilles, &c. Schol. in Aristoph. Lysistr. 646. Μεθερμηνευεται το θριον ποτισμος και κινησις (lege γεννησις vel κυησις) παντων, και δοκει γεννητικῳ μοριῳ την φυσιν εοικεναι. Plutarch de Is. et Osir. p. 305.

from the stimulating and intoxicating quality of the liquor extracted from them ;¹ or, more probably, from a fancied resemblance to the object, which is much heightened in the representations of them upon some coins, where they are employed as accessary symbols in the same manner as fig-leaves are upon others.² Barley was also thrown upon the altar with salt, the symbol of the preserving power, at the beginning of every sacrifice, and thence denominated *ουλοχυται*.³ The thighs of the victim, too, were sacrificed in preference to every other part, on account of the generative attribute ; of which they were supposed to be the seat :⁴ whence, probably, arose the fable of Bacchus being nourished and matured in the thigh of Jupiter.

49. Instead of beads, wreaths of foliage, generally of laurel, olive, myrtle, ivy, or oak, appear upon coins ; sometimes encircling the symbolical figures, and sometimes as chaplets on their heads. All these were sacred to some particular personifications of the deity, and significant of some particular attributes, and, in general, all evergreens were dionysiac plants :⁵ that is, symbols of the generative power, signifying perpetuity of youth and vigour ; as the circles of beads and diadems signified perpetuity of existence. Hence the crowns of laurel, olive, &c. with which the victors in the Roman triumphs and Grecian games were honored, may properly be considered as emblems of consecration to immortality, and not as mere transitory marks of occasional distinction. In the same sense, they were worn in all sacrifices and feasts in honor of the gods ; whence we find it observed by one of the guests at

---

¹ Οινω δ' εκ κριθεων πεποιημενω διαχρεωνται· ου γαρ σφι εισι εν τη χωρη αμπελοι. Herodot. de Ægypt. lib. ii. s. 77.

² See coins of Gela, Leontium, Selinus ; and Eustath. p. 1400. 28.

³ Eustath. in Il. A. p. 132 and 3. and in p. 1400. 28.

⁴ Τους μηρους, ως τι τιμιον, ὁλοκαυτουν, εξαιρουντες απο των αλλων του ζωου μερων, δια το συντελειν τοις ζωοις εις βαδισιν τε και εις γενεσιν τη προεσει του σπερμα-τος. Eustath. p. 134.

⁵ ————φησιν (ο Μεγασθενης) υμνητας ειναι του Διονυσου, δεικνυτας τεκμηρια, την ᾳμπελον, ————και κιττον, και δαφνην, και μυρρινην, και πυξον, και αλλα των αειθαλων. Strabo Lib. xv. p. 711.

an entertainment of this kind, that the host, by giving crowns of flowers instead of laurel, not only introduced an innovation, but made the wearing of them a matter of luxury instead of devotion.[1] It was also customary, when any poems sacred to the deity, such as those of a dramatic kind, were recited at private tables, for the person reciting to hold a branch of laurel in his hand,[2] to signify that he was performing an act of devotion, as well as of amusement.

50. The Scandinavian goddess Freya had, like the Paphian Venus, the characteristics of both sexes;[3] and it seems probable that the fable of the Amazons arose from some symbolical composition; upon which the Greek poets engrafted, as they usually did, a variety of amusing fictions. The two passages in the Iliad, in which they are slightly mentioned, appear to us to be interpolations;[4] and of the tales which have been circulated in later times concerning them, there is no trace in either of the Homeric poems, though so intimately connected with the subjects of both. There were five figures of Amazons in the temple of Diana at Ephesus, the rival works of five of the most eminent Greek sculptors;[5] and notwithstanding the contradictory stories of their having placed the ancient statue of the goddess, and been suppliants at her altar,[6] we suspect that they were among her symbolical attendants; or personifications of her subordinate attributes. In the great sculptured caverns of the island of Elephanta near Bombay, there is a figure, evidently symbolical, with a large prominent female breast on the left side, and none on the right; a peculiarity, which is said to have distinguished the Amazons, and given them their Greek name; the growth of the right breast having been artificially prevented, that they might have the free use of that

---

Τον στεφανον·ηδονης ποιων, ουκ ευσεβειας. Plutarch. Sympos. lib. viii. probl. xx.

[2] Aristoph. Neph. 1364, et Schol.

[3] Mallet Hist. de Danemarc. Introd. c. vii. p. 116.

[4] Γ. 188 and 9, and Ζ. 186.

[5] Plin. lib. xxxiv. c. viii.

[6] Pausan. lib. v. c. xxx. and lib. vii. c. i.

arm in war. This figure has four arms; and, of those on the right side, one holds up a serpent, and the other rests upon the head of a bull ; while, of those on the left, one holds up a small buckler, and the other something which cannot be ascertained.[1] It is probable that, by giving the full prominent form of the female breast on one side, and the flat form of the male on the other, the artist meant to express the union of the two sexes in this emblematical composition ; which seems to have represented some great deity of the people, who wrought these stupendous caverns ; and which, probably, furnished the Greeks with their first notion of an Amazon. Hippocrates however states that the right breast of the Sarmatian women was destroyed in their infancy, to qualify them for war, in which they served on horseback ; 'and none was qualified to be a wife, till she had slain three enemies.[2] This might have been the foundation of some of the fables concerning a nation of female warriors. The fine figure, nevertheless, of an Amazon in Lansdowne House, probably an ancient copy of one of those above mentioned, shows that the deformity of the one breast was avoided by their great artists, though the androgynous character is strongly marked throughout, in the countenance, limbs, and body. On gems, figures of Amazons, overcome by Hercules, Theseus, or Achilles, are frequent ; but we have never observed any such compositions upon coins.

51. This character of the double sex, or active and passive powers combined, seems to have been sometimes signified by the large aquatic snail or buccinum ; an androgynous insect, which we often find on the mystic monuments of the Greeks,[3] and of which the shell is represented radiated in the hands of several Hindoo idols, to signify fire and water, the principles from which this double power in nature sprang. The tortoise is, however, a more frequent symbol of this attribute ; though it might also have signified

---

[1] Niebuhr Voyages, T. ii. tab. vi.

[2] Περι αερ. κ. τ. λ. s. xlii.

[3] See silver coins of Panormus and Segesta, and brass of Agrigentum in Sicily.

[4] See Sonnerat's, and other collections of Hindoo Idols.

another: for, like the serpent, it is extremely tenacious of life; every limb and muscle retaining its sensibility long after its sepa-ration from the body.[1] It might, therefore, have meant immortality, as well as the double sex : and we accordingly find it placed under the feet of many deities, such as Apollo, Mercury, and Venus ;[2] and also serving as a foundation or support to tripods, pateras, and other symbolical utensils employed in religious rites.   Hence, in the figurative language of the poets and theologists, it might have been properly called the *support of the Deity;* a mode of expression, which probably gave rise to the absurd fable of the world's being supported on the back of a tortoise; which is still current among the Chinese and Hindoos, and to be traced even among the savages of North America.[3]   The Chinese have, in-deed, combined the tortoise with a sort of flying serpent or dragon; and thus made a composite symbol expressive of many attributes.[4]

52. At Momemphis in Ægypt, a sacred cow was the symbol of Venus,[5] as the sacred bull Mnevis and Apis were of the male personifications at Heliopolis and Memphis.   The Phœnicians employed the same emblem :[6] whence the Cadmeians are said to have been conducted to the place of their settlement in Bœotia by a cow; which pointed out the spot for building the Cadmeion or citadel of Thebes, by lying down to rest upon it.[7] This cow was probably no other than the symbolical image

---

[1] Ælian. de Animal. lib. iv. c. xxviii.

[2] Την Ηλειων ὁ Φειδιας Αφροδιτην εποιησε χελωνην πατουσαν, οικουριας συμβολον, ταις γυναιξι, και σιωπης. Plutarch. Conj. Priap. 138.
The reason assigned is to serve the purpose of the author's own moral argument; and is contradicted by the other instances of the use of the symbol.

[3] Lafitan Mœurs des Sauvages. T. i. p. 99.

[4] Kercher. China illustrata, p. 187. col. 2.

[5] Οἱ δε Μωμεμφιται την Αφροδιτην τιμωσι, και τρεφεται θηλεια βους ιερα, καθαπερ εν Μεμφει ὁ Απις, εν Ἡλιου δε πολει ὁ Μνευις. Strabo. lib. xvii. p. 552. See also eund. p. 556. and Ælian. de Anim. lib. xi. c. 27.

[6] Porphyr. de Abstinen. lib. ii. p. 158.

[7] Pausan. lib. ix. p. 773.   Schol. in Aristoph. Βατραχ. 1256. Ovid. Metamorph.

of their deity, which was borne before them, till fixed in the place chosen for their residence ; to which it gave the name of Thebes; *Thebah* in the Syrian language signifying a cow.[1] Hence we may perceive the origin of the fable of Bacchus being born at Thebes : for that city, being called by the same name as the symbol of nature, was easily confounded with it by the poets and mythologists; by which means the generator Bacchus, the first-begotten *Love*, and primary emanation of the all-pervading Spirit, became a deified mortal, the son of a Cadmeian damsel.

53. The cow is still revered as a sacred symbol of the deity, by the inhabitants of the gold-coast of Africa ;[2] and more particularly by the Hindoos ; among whom there is scarcely a temple without the image of one; and where the attribute expressed by it so far corresponds with that of the Grecian goddess Venus, as to be reputed the mother of the God of Love. It is also frequently found upon ancient Greek coins ;[3] though we do not find that any public worship was ever paid it by that people : but it appears to have been held sacred by all the African tribes adjoining Ægypt, as far as the Tritonian Lake ;[4] among whom the Greek colonies of Barcè and Cyrenè were settled at an early period. In the Scandinavian mythology, the sun was fabled to recruit his strength during winter by sucking the white cow Adumbla, the symbol of the productive power of the earth, said to have been the primary result of warmth operating upon ice, which the ancient nations of the north held to be the source of all organised being.[5] On the Greek coins, the cow is most commonly represented suckling a calf or

---

[1] Θηβα γαρ ή βους κατα Συρους. Schol. in Lycophr. v. 1206. See also Etymol. Magn.

[2] Hist. gén. des Voyages, T. iii. p. 392.

[3] See those of Dyrrachium, Corcyra, &c.

[4] Μεχρι της Τριτωνιδος λιμνης απ' Αιγυπτου νομαδες εισι κρεοφαγοι και γαλακτοποται Λιβυες· και θηλεων τε βοων ουτι γευομενοι, διοτι περ ουδε Αιγυπτιοι, και ύς ου τρεφοντες. Herodot. lib. iv. c. 186.

[5] Ol. Rudbeck. Atlant. p. 11. c. v. p. 235-253. & c. vi. p. 455.

young bull;[1] who is the mystic god Epaphus, the Apis of the Ægyptians, fabled by the Greeks to have been the son of Jupiter and Io.[2]

54. As men improved in the practice of the imitative arts, they gradually changed the animal, for the human form ; preserving still the characteristic features, which marked its symbolical meaning. Of this, the most ancient specimens now extant are the heads of Venus or Isis, (for they were in many respects the same personification,)[3] upon the capitals of one of the temples of Philæ, an island in the Nile between Ægypt and Æthiopia : and in these we find the horns and ears of the cow joined to the beautiful features of a woman in the prime of life.[4] In the same manner the Greek sculptors of the finest ages of the art represented Io ;[5] who was the same goddess confounded with an historical or poetical personage by the licentious imaginations of the Greek mythologists; as we shall further show in the sequel. Her name seems to have come from the north ; there being no obvious etymology for it in the Greek tongue : but, in the ancient Gothic and Scandinavian, Io and Gio signified the earth ; as Isi and Isa signified ice, or water in its primordial state ; and both were equally titles of the goddess, that represented the productive and nutritive power of the earth ; and, therefore, may afford a more probable etymology for the name Isis, than any that has hitherto been given.[6] The god or goddess of Nature is

---

[1] See those of Dyrrachium and Parium.

[2] Euripid. Phœniss. 688. ed. Porson.

[3] Ἡ γαρ Ισις εστι μεν το της φυσεως θηλυ, και δεκτικον ἁπασας γενεσεως, καθο τιθηνη και πανδεχης ὑπο Πλατωνος, ὑπο δε των πολλων μυριωνυμος κεκληται, δια το πασας ὑπο του λογου τρεπομενη μορφας δεχεσθαι και ιδεας. Plutarch. de Is. & Osir. p. 372.

Isis junctâ religione celebratur, quæ est vel terra, vel natura rerum Soli subjacens. Macrob. Sat. 1. c. xx.

[4] Norden's Ægypt.

[5] Το γαρ της Ισιος αγαλμα, εον γυναικηιον βουκερων εστι, καταπερ Ἑλληνες την Ιουν γραφουσι. Herodot. lib. ii.

[6] Ol. Rudbeck. Atlant. p. 1. c. xviii. & xx. p. 854. p. 11. c. v. p. 208-214, 340, & 451.

Edda Snorron. Myth. iv.

however called Isa in the Sanscrit;¹ and many of the Ægyptian
symbols appear to be Indian; but, on the contrary, it seems equally
probable that much of the Hindoo mythology, and, as we suspect,
all their knowledge of alphabetic writing, as well as the use of
money, came from the Greeks through the Bactrian and Parthian
empires; the sovereigns of both which appear to have employed
the Grecian letters and language in all their public acts.²

55. The Ægyptians, in their hymns to Osiris, invoked that god,
*as the being who dwelt concealed in the embraces of the Sun;*³ and
several of the ancient Greek writers speak of the great luminary
itself as *the generator and nourisher of all things, the ruler of the
world, the first of the deities, and the supreme Lord of all mutable
or perishable being.*⁴ Not that they, any more than the Ægyptians,
deified the Sun considered merely as a mass of luminous or fervid
matter; but as the centre or body, from which the pervading Spirit,
the original producer of order, fertility, and organisation, amidst
the inert confusion of space and matter, still continued to emanate
through the system, to preserve the mighty structure which it had
formed.⁵ This primitive pervading Spirit is said to have made the

¹ Sacontala. There were two goddesses of the name of Isis worshipped
in Greece, the one Pelasgian and the other Ægyptian, before the Pantheic
Isis of the latter ages.

Εστιν Ισιδος τεμενη· ὧν την μεν Πελασγιαν, την δε Αιγυπτιαν αυτων επονομαζουσι·
και δυο Σεραπιδος, εν Κανωβῳ καλουμενου το ἑτερον. Pausan. in Cor. c. iv. s. 7.

² Οἱ δε ες την Ινδικην εσπλεοντες φορτιων φασιν 'Ελληνικων τους Ινδους αγωγιμα αλλα
ανταλλασσεσθαι, νομισμα δε ουκ επιστασθαι, και ταυτα χρυσου τε αφθονου και χαλκου
παροντος σφισι. Pausan. in Lacon. c. xii. s. 3.

³ Εν δε τοις ἱεροις ὑμνοις του Οσιριδος ανακαλουνται τον εν ταις αγκαλαις κρυπτομενον
του ἡλιου. Plutarch. de Is. et Osir.

⁴ 'Ηλιος παγγενετωρ. Orph.
—— την γουν παντα βοσκουσαν φλογα
αιδεισθ' ανακτος ἡλιου. Sophocl. Œd. Tyr. v. 1424.
ου, τον παντων θεων
θεον προμον ἁλιον. Sophocl. Œd. Tyr. v. 674.
—— τον κυριον και ἡγεμονα της ρευστης ουσιας ἁπασης. Plutarch. Quæst. Rom.

⁵ See Plutarch. Qu. Rom. p. 138. & Fragm. Orphic.

Sun to guard and govern all things ;[1] it being thought the instrumental cause, through which the powers of reproduction, implanted in matter, continued to exist : for, without a continued emanation from the active principle of generation, the passive, which was derived from it, would of itself become exhausted.

56. This continued emanation, the Greeks personified into two distinct personages ; the one representing celestial love, or attraction ; and the other, animal love, or desire : to which the Ægyptians added a third, by personifying separately the great fountain of attraction, from which both were derived. All the three were, however, but one ; the distinctions arising merely out of the metaphysical subtilty of the theologists, and the licentious allegories of the poets ; which have a nearer resemblance to each other, than is generally imagined.

57. This productive ætherial spirit being expanded through the whole universe, every part was in some degree impregnated with it ; and therefore every part was, in some measure, the seat of the Deity ; whence local gods and goddesses were every where worshipped, and consequently multiplied without end. "Thousands of the immortal progeny of Jupiter," says Hesiod, "inhabit the fertile earth, as guardians to mortal men."[2] An adequate knowledge, either of the number or attributes of these, the Greeks never presumed to think attainable ; but modestly contented themselves with revering and invoking them whenever they felt or wanted their assistance.[3] If a shipwrecked mariner were cast upon an unknown shore, he immediately offered up his prayers to the gods of the

---

[1] Και φυλακ' αυτον ετευξε, κελευσε δε πασιν ανασσειν. Fragm. Orphic. No. xxv. ed. Gesn.

[2] Τρις γαρ μυριοι εισιν επι χθονι πουλυβοτειρη
Αθανατοι Ζηνος, φυλακες θνητων ανθρωπων.
   Εργα κ. ήμ. v. 252. See also Max. Tyr. Diss. xiv. s. 8.

[3] Θεον νομιζε και σεβου, ζητει δε μη,
πλειον γαρ ουδεν αλλο η ζητειν εχεις·
ει τ' εστιν, ει τ' ουκ εστιν μη βουλου μαθειν,
ως οντα τουτον και παροντ' αει σεβου. Philemon. Fragm. incert. No. 5.
Τις εστιν ὁ θεος, ου θελης συ μανθανειν·
ασεβεις τον ου θελοντα μανθανειν θελων. Menandr. Fragm. incerta. No. 246.

country, whoever they were ;[1] and joined the inhabitants in whatever modes of worship they employed to propitiate them ;[2] concluding that all expressions of gratitude and submission must be pleasing to the Deity ; and as for other expressions, he was not acquainted with them ; cursing, or invoking the divine wrath to avenge the quarrels of men, being unknown to the public worship of the ancients. The Athenians, indeed, in the fury of their resentment for the insult offered to the mysteries, commanded the priestess to curse Alcibiades: but she had the spirit to refuse ; saying, *that she was the priestess of prayers, and not of curses.*[3]

58. The same liberal and humane spirit still prevails among those nations whose religion is founded in the same principles. " The Siamese," says a traveller of the seventeenth century, " shun disputes, and believe that almost all religions are good."[4] When the ambassador of Lewis XIV. asked their king, in his master's name, to embrace Christianity, he replied, *that it was strange that the king of France should interest himself so much in an affair which concerned only God; whilst He, whom it did concern, seemed to leave it wholly to our discretion. Had it been agreeable to the Creator that all nations should have had the same form of worship, would it not have been as easy to his Omnipotence to have created all men with the same sentiments and dispositions; and to have inspired them with the same notions of the true Religion, as to endow them with such different tempers and inclinations? Ought they not rather to believe that the true God has as much pleasure in being honored by a variety of forms and ceremonies, as in being praised and glorified by a number of different creatures? Or why should that beauty and variety, so admirable in the natural order of things, be less admirable, or less worthy of the wisdom of God, in the supernatural?*[5]

---

[1] Odyss. E. 415.

[2] Ib. Γ.

[3] Ουδ' αλλοις επαρασθαι νομιζεται τους ιερεις (των Ρωμαιων) επηνεθη γουν Αθηνησι η ιερεια μη θελησασα καταρασασθαι τω Αλκιβιαδη, του δημου κελευοντος· εφη γαρ, ευχης, ου καθαρας, ιερεια γεγονεναι. Plutarch. Qu. Rom.

[4] Journal du Voyage du Siam.

[5] Voyage de Siam, lib. v.

59. The Hindoos profess exactly the same opinion. " They would readily admit the truth of the Gospel," says a very learned writer, long resident among them, " but they contend that it is perfectly consistent with their Sastras. The Deity, they say, has appeared innumerable times in many parts of this world, and of all worlds, for the salvation of his creatures : and though we adore him in one appearance, and they in others ; yet we adore, they say, the same God; to whom our several worships, though different in form, are equally acceptable, if they be sincere in substance." [1]

60. The Chinese sacrifice to the spirits of the air, the mountains, and the rivers ; while the emperor himself sacrifices to the sovereign Lord of Heaven ; to whom these spirits are subordinate, and from whom they are derived.[2] The sectaries of Foe have, indeed, surcharged this primitive elementary worship with some of the allegorical fables of their neighbours; but still as their creed, like that of the Greeks and Romans, remains undefined, it admits of no dogmatical theology, and, of course, of no persecution for opinion. Obscene and sanguinary rites have, indeed, been wisely proscribed on many occasions ; but still as *actions,* and not as *opinions.*[3] Atheism is said to have been punished with death at Athens : but, nevertheless, it may be reasonably doubted, whether the atheism, against which the citizens of that republic expressed such fury, consisted in a denial of the existence of the gods : for Diagoras, who was obliged to fly for this crime, was accused of revealing and calumniating the doctrines taught in the mysteries ;[4] and, from the opinions ascribed to Socrates, there is reason to believe that his offence was of the same kind, though he had not been initiated.

61. These two were the only martyrs to religion among the ancient Greeks, except such as were punished for actively violating

---

[1] Asiatic Researches, vol. i. p. 274.

[2] Du Halde, vol. i. p. 32.

[3] See the proceedings against the Bacchanalians at Rome. Liv.His.xxxix. 9.

[4] Διαγορας Αθηναιος ην, αλλα τουτον εξορχησαμενον τα παρ' Αθηναιοις μυστηρια, τετιμωρηκατε. Tatian. ad. Græc.

or insulting the mysteries ; the only part of their worship which seems to have possessed any energy : for, as to the popular deities, they were publicly ridiculed and censured with impunity, by those who dared not utter a word against the very populace that worshipped them ;[1] and, as to forms and ceremonies of devotion, they were held to be no otherwise important, than as they constituted a part of the civil government of the state ; the Pythian priestess having pronounced from the tripod, *that whoever performed the rites of his religion according to the laws of his country, performed them in a manner pleasing to the Deity.*[2] Hence the Romans made no alterations in the religious institutions of any of the conquered countries ; but allowed the inhabitants to be as absurd and extravagant as they pleased ; and even to enforce their absurdities and extravagancies, wherever they had any pre-existing laws in their favor. An Ægyptian magistrate would put one of his fellow-subjects to death for killing a cat or a monkey ;[3] and though the religious fanaticism of the Jews was too sanguinary and violent to be left entirely free from restraint, a chief of the synagogue could order any one of his congregation to be whipped for neglecting or violating any part of the Mosaic Ritual.[4]

62. The principle of the system of emanations was, that all things were of one substance ; from which they were fashioned, and into which they were again dissolved, by the operation of one plastic spirit universally diffused and expanded.[5] The liberal and

---

[1] See the Prometheus of Æschylus, and the Plutus and Frogs of Aristophanes, which are full of blasphemies ; the former serious, and the latter comic, or rather farcical.

[2] Xenoph. Memorab. lib. 1. c. iii. s. i.

[3] Tertullian. Apol. c. xxiv.

[4] See Acta Apost.

[5] Των δη πρωτων φιλοσοφησαντων, οἱ πλειστοι τας εν ὑλης ειδει μονον ῳηθησαν αρχας ειναι παντων· εξ οὗ γαρ εστιν ἁπαντα τα οντα, και εξ οὗ γιγνεται πρωτον, και εις ὁ φθειρεται τελευταιον, της μεν ουσιας ὑπομενουσης, τοις δε παθεσι μεταβαλλουσης, τουτο στοιχειον και ταυτην την αρχην ειναι των οντων· και δια τουτο, ουτε γιγνεσθαι ουθεν οιονται, ουτε απολλυσθαι, ὡς της τοιαυτης φυσεως αει σωζομενης. Aristot. Metaphys. A. μειζ. c. iii.

candid polytheist of ancient Greece and Rome thought, like the modern Hindoo, that all rites of worship and forms of devotion were directed to the same end ; though in different modes, and through different channels. " Even they who worship other gods," says the incarnate Deity in an ancient Indian poem, " worship me although they know it not."[1]

63. By this universal expansion of the creative Spirit, every production of earth, water, and air, participated in its essence ; which was continually emanating from, and reverting back to its source in various modes and degrees of progression and regression, like water to and from the ocean. Hence not only men, but all animals, and even vegetables, were supposed to be impregnated with some particles of the Divine nature ; from which their various qualities and dispositions, as well as their powers of propagation, were thought to be derived. These appeared to be so many different emanations of the Divine power operating in different modes and degrees, according to the nature of the substances with which they were combined : whence the characteristic properties of particular animals and plants were regarded, not only as symbolical representations, but as actual emanations of the supreme Being, consubstantial with his essence, and participating in his attributes.[2] For this reason, the symbols were treated with greater respect and veneration, than

νουν δε τις ειπων ειναι, καθαπερ εν τοις ζωοις και εν τη φυσει, τον αιτιον και του κοσμου και της ταξεως πασης. Ibid.

αρχαιος μεν ουν τις λογος και πατριος εστι πασιν ανθρωποις, ως εκ θεου τα παντα και δια θεου ημιν συνεστηκεν· ουδεμια δε φυσις αυτη καθ' ἑαυτην αυταρκης, ερημωθεισα της εκ τουτου σωτηριας διο και των παλαιων ειπειν τινες προηχθησαν, ὁτι ταυτα εστι παντα θεων πλεα, κ. τ. λ. Pseud. Aristot. de Mundo. c. vi.

Principio cœlum ac terras, camposque liquentes,
Lucentemque globum Lunæ, Titaniaque astra,
Spiritus intus alit ; totamque infusa per artus
Mens agitat molem, et magno se corpore miscet.
Inde hominum pecudumque genus, vitæque volantum,
Et quæ marmoreo fert monstra sub æquore pontus.
Virgil. Æneid. vi. 724.
See also Plutarch. in Rom. p. 76. & Cicer. de Divinit. lib. ii. c. 49.

[1] Bagvatgeeta.
[2] Proclus in Theol. lib. i. p. 56 & 7.

if they had been merely signs and characters of convention ; and, in some countries, were even substituted as objects of adoration, instead of the deity, whose attributes they were meant to signify.

64. Such seems to have been the case in Ægypt ; where various kinds of animals, and even plants, received divine honors ; concerning which, much has been written, both in ancient and modern times, but very little discovered. The Ægyptians themselves would never reveal any thing concerning them, as long as they had any thing to reveal, unless under the usual ties of secrecy ; wherefore Herodotus, who was initiated, and consequently understood them, declines entering into the subject, and apologises for the little which the general plan of his work has obliged him to say.[1] In the time of Diodorus Siculus the priests pretended to have some secret concerning them ;[2] but they probably pretended to more science than they really possessed, in this, as well as in other instances : for Strabo, who was contemporary with Diodorus, and much superior to him in learning, judgment, and sagacity, says that they were mere sacrificers without any knowledge of their ancient philosophy and religion.[3] The symbolical characters, called Hieroglyphics, continued to be esteemed more holy and venerable than the conventional signs for sounds : but, though they pretended to read, and even to write them,[4] the different explanations which they gave to different travellers, induce us to suspect that it was all imposture ; and that the knowledge of the ancient hieroglyphics, and consequently of the symbolical meaning of the sacred animals, perished with their Hierarchy under the Persian and Macedonian kings. We may indeed safely conclude, that all which they told of the exten-

---

[1] Των δε είνεκεν ανειται τα ιρα (θηρια) ει λεγοιμι, καταβαιην τῳ λογῳ ες τα θεια πρηγματα, τα εγω φευγω μαλιστα απηγεεσθαι· τα δε και ειρηκα αυτων επιψαυσας, αναγκαιῃ καταλαμβανομενος ειπον. Herodot. l. ii. s. 65.

[2] Οἱ μεν ουν ἱερεις αυτων (των Αιγυπτιων) απορρητον τι δογμα περι τουτων εχουσιν. lib. i. p. 96. ed. Wess.

[3] Strabo lib. xvii. p. 806.

[4] See the curious inscription in honor of Ptolemy V. published by the Society of Antiquaries of London, 1803.

D

sive conquests and immense empire of Sesostris, &c., was entirely fiction; since Palestine must from its situation have been among the first of those acquisitions; and yet it is evident from the sacred writings, that at no time, from their emigration to their captivity, were the ancient Hebrews subject to the kings of Ægypt; whose vast resources were not derived from foreign conquests, but from a river, soil, and climate, which enabled the labor of few to find food for many, and which consequently left an immense surplus of productive labor at the disposal of the state or of its master.[1]

65. As early as the second century of Christianity, we find that an entirely new system had been adopted by the Ægyptian priesthood, partly drawn from the writings of Plato and other Greek and oriental sophists, and partly invented among themselves. This they contrived to impose, in many instances, upon Plutarch, Apuleius, and Macrobius, as their ancient creed; and to this Iamblichus attempted to adapt their ancient allegories, and Hermapion and Horapollo, their symbolical sculptures; all which they very readily explain, though their explanations are wholly inconsistent with those given to Herodotus, Diodorus, and Germanicus; which are also equally inconsistent with each other. That the ancient system should have been lost, is not to be wondered at, when we consider the many revolutions and calamities, which the country suffered during the long period that elapsed from the conquest of it by Cambyses, to that by Augustus. Two mighty monarchs of Persia employed the power of that vast empire to destroy their temples and extinguish their religion; and though the mild and steady government of the first Ptolemies afforded them some relief, yet, by introducing a new language, with new princip es of science and new modes of worship, it tended perhaps to obliterate the ancient learning of Ægypt, as much as either the bigotry of their predecessors, or the tyranny of their successors.

66. It is probable, that in Ægypt, as in other countries, zeal and knowledge subsisted in inverse proportions to each other: where-

---

[1] See Herodot. lib. ii. c. 15.

fore those animals and plants, which the learned respected as sym
bols of Divine Providence acting in particular directions, because they
appeared to be impregnated with particular emanations, or endowed
with particular properties, might be worshipped with blind adoration
by the vulgar, as the real images of the gods. The cruel persecutions
of Cambyses and Ochus must necessarily have swept off a large proportion of the former class : whence this blind adoration probably
became general ; different cities and districts adopting different animals for their tutelar deities, in the same manner as those of modern
Europe put themselves under the protection of different saints ; or
those of China under that of particular subordinate spirits, supposed
to act as mediators and advocates with the supreme God.[1]

67. From the system of emanations, came the opinion, so pre-
valent among the ancients, that future events might be predicted by
observing the instinctive motions of animals, and more especially
those of birds ; which, being often inexplicable from any known
principles of mental operation, were supposed to proceed from the
immediate impulse of the Deity. The skill, foresight, and contrivance, which many of them display in placing and constructing
their nests is wholly unaccountable ; and others seem to possess a
really prophetic spirit, owing to the extreme sensibility of their
organs, which enables them to perceive variations in the state of the
atmosphere, preceding a change of weather, long before they are
perceptible to us.[2] The art of interpreting their various flights and
actions, seems to have been in repute during the Homeric times ;
but to have given way, by degrees, to the oracular temples ; which
naturally acquired pre-eminence by affording a permanent establish-
ment, and a more lucrative trade, to the interpreters and deliverers
of predictions.

68. The same ancient system, that produced augury, produced
oracles : for the human soul, as an emanation of the Divine Mind,

---

[1] Du Halde, vol. ii. p. 49.

[2] Virgil. Georgic. i. 415.   Ammian. Marcellin. lib. xxi. c. 1.

was thought by many to be in its nature prophetic ; but to be blunted and obscured by the opaque incumbrance of the body; through which it, however, pierced in fits of ecstasy and enthusiasm; such as were felt by the Pythian priestesses and inspired votaries of Bacchus.[1] Hence proceeded the affected madness and assumed extravagance of those votaries ; and also the sanctity attributed to wine ; which, being the means of their inspiration, was supposed to be the medium of their communion with the deity ; to whom it was accordingly poured out upon all solemn occasions, as the pledge of union and bond of faith; whence treaties of alliance and other public covenants were anciently called libations.[2] Even drinking it to intoxication, was in some cases an act of devotion ;[3] and the vine was a favorite symbol of the deity, which seems to have been generally employed to signify the generative or preserving attribute ;[4] intoxicating liquors being stimulative, and therefore held to be aphrodisiac. The vase is often employed in its stead, to express the same idea, and is usually accompanied by the same accessary symbols.[5]

69. It was for the same reason, probably, that the poppy was consecrated to Ceres, and her statues crowned with it ;[6] and that

---

[1] Plutarch. de Orac. Defect. p. 481.

Το γαρ βακχευσιμον,
Και το μανιωδες, μαντικην πολλην εχει.
'Οταν γαρ ὁ θεος εις το σωμ' ελθη πολυς,
Λεγειν το μελλον τους μεμηνοτας ποιει.

[2] ΣΠΟΝΔΑΙ. Il. 8. &c.

[3] —— διο και θοινας και θαλιας και μεθυς ωνομαζον' τας μεν ὁτι δια θεους οινουσθαι δειν υπελαμβανον' τας δ' ὁτι θεων χαριν ηυλιζοντο και συνηεσαν' τουτο γαρ εστι δαιτα θαλειαν· το δε μεθυειν, φησιν Αριστοτελης, το μετα το θυειν αυτῳ χρησθαι. Seleuc. apud Athenæ. Deipnos. lib. ii. c. 3.

Πινειν δ' εις μεθην ουδαμου πρεπον ελεγε (ὁ Πλατων), πλην εν ταις ἑορταις, του και τον οινον διδοντος θεου. Diog. Laert. lib. iii. s. 39.

[4] See coins of Maronea, Soli, Naxus, &c.

[5] See coins of Thebes, Haliartus, Hipponium, &c.

[6] Cereale papaver. Virg.   See coins of Seleucus IV.

Venus was represented holding the cone of it in one hand, while the other held an apple, and the πολος or modius decorated her head :[1] for the juice of the poppy is stimulative and intoxicating to a certain degree, though narcotic when taken to excess.

70. By yielding themselves to the guidance of wild imagination, and wholly renouncing common sense, which evidently acted by means of corporeal organs, men hoped to give the celestial faculties of the soul entire liberty, and thus to penetrate the darkness of futurity ; in which they often believed themselves successful, by mistaking the disorderly wanderings of a distempered mind, for the ecstatic effusions of supernatural perception. This sort of prophetic enthusiasm was sometimes produced, or at least supposed to be produced, by certain intoxicating exhalations from the earth ; as was the case at Delphi; where the design of setting up an oracle was first suggested by the goats being observed to skip about and perform various extravagant gesticulations, as often as they approached a certain fissure in the rock.[2] It is said to have been founded by some Hyperboreans ; and principally by the bard Olen, a priest and prophet of Apollo :[3] but women had officiated there as far back as any certain traditions could be traced ;[4] they having, probably, been preferred on account of the natural weakness of the

---

[1] Το μεν δη αγαλμα (Αφροδιτης) καθημενον Καναχος Σικυωνιος εποιησεν. ———— πεποιηται δ' εκ χρυσου τε και ελεφαντος φερουσα επι τη κεφαλη πολον, των χειρων δε εχει τη μεν μηκωνα, τη δε ετερα μηλον. Pausan. in Cor. c. x. s. 4.

Figures holding the poppy in one hand and the patera in the other, are upon the medals of Tarentum and Locri in Italy.

The laurel was also supposed to have a stimulative and intoxicating quality, and therefore the proper symbol for the god of poetry and prophecy.

ἡ δαφνη ενεργει προς τους ενθουσιασμους. Σοφοκλης·
   Δαφνην φαγων οδοντι πριε το στομα.
και Λυκοφρων·
   Δαφνηφαγον φοιβαζεν εκ λαιμων οπα.
       Schol. in Hesiod. Theogon. v. 30.

[2] Plutarch. de Orac. Defect. p. 434.

[3] Pausan. lib. x. c. v.

[4] Ibid.

sex, which rendered them more susceptible of enthusiastic delirium ; to promote which, all the rites practised before the responses were given, particularly tended.

71. The inspiring exhalation was at first attributed to the Earth only ; then to the Earth in conjunction with Neptune or the Sea; and lastly to Apollo or the Sun.[1] These were, however, only different modifications of one cause, always held to be unalterably the same, though supposed to act, at different times, in different ways and by different means. This cause was Jupiter, the all-pervading spirit of the universe, who had the title of All-prophetic, because the other deities presiding over oracular temples were merely personifications of his particular modes of action.[3] The Pelasgian, or rather Druidical oracle of Dodona, the most ancient known, immediately belonged to him ; the responses having been originally delivered by certain priests, who pretended that they received them from the oaks of the sacred grove ;[4] which, being the largest and

---

[1] Pausan. lib. x.

[2] Πανομφαιος.

[3] See Pindar. Olymp. viii. 58. Lucan has expressed this ancient mystic dogma in the language of the Stoics; and modified it to their system, according to the usual practice of the Syncretic sects.

Forsan terris inserta regendis
Aëre libratum vacuo quæ sustinet orbem,
Totius pars magna Jovis Cirrhæa per antra
Exit, et ætherio trahitur connexa Tonanti.
Hoc ubi virgineo conceptum est pectore numen,
Humanam feriens animam sonat, oraque vatis
Solvit.   Pharsal. lib. v. ver. 93

See also Ammian. Marcellin. lib. xxi. c. 1.

[4] Ζευ ανα, Δωδωναιε, Πελασγικε, τηλοθε ναιων,
Δωδωνης μεδεων δυσχειμερου· αμφι δε Σελλοι
Σοι ναιουσ' υποφηται, ανιπτοποδες, χαμαιευναι.
                              Iliad. Π. v. 233

Æschylus has only commented upon Homer.

'Α των αρειων και χαμαι κοιτων εγω
Σελλων εσελθων αλσος εισεγραψαμην
Προς της πατρωας και πολυγλωσσου δρυος.

strongest vegetable productions of the North, were employed by
the Celtic nations as symbols of the supreme God;[1] whose primary emanation, or operative Spirit, seems to have been signified
by the misletoe which grew from its bark; and, as it were, emanated from its substance; whence probably came the sanctity attributed to that plant.

72. Such symbols seem once to have been in general use; for
among the vulgar, the great preservers of ancient customs, they
continued to be so down to the latest periods. of Heathenism.
" The shepherd," says Maximus Tyrius, " honors Pan by conse-
crating to him the high fir, and deep cavern, as the husband-
man does Bacchus by sticking up the rude trunk of a tree."[2] Art
and refinement gradually humanised these primitive emblems, as
well as others; but their original meaning was still preserved in the
crowns of oak and fir, which distinguished the statues of Jupiter
and Pan, in the same manner as those of other symbolical plants
did those of other personifications.[3]

73. The sanctity, so generally attributed to groves by the barbarians of the North, seems to have been imperfectly transmitted
from them to the Greeks: for the poets, as Strabo observes, call
any sacred place a grove, though entirely destitute of trees;[4] so
that they must have alluded to these obsolete symbols and modes
of worship. The ΣΕΛΛΟΙ, the priests of Dodona, mentioned
in the Iliad, had disappeared, and been replaced by women long
before the time of Herodotus, who relates some absurd tales,
which he heard in Ægypt, concerning their having come from that

[1] Maxim. Tyr. Dissert. viii. s. 8.

[2] See ibid. p. 79.; also Plin. lib. ii. c. 1., and Tacit. de M. Germ. Even as
late as the eighth century of Christianity, it was enacted by Luitprand, king
of the Lombards, that whoever paid any adoration or performed any incan-
tation to a tree should be punished by fine. Paul. Diacon. de Leg. Longo-
bard.

[3] See heads of Jupiter of Dodona on the coins of Pyrrhus.

[4] Οἱ δε ποιηται κοσμουσιν, αλση καλουντες τα ιερα παντα κᾳν ῃ ψιλα. Strab. l. ix.
p. 599. ed. Oxon.

country.[1] The more prompt sensibility of the female sex was more susceptible of enthusiastic emotions, and consequently better adap ed to the prophetic office which was to express inspiration rather than convey meaning.

74. Considering the general state of reserve and restraint in which the Grecian women lived, it is astonishing to what an excess of extravagance their religious enthusiasm was carried on certain occasions; particularly in celebrating the orgies of Bacchus. The gravest matrons and proudest princesses suddenly laid aside their decency and their dignity, and ran screaming among the woods and mountains, fantastically dressed or half-naked, with their hair dishevelled and interwoven with ivy or vine, and sometimes with living serpents.[2] In this manner they frequently worked themselves up to such a pitch of savage ferocity, as not only to feed upon raw flesh.[3] but even to tear living animals to pieces with their teeth, and eat them warm and palpitating.[4]

75. The enthusiasm of the Greeks was, however, generally of the gay and festive kind; which almost all their religious rites tended to promote.[5] Music and wine always accompanied devotion, as tending to exhilarate men's minds, and assimilate them with the Deity; to imitate whom, was to feast and rejoice; to cultivate the elegant and useful arts; and thereby to give and receive happiness.[6] Such were most of the religions of antiquity, which

[1] Lib. ii. 54. &c. His story of the pigeons probably arose from the mystic dove on the head of Dione, the goddess of Dodona.

[2] Plutarch. in Alexandr.

[3] Apollon. Rhod. lib. i. 636., and Schol.

[4] Jul. Firmic. c. 14. Clement. Alex. Cohort. p. 11. Arnob. lib. v.

[5] Δοκεις τοις σοισι δακρυοις,
Μη τιμουσα θεους, κρατησειν
Εχθρων; ουτοι στοναχαις,
Αλλ' ευχαις, θεους σεβιζουσ',
Εξεις ευμεριαν, ω παι.   Eurip. Electra. 193.

[6] Strabo. lib. x. p. 476.

were not, like the Ægyptian and Druidical, darkened by the gloom of a jealous hierarchy, which was to be supported by inspiring terror rather than by conciliating affection. Hence it was of old observed, *that the Ægyptian temples were filled with lamentations and those of the Greeks with dances;*[1] the sacrifices of the former being chiefly expiatory, as appears from the imprecations on the head of the victim ;[2] and those of the latter almost always propitiatory or gratulatory.[3] Wine, which was so much employed in the sacred rites of the Greeks, was held in abomination by the Ægyptians; who gave way to none of those ecstatic raptures of devotion; which produced Bacchanalian phrensy and oracular prophecy ;[4] but which also produced Greek poetry, the parent of all that is sublime and elegant in the works of man. The poetry of Delphi and Dodona does not seem, indeed, to have merited this character: but the sacerdotal bards of the first ages appear to have been the polishers and methodisers of that language, whose copiousness, harmony, and flexibility, afforded an adequate vehicle for the unparalleled effusions of taste and genius, which followed.

76. Oracles had great influence over the public counsels of the different states of Greece and Asia during a long time ; and as they were rarely consulted without a present, the most celebrated of them acquired immense wealth. That of Delphi was so rich, when plundered by the Phocians, that it enabled them to support an army of twenty thousand mercenaries upon double pay during nine years, besides supplying the great sums employed in bribing

---

[1] Ægyptiaca numinum fana plena plangoribus, Græca plerumque choreis. Apul. de Genio. Socrat.

[2] Herodot. lib. ii. 39.

[3] Expiatory sacrifices were occasionally performed by individuals, but seem not to have formed any part of the established worship among the Greeks ; hence we usually find them mentioned with contempt. See Plat. de Repub. lib. ii. p. 595. E. ed. Fic. 1620.

[4] Plutarch. de Is. et Osir. p. 353.

the principal states of Greece to support or permit their sacrilege.[1] Too great eagerness to amass wealth was, however, the cause of their falling into discredit; it having been discovered that, on many occasions, those were most favored, who paid best;[2] and, in the time of Philip, the Pythian priestess being observed to be as much under the influence of Macedonian gold, as any of his pensioned orators.[3]

77. The Romans, whose religion, as well as language, was a corruption of the Greek, though immediately derived from the Etruscans, revived the ancient mode of divination by the flights of birds, and the motions and appearances of animals offered in sacrifice; but though supported by a college of augurs chosen from the most eminent and experienced men in the republic, it fell into disregard, as the steady light of human science arose to show its fallacy. Another mode, however, of exploring future events arose at the same time; and, as it was founded upon extreme refinement of false philosophy, it for a long time triumphed over the common sense of mankind, even during the most enlightened ages. This was judicial astrology; a most abject species of practical superstition, arising out of something extremely like theoretical atheism.

78. The great active principle of the universe, though personified by the poets, and dressed out with all the variable attributes of human nature, was supposed by the mystic theologists to act by the permanent laws of pre-established rule; and not by the fluctuating impulses of any thing analogous to the human will; the very exertion of which appeared to them to imply a sort of mutability of intention, that could only arise from new ideas or new sentiments, both equally incompatible with a mind infinite in its

---

[1] Diodor. Sic. lib. xvi. s. 37. et seq.

[2] Το μαντικον γαρ παν φιλαργυρον γενος.

Sophocl. Antigon. v. 1069.

See also Herodot. lib. vi.

[3] See Demosth. Philip. &c.

powers of action and perception : for, to such a mind, those events which happened yesterday, and those which are to happen during the immeasurable flux of time, are equally present, and its will is necessarily *that* which is, because all that is arose from its will. The act that gave existence, gave all the consequences and effects of existence, which are therefore all equally dependent upon the first cause ; and, how remote soever from it, still connected with it by a regular and indissoluble chain of gradation : so that the movements of the great luminaries of heaven, and those of the smallest reptiles that elude the sight, have some mutual relation to each other, as being alike integral parts of one great whole.

79. As the general movement of this great whole was supposed to be derived from the first divine impulse, which it received when constructed ; so the particular movements of each subordinate part were supposed to be derived from the first impulse, which that particular part received, when put into motion by some more principal one. Of course the actions and fortunes of individual men were thought to depend upon the first impulse, which each received upon entering the world : for, as every subsequent event was produced by some preceding one, all were really produced by the first. The moment therefore of every man's birth being supposed to determine every circumstance of his life, it was only necessary to find out in what mode the celestial bodies, supposed to be the primary wheels of the universal machine, operated at that moment, in order to discover all that would happen to him afterwards.

80. The regularity of the risings and settings of the fixed stars, though it announced the changes of the seasons, and the orderly variations of nature, could not be adapted to the capricious mutability of human actions, fortunes, and adventures : wherefore the astrologers had recourse to the planets ; whose more complicated revolutions offered more varied and more extended combinations. Their different returns to certain points of the zodiac ; their relative positions, and conjunctions with each other ; and the particular character and aspect of each, were supposed to influence the affairs of men ; whence daring impostors presumed to foretell,

not only the destinies of individuals; but also the rise and fall of empires, and the fate of the world itself.[1]

81. This mode of prediction seems to have been originally Chaldæan; and to have been brought from Babylon by the Greeks together with the little astronomy that they knew :[2] but the Chaldæans continued to be the great practitioners of it; and by exciting the hopes of aspiring individuals, or the fears of jealous tyrants, contrived to make themselves of mischievous importance in the Roman empire;[3] the principles of their pretended science being sufficiently specious to obtain credit, when every other of the kind had been exploded. The Greeks do not seem ever to have paid much attention to it; nor, indeed, to any mode of prediction after the decline of their oracles :[4] neither is it ever mentioned among the superstitions of the ancient Ægyptians, though their creed certainly admitted the principle upon which it is founded.[5] It is said to have been believed by only a certain sect among the Chaldæans;[6] the general system of whose religion seems to have been the same as that of most other nations of the northern hemisphere; and to have taught the existence of an universal pervading Spirit, whose subordinate emanations diffused themselves through the world,[7] and presented themselves in different places, ranks, and offices, to the adoration of men; who, by their mediation, were

---

[1] See Baillie Discours sur l'Astrologie.

[2] Herodot. l. ii. c. 109. Πολον μεν γαρ, και γνωμονα, και τα δυωδεκα μερεα της ἡμερης παρα Βαβυλωνιων εμαθον Ἑλληνες.

[3] Genus hominum potentibus infidum, sperantibus fallax. See Tacit. Ann. lib. ii. c. 32. lib. xii. c. 52. and Hist. lib. i. c. 22.; also Plin. lib. xxx. c. 1.

[4] Pindar. Olymp. xii. 10.

[5] Herodot. lib. ii. 82.

[6] Προσποιουνται δε τινες (των Χαλδαιων) γενεθλιαλογειν, ους ου καταδεχονται οἱ ἑτεροι. Strabo. lib. xvi.

[7] Fons omnium spirituum, cujus essentiam per universum mundum tanquam animam diffusam esse, &c. &c.—non Chaldæa tantum et Ægyptus, sed universus fere gentilismus vetustissimus credidit. Brucker. Hist. Crit. Philos. lib. i. c. 2. See also Euseb. Præp. Evang. lib. iv. c. 5.

enabled to approach the otherwise inaccessible light of the supreme and ineffable First Cause.[1]

82. Like the Greeks, they personified these subordinate emanations, and gave them names expressing their different offices and attributes; such as Michael, Raphael, Uriel, Gabriel, &c.; which the Jews having adopted during the captivity, and afterwards engrafted upon the Mosaic system, they have still retained their primitive sanctity, and are solemnly invoked in many parts of Europe by persons, who would think themselves guilty of the most flagitious impiety, if they invoked the same personifications by their Greek or Latin titles of Mars, Mercury, Hermes, or Apollo. The generative or creative attribute seems to have held the highest rank; but it was not adopted with the others by the Jews: for as the true Creator had condescended to become their national and peculiar God, they naturally abhorred all pretenders to his high office.

83. At Babylon, as in other countries, this attribute was divided into two distinct personifications, the one male, and the other female, called Beel and Mylitta by the Assyrians, and Ζευς and Αφροδιτη by the Greeks:[2] but, as the latter people subdivided their personified attributes and emanations much more than any other, the titles of their deities cannot be supposed to express the precise meaning of those of Assyria. Beel, or as the Greeks write it Βηλος, was certainly the same title differently pronounced, as the Baal of the Phœnicians, which signified lord or master; and Mylitta seems to have been in all respects the same as the Venus of the Greeks; she having been honored with rites equally characteristic and appropriate. The Babylonian women of every rank and condition he d it to be an indispensable duty of religion to prostitute themselves, once in their lives, in her temple, to any stranger who came and offered money; which, whether little or much, was accepted and applied to sacred purposes. Numbers

[1] Summum universi regem in luce inaccessibili habitare, nec adiri posse nisi mediantibus spiritibus mediatoribus, universi fere Orientis dogma fuit. Brucker. ibid.

[2] Herodot. lib. i.

of these devout ladies were always in waiting, and the stranger had the liberty of choosing whichever he liked, as they stood in rows in the temple ; no refusal being allowed.[1]

84. A similar custom prevailed in Cyprus,[2] and probably in many other countries ; it being, as Herodotus observes, the practice of all mankind, except the Greeks and Ægyptians, to take such liberties with their temples, which, they concluded, must be pleasing to the Deity, as birds and animals, acting under the guidance of instinct, or by the immediate impulse of Heaven, did the same.[3] The exceptions he might safely have omitted, at least as far as relates to the Greeks : for there were a thousand sacred prostitutes kept in each of the celebrated temples of Venus at Eryx and Corinth ; who, according to all accounts, were extremely expert and assiduous in attending to the duties of their profession ;[4] and it is not likely that the temple, which they served, should be the only place exempted from being the scene of them. Dionysius of Halicarnassus claims the same exception in favor of the Romans ; but, as we suspect, equally without reason : for Juvenal, who lived only a century later, when the same religion, and nearly the same manners prevailed, seems to consider every temple in Rome as a kind of licensed brothel.[5]

85. While the temples of the Hindoos possessed their establishments, most of them had bands of consecrated prostitutes, called the Women of the Idol, selected in their infancy by the Bramins for the beauty of their persons, and trained up with every elegant

---

[1] Herodot. lib. i.

[2] Ibid. c. 199.

[3] Lib. ii. 64.

[4] Strabo, lib. viii. Diodor. Sic. lib. iv. Philodemi Epigr. in Brunck. Analect. vol. ii. p. 85.

[5] Nuper enim, ut repeto, fanum Isidis et Ganymeden,
    Pacis, et advectæ secreta palatia matris,
    Et Cererem (nam quo non prostat femina templo ?)
    Notior Aufidio mœchus celebrare solebas.   Sat. ix. 22.

accomplishment that could render them attractive, and ensure success in the profession ; which they exercised at once for the pleasure and profit of the priesthood. They were never allowed to desert the temple ; and the offspring of their promiscuous embraces were, if males, consecrated to the service of the deity in the ceremonies of his worship ; and, if females, educated in the profession of their mothers.[1]

86. Night being the appropriate season for these mysteries, and being also supposed to have some genial and nutritive influence in itself,[2] was personified, as the source of all things, the passive productive principle of the universe,[3] which the Ægyptians called by a name, that signified Night.[4] Hesiod says, that the nights belong to the blessed gods ; it being then that dreams descend from Heaven to forewarn and instruct men.[5] Hence night is called ευφρονη, *good*, or *benevolent*, by the ancient poets ; and to perform any unseemly act or gesture in the face of night, as well as in the face of

---

[1] Maurice Antiq. Ind. vol. i. pt. 1. p. 341.

A devout Mohammedan, who in the ixth. century travelled through India, solemnly thanks the Almighty that *he* and *his* nation were delivered from the errors of infidelity, and unstained by the horrible enormities of so criminal a system of superstition.

The devout Bramin might, perhaps, have offered up more acceptable thanks, that *he* and *his* nation were free from the errors of a sanguinary fanaticism, and unstained by the more horrible enormities of massacre, pillage, and persecution ; which had been consecrated by the religion of Mohammed; and which every where attended the progress of his followers, spreading slavery, misery, darkness, and desolation, over the finest regions of the earth; of which the then happy Indians soon after felt the dire effects : —effects, which, whether considered as moral, religious, or political evils, are of a magnitude and atrocity, which make all the licentious abuses of luxury, veiled by hypocrisy, appear trifling indeed !

[2] Diodor. Sic. l. i. c. vii.

[3] Νυξ γενεσις παντων ην και Κυπριν καλεσωμεν.

Orph. Hymn. ii. 2.

[4] Αθυρ or Αθωρ, called Athorh still in the Coptic. Jablonski Panth. Ægypt. lib. i. c. 1. s. 7.

[5] Μακαρων τοι νυκτες εασιν.

Hesiod. Εργ. 730.

the sun, was accounted a heinous offence.[1] This may seem, indeed, a contradiction to their practice: but it must be remembered that a free communication between the sexes was never reckoned criminal by the ancients, unless when injurious to the peace or pride of families; and as to the foul and unnatural debaucheries imputed to the Bacchanalian societies suppressed by the Romans, they were either mere calumnies, or abuses introduced by private persons, and never countenanced by public authority in any part of the world. Had the Christian societies sunk under the first storms of persecution, posterity would have believed them guilty of similar crimes; of which they were equally accused by witnesses more numerous and not less credible.[2] We do, indeed, sometimes find indications of unnatural lusts in ancient sculptures: but they were undoubtedly the works of private caprice; or similar compositions would have been found upon coins; which they never are, except upon the Spinthriæ of Tiberius, which were merely tickets of admission to the scenes of his private amusement. Such preposterous appetites, though but too observable in all the later ages of Greece, appear to have been wholly unknown to the simplicity of the early times; they never being once noticed either in the Iliad, the Odyssey, or the genuine poem of Hesiod; for as to the lines in the former poem alluding to the rape of Ganymede, they are manifestly spurious.[3]

87. The Greeks personified night under the title of *ΛΗΤΩ*, or Latona, and *ΒΑΥΒΩ*; the one signifying *oblivion,* and the other *sleep,* or quietude;[4] both of which were meant to express the unmoved tranquillity prevailing through the infinite variety of unknown darkness, that preceded the Creation, or first emanation of light.

---

[1] Hesiod. Εργ. 727.

[2] Liv. Hist. l. xxxix. c. 9. &c. Mosheim, Gibbon, &c.

[3] Il. E. 265, &c. T. 230, &c.

[4] Νυξ δε ἡ Λητω, ληθω τις ουσα των εις ὑπνον τρεπομενων.
Plutarch. apud Euseb. Præp. Evang. lib. iii. c. 1.
βαυβᾷ κοιμιζει. βαυβᾷν καθευδειν. Hesych. It is the same word as ιαυειν, in a different dialect.

Hence she was said to have been the first wife of Jupiter, [1] the mother of Apollo and Diana, or the Sun and Moon, and the nurse of the Earth and the stars. [2] The Egyptians differed a little from the Greeks, and supposed her to be the nurse and grandmother of Horus and Bubastis, their Apollo and Diana ; [3] in which they agreed more exactly with the ancient naturalists, who held that heat was nourished by the humidity of night. [4] Her symbol was the Mygalè, or Mus Araneus, anciently supposed to be blind ; [5] but she is usually represented, upon the monuments of ancient art, under the form of a large and comely woman, with a veil upon her head. [6] This veil, in painting, was always black ; and in gems, the artists generally avail themselves of a dark-coloured vein in the stone to express it; it being the same as that which was usually thrown over the symbol of the generative attribute, to signify the nutritive power of Night, fostering the productive power of the pervading Spirit ; whence Priapus is called, by the poets, *black-cloaked.* [7] The veil is often stellated, or marked with asterisks, [8] and is occasionally given to all the personifications of the generative attribute, whether male or fe-

---

[1] Odyss. Λ. 579.

[2] ΒΑΥΒΩ· τιθηνη Δημητρος. Hesych.
Ω νυξ μελαινα χρυσεων αστρων τροφε. Euripid. Electra.

[3] Herodot. lib. ii. 156.

[4] Omnium autem physicorum assertione constat calorem humore nutriri. Macrob. Sat. i. c. 23.

[5] Plutarch. Symposiac. lib. iv. q. v. p. 670. Anton. Liberal. Fab. xxviii.

[6] See medals of the Brettii, Siciliotæ, King Pyrrhus, &c.
The animal symbol rarely occurs; but upon a beautifully-engraved gem, belonging to Mr. Payne Knight, is the head of a Boar, the symbol of Mars the destroyer, joined to the head of a Ram, the symbol of Bacchus or Ammon the generator; upon which repose a Dog, the symbol of Mercury, or presiding Mind; and upon the back of the dog is the Mygalè, the symbol of Latona, or Night.

[7] Μελαγχλαινοι·τε Πριηποι. Mosch. Epitaph. Bion. 27.

[8] See medals of Syracuse.

E

male ; [1] and likewise to portraits of persons consecrated, or represented in a sacred or sacerdotal character, which, in such cases, it invariably signifies. [2]

88. The Egyptian Horus is said to have been the son of Osiris and Isis, and to have been born while both his parents were in the womb of their mother Rhea ; [3] a fable which means no more than that the active and passive powers of production joined in the general concretion of substance, and caused the separation or delivery of the elements from each other : for the name Apollo is evidently a title derived from a Greek verb, signifying *to deliver from;* [4] and it is probable that Horus (or whatever was the Ægyptian name of this deity) had a similar meaning, it being manifestly intended to signify a personified mode of action of Osiris ; [5] in the same manner as Liber, the corresponding title in the Latin tongue, signified a personified mode of action of the generator Bacchus. [6] His statue at Coptos had the symbol of the generative attribute in his hand, said to be taken from Typhon, the destroying power ; [7] and there are small statues of him now extant, holding the circle and cross, which seems to have been the symbol meant. Typhon is said to have

---

[1] See heads of Venus on the gold coins of Tarentum, silver of Corinth—of Bacchus on those of Lampsacus, &c.

[2] See medals of Julius Cæsar, Livia, the Queens of Syria and Egypt, bust of Marcus Aurelius in the Townley collection, &c.

[3] Ἡ μεν γαρ, ετι των θεων εν γαστρι της Ῥεας οντων, εξ Ισιδος και Οσιριδος γενομενη γενεσις Απολλωνος, &c. Plutarch. de Is. et Osir. p. 373. We only quote Plutarch's facts, his explanations and etymologies being oftener from the School of Plato, than from ancient Egypt.

[4] Απολυω, anciently written ΑΠΟΛΥΓΩ.

[5] Εστι δ' ουτος ('Ωρος) ὁ περιγειος κοσμος, ουτε φθορας απαλλαττομενος πανταπασιν, ουτε γενεσεως. Plutarch. de Is. et Osir. p. 371.
Plutarch, in this explanation, has only mistaken the effect for the cause.

[6] The Latin adjective liber comes from the Greek verb ΛΥΓΩ ; by a well-known variation of dialect, from the Υ to the I, and from the F to the B.

[7] Εν Κοπτῳ το αγαλμα του 'Ωρου εν ἑτερᾳ χειρι Τυφωνος αιδοια κατεχει. Plutarch. de Is. et Osir. p. 470.

struck out and swallowed one of his eyes; [1] whence the itinerant priests and priestesses of the Ægyptian religion, under the Roman emperors, always appeared with this deformity: [2] but the meaning of the fable cannot now be ascertained, any more than that of the single lock of hair, worn on the right side of the head, both by Horus and his priests.

89. According to Manethos, the Ægyptians called the loadstone, the *bone of Osiris:* [3] by which it should seem that he represented the attractive principle; which is by no means incompatible with his character of separator and deliverer of the elements; for this separation was supposed to be produced by attraction. The Sun, according to the ancient system, learnt by Pythagoras from the Orphic, and other mystic traditions, being placed in the centre of the universe, with the planets moving round, [4] was, by its attractive force, the cause of all union and harmony in the whole, and, by the emanation of its beams, the cause of all motion and activity in the parts. This system, so remote from all that is taught by common sense and observation, but now so fully proved to be true, was taught secretly by Pythagoras; who

---

[1] Και λεγουσιν ότι του Ὡρου νυν μεν επαταξε, νυν δ᾽ εξελων κατεπιεν ὁ Τυφων τον οφθαλμον. Plutarch. de Is. et Osir.

[2] Lusca sacerdos, Juv. A bronze head of an Agyrtes, with this deformity, belongs to Mr. P. Knight.

[3] Ετι την σιδηριτιν λιθον οστεον Ὡρου, (καλουσι)—ὡς ἱστορει Μανεθος. Plutarch de Is. et Osir. p. 376.

[4] Εναντιως οἱ περι την Ιταλιαν, καλουμενοι δε Πυθαγορειοι, λεγουσιν επι γαρ του μεσου πυρ ειναι φασι, την δε γην ἐν των αστξων ουσαν κυκλῳ φερομενην π'ερι το μεσον, νυκτα τε και ἡμεραν ποιειν. Aristot. de Cœl. lib. ii. c. 13.

The author of the trifling book on the tenets of the Philosophers, falsely attributed to Plutarch, understands the central fire, round which the Earth and planets were supposed to move, not to be the Sun; in which he has been followed by Adam Smith and others: but Aristotle clearly understands it to be the Sun, or he could not suppose it to be the cause of day and night; neither could the Pythagoreans have been so ignorant as to attribute that cause to any other fire. This system is alluded to in an Orphic Fragment: Το απειρεσιον κατα κυκλον Απρυτως εφορειτο, No. xxxiii. ed. Gesner; and by Galen: Ἡρακλειδης δε και οἱ Πυθαγορειοι ἑκαστον των αστερων κοσμον ειναι νομιζουσι, γην παρεχοντα και αιθερα εν τῳ απειρῳ αερι. ταυτα δε τα δογματα εν ενιοις Ορφικοις φερεσθαι λεγουσι. Hist. Phil. c. xiii.

was rather the founder of a religious order for the purposes of ambition, than of a philosophical sect for the extension of science. After a premature discovery had caused the ruin of him and his society, Philolaus, one of his disciples, published this part of his doctrines, and Aristarchus of Samos openly attempted to prove the truth of it; [1] for which he was censured by Cleanthes, as being guilty of impiety: [2] but speculative theories were never thought impious by the Greeks, unless they tended to reveal the mystic doctrines, or disprove the existence of a Deity. That of Aristarchus could not have been of the latter class, and therefore must have been of the former; though his accuser could not specify it without participating in the imputed criminality. The crimes of Socrates and Diagoras appear to have been, as before observed, of the same kind: whence Aristophanes represents them attributing the order and variety of the universe to circular motion, called $\Delta INO\Sigma$; and then humorously introduces Strepsiades mistaking this Dinos for a new god, who had expelled Jupiter. [3] Among the symbols carried in the mystic processions was a wheel; [4] which is also represented on coins, [5] probably to signify the same meaning as was expressed by this word.

90. The great system to which it alluded was, however, rather believed than known; it having been derived from ancient tradition, and not discovered by study and observation. It was therefore supported by no proof; nor had it any other credit than what it derived from the mystic veneration paid to a vague notion, in some degree connected with religion, but still not sufficiently so to become an article of faith, even in the lax and comprehensive creed of

---

[1] Dutens Découvertes attribuées aux Modernes; and authorities there cited.

[2] Plutarch. de Fac. in orbe Lunæ, p. 922-3. The words of Plutarch are here decisive of the sense of those of Aristotle above cited. Αρισταρχον ωετο δειν Κλεανθης τον Σαμιον ασεβειας προκαλεισθαι τους Ελληνας, ὡς κινουντα του κοσμου την ἑστιαν, ὁτι φαινομενα σωζειν ανηρ επειρατο, μενειν τον ουρανον υποτιθεμενος, εξελιττεσθαι δε κατα λοξου κυκλου την γην, ἁμα και περι τον αὑτης αξονα δινουμενην.

[3] Nub. 826.

[4] Epiphan. p. 1092.

[5] See medals of Phliasus, Cyrene, Luceria, Vetulonia, &c.

Polytheism. Common observation might have produced the idea of a central cause of motion in the universe, and of a circular distribution of its parts; which might have led some more acute and discerning minds to imagine a solar system, without their having been led to it by any accurate or regular progress of discovery; and this we conceive to be a more easy and natural way of accounting for it, than supposing it to be a wreck or fragment of more universal science that had once existed among some lost and unknown people. [1]

91. Of this central cause, and circular distribution, the primitive temples, of which we almost every where find vestiges, appear to have been emblems : for they universally consist of circles of rude stones; in the centre of which seems to have been the symbol of the deity. Such were the pyrætheia of the Persians, [2] the Celtic temples of the North, and the most ancient recorded of the Greeks; one of which, built by Adrastus, a generation before the Trojan war, remained at Sicyon in the time of Pausanias. [3] It seems that most of the places of worship known in the Homeric times were of this kind; for though temples and even statues are mentioned in Troy, the places of worship of the Greeks consisted generally of an area and altar only. [4]

92. The Persians, who were the primitists, or puritans of Heathenism, thought it impious or foolish to employ any more complicated structures in the service of the Deity; [5] whence they destroyed, with unrelenting bigotry, the magnificent temples of Egypt and Greece. [6] Their places of worship were circles of stones, in the centre of which they kindled the sacred fire, the only symbol of their god: for they abhorred statues, as well as temples and altars; [7]

---

[1] See Baillie Hist. de l'Astronomie Ancienne.
[2] Pausan. lib. vii. c. xxii. and lib. ix.
[3] Ibid. p. 747.
[4] Τεμενος και βωμος.
[5] Herodot. lib. i. 131.
[6] Ib.
[7] Strabo, lib. xv. p. 1064, &c.

thinking it unworthy of the majesty of the Deity to be represented by any definite form, or to be circumscribed in any determinate space. The universe was his temple, and the all-pervading element of fire his only representative; whence their most solemn act of devotion was, kindling an immense fire on the top of a high mountain, and offering up, in it, quantities of wine, honey, oil, and all kinds of perfumes; as Mithradates did, with great expense and magnificence, according to the rites of his Persian ancestors, when about to engage in his second war with the Romans; the event of which was to make him lord of all, or of nothing. [1]

93. These offerings were made to the all-pervading Spirit of the universe, (which Herodotus calls by the Greek name of Jupiter), and to his subordinate emanations, diffused through the Sun and Moon, and the terrestrial elements, fire, air, earth, and water. They afterwards learned of the Syrians to worship their Astartè, or celestial Venus; [2] and by degrees adopted other superstitions from the Phœnicians and other neighbouring nations; who probably furnished them with the symbolical figures observable in the ruins of Persepolis, and the devices of their coins. We must not, however, as Hyde and Anquetil have done, confound the Persians of the first with those of the second dynasty, that succeeded the Parthians; nor place any reliance upon the pretended Zendavesta, which the latter produced as the work of Zoroaster; but which is in reality nothing more than the ritual of the modern Guebers or Parsees. That it should have imposed upon Mr. Gibbon, is astonishing; as it is manifestly a compilation of no earlier date than the eighth or ninth century of Christianity, and probably much later.

94. The Greeks seem originally to have performed their acts of devotion to the ætherial Spirit upon high mountains; from which new titles, and consequently new personifications, were derived; such as those of Olympian, Dodonæan, Idæan, and Casian Jupiter. [3] They

---

[1] Appian. de Bello Mithrad. p. 361.

[2] Herodot. l. i. 131.

[3] See Maxim. Tyr. Dissert. viii.

were also long without statues;[1] which were always considered, by
the learned among them, as mere symbols, or the invention of human
error to console human weakness.[2] Numa, who was deeply
skilled in mystic lore, forbade the Romans to represent the gods
under any forms either of men or beasts;[3] and they adhered to his
instructions during the first hundred and seventy years of the
republic:[4] nor had the Germans, even in the age of Tacitus, re-
nounced their primitive prejudices, or adopted any of the refinements of their neighbours on this subject.

95. In some instances, the circular area above mentioned is in-
closed in a square one; and we are told that a square stone was the
primitive symbol of several deities, more especially of the celestial
Venus, or passive productive power, both among the ancient Greeks
and ancient Arabians.[5] Upon most of the very early Greek coins,
too, we find an inverse or indented square, sometimes divided into
four, and sometimes into a greater number of compartments; and
latterly, with merely the symbol of the deity forming the device, in
the centre. Antiquaries have supposed this incuse to be merely the
impression of something put under the coin to make it receive the
stroke of the die more steadily:[6] but in all that we have seen of

---

[1] Pausan. lib. viii. c. xxii. and lib. ix.

[2] Θνητοι δε πολλοι καρδια πλανωμενοι,
'Ιδρυσαμεσθα, πηματων παραψυχην
Θεων αγαλματ' εκ λιθων τε και ξυλων.
Sophocl. apud Justin. Martyr. Cohort. ad Gent. p. 10.
There is another line, but it is a scholion on the preceding one. See Toup.
Emend. in Suid. vol. ii. p. 526. The whole may possibly be the production
of an Alexandrine Jew.

[3] Plutarch. in Numa.

[4] Varro apud Augustin. de Civ. Dei. lib. iv. c. vi.

[5] Maxim. Tyr. Dissert. xxxviii. Clem. Alex. Protrept.
'Εστηκασι δε εγγυτα του αγαλματος τετραγωνοι λιθοι τριακοντα μαλιστα αριθμον·
τουτους σεβουσιν οι Φαρεις εκαστω θεου τινος ονομα επιλεγοντες· τα δε ετι παλαιοτερα και
τοις πασιν 'Ελλησι τιμας θεων αντι αγαλματων ειχον αργοι λιθοι. Pausan. in Achaic.
c. xxii. s. 3.
Ταυτης (της Αφροδιτης) γαρ σχημα μεν τετραγωνον κατα ταυτα και τοις 'Ερμαις· το δε
επιγραμμα σημαινει την Ουρανιαν Αφροδιτην των καλουμενων Μοιρων ειναι πρεσβυτατην.
Pausan. in Att. c. xix. s. 2.

[6] Abbé Barthelemi Mémoires de l'Académie des Inscr. t. xxiv. p. 30. D'An-
carville Recherches sur les Arts, lib. i. c. iv. p. 412.

this kind, amounting to some hundreds, the coin has been driven into the die, and not struck with it, and the incuse impression been made either before or after the other, the edges of it being always beaten in or out. Similar impressions also occur on some of the little Egyptian amulets of paste, found in mummies, which were never struck, or marked with any impression on the reverse.

96. In these square areas, upon different coins almost every different symbol of the deity is to be found : whence, probably, the goddess represented by this form, acquired the singular titles of *the Place of the Gods,* [1] and the *mundane House of Horus.* [2] These titles are both Egyptian : but the latter is signified very clearly upon Greek coins, by an asterisk placed in the centre of an incuse square : [3] for the asterisk being composed of obelisks, or rays diverging from a globe or common centre, was the natural representation of the Sun ; and precisely the same as the radiated head of Apollo, except that, in the latter, the globe or centre was humanised. Upon the ancient medals of Corinth and Cnossus, the square is a little varied, by having the angles drawn out and inverted ; [4] particularly upon those of the latter city, which show a progressive variation of this form from a few simple lines, which, becoming more complicated and inverted, produce at length the celebrated Labyrinth [5] which Dædalus is said by the mythologists to have built for Minos, as a prison to confine a monster begotten upon his wife Pasiphaë, by a bull, and therefore called the Minotaur. Pasiphaë is said to have been the daughter of the Sun; and her name, signifying *all-splendid,* is evidently an ancient epithet of that luminary. The bull is said to have been sent by Neptune, or the Sea ; [6] and the title which distin-

---

[1] Διο και την Συριαν Αταργατην τοπον θεων καλουσιν, και την Ισιν οἱ Αιγυπτιοι, ὡς πολλων θεων ιδιοτητας περιεχουσας. Simplic. in Aristot. lib. iv. Auscult. Phys. p. 150. ed. Ald. Hence Plutarch says that Osiris was the beginning, Isis the receptacle, and Orus the completion. De Is. et Osir. p. 374.

[2] Ἡ δ' Ισις, εστιν οτε και Μουθ, και παλιν Αθυρι, και Μεθυερ προσαγορευουσι· Σημαινουσι δε τῳ πρωτῳ των ονοματων μητερα, τῳ δε δευτερῳ οικον Ὡρου κοσμιον. Plutarch. ibid.

[3] See small brass coins of Syracuse, which are very common.

[4] See Mus. Hunterian.

[5] Ibid.

[6] Apollodor. lib. iii. c. i.

guished the offspring is, in an ancient inscription, applied to Attis, the Phrygian Bacchus : [1] whence the meaning of the whole allegory distinctly appears ; the Minotaur being only the ancient symbol of the bull, partly humanised ; to whom Minos may have sacrificed his tributary slaves, or, more probably, employed them in the service of the deity.

97. In the centre of one of the more simple and primitive labyrinths on the Grecian coins above cited, is the head of a bull; [2] and in others of a more recent style, the more complicated labyrinth is round. [3] On some of those of Camarina in Sicily, the head of the god, more humanised than the Minotaur, yet still with the horns and features of the bull, is represented in the centre of an indented scroll, [4] which other coins show to have been meant to represent the waters, by a transverse section of waves. [5] On the coins, too, of Magnesia upon the Meander, the figure of Apollo is represented as leaning upon the tripod, and standing upon some crossed and inverted square lines, similar to the primitive form of the labyrinth on the coins of Corinth above cited. [6] These have been supposed to signify the river Meander: but they more probably signify the waters in general; as we find similar crossed and inverted lines upon coins struck in Sicily, both Greek and Punic ; [7] and also upon rings and fibulæ, which are frequently adorned with symbolical devices, meant to serve as amulets or charms. The bull however, both in its natural form, and humanised in various degrees, so as in some instances to leave only the horns of the animal symbol, is perpetually employed upon coins to signify particular rivers or streams; which being all derived from the Bacchus Hyes, as the Nile was from Osiris, were all represented under the same form. [8]

---

[1] ATTIDI MINOTAURO. Gruter. vol. i. p. xxviii. No. 6.

[2] In the cabinet of Mr. Payne Knight.

[3] In the same. Also in the British Museum.

[4] Mus. Hunter. tab. 14. No. ix.

[5] Ib. tab. 56. No. iii.

[6] Ib. tab. 35. No. ix.

[7] See a specimen of them on the reverse of a small coin, Mus. Hunter. tab. 67. No. v.

[8] See coins of Catania, Selinus, Gela, Sybaris, &c.

98. It appears, therefore, that the asterisk, bull, or Minotaur, in the centre of the square or labyrinth, equally mean the same as the Indian lingam—that is, the male personification of the productive attribute placed in the female, or heat acting upon humidity. Sometimes the bull is placed between two dolphins, [1] and sometimes upon a dolphin or other fish; [2] and in other instances the goat or the ram occupy the same situation; [3] which are all different modes of expressing different modifications of the same meaning in symbolical or mystical writing. The female personifications frequently occupy the same place; in which case the male personification is always upon the reverse of the coin, of which numerous instances occur in those of Syracuse, Naples, Tarentum, and other cities.

99. Ariadne, the fabled wife of Bacchus, is a personage concerning whom there has been more confusion of history and allegory than concerning almost any other. Neither she, nor Bacchus, nor Theseus, appear to have been known to the author of the Iliad; the lines concerning them all three being manifestly spurious: but in the Odyssey, she is said to have been the daughter of Minos, and to have been carried away from Crete by Theseus to Athens, where she was killed by Diana—that is, died suddenly, before he enjoyed her. [4] Such appears to have been the plain sense of the passage, according to its true and original reading: but Theseus having become a deified and symbolical personage, in a manner hereafter to be explained, Ariadne became so likewise; and was therefore fabled to have been deserted by him in the island of Naxus; where Bacchus found and married her; in consequence of which she became the female personification of the attribute which he represented; and as such constantly appears in the symbolical monuments of art, with

---

[1] See brass coins of Syracuse.

[2] On a gold coin of Eretria in the cabinet of Mr. Payne Knight. Hence the curious hymn or invocation of the women of Elis to Bacchus :— Εχει δ' ουτως ὁ ὑμνος (των Ηλειων γυναικων) " Ελθειν ἥρω, Διονυσε, ἁλιον ες ναον ἁγνον, συν χαριτεσσιν ες ναον τῳ βοεῳ ποδι θυων." Ειτα δις επᾳδουσιν· " Αξιε ταυρε." Plutarch. Quæst. Græc.

[3] On gold coins of Ægæ and Clazomenæ, in the same collection.

[4] Λ. 320.

ull the accessary and characteristic emblems. Some pious heathen, too, made a bungling alteration, and still more bungling interpolation, in the passage of the Odyssey, to reconcile historical tradition with religious mythology. [1]

100. In many instances, the two personifications are united in one; and Bacchus, who on other occasions is represented as a bearded venerable figure, [2] appears with the limbs, features, and character of a beautiful young woman; [3] sometimes distinguished by the sprouting horns of the bull, [4] and sometimes without any other distinction than the crown or garland of vine or ivy. [5] Such were the Phrygian Attis, and Syrian Adonis; whose history, like that of Bacchus, is disguised by poetical and allegorical fable; but who, as usually represented in monuments of ancient art, are androgynous personifications of the same attribute, [6] accompanied, in different instances, by different accessary symbols. Considered as the pervading and fertilizing spirit of the waters, Bacchus differs from Neptune in being a general emanation, instead of a local division, of the productive power; [7] and also in being a personification derived from a more refined and philosophical system of religion, engrafted upon the old elementary worship, to which Neptune belonged.

101. It is observed by Dionysius the geographer, that Bacchus was worshipped with peculiar zeal and devotion by the ancient

---

[1] Εσχε for εκτα (which is preserved in some Mss. and Scholia), and by adding the following line, v. 524; a most manifest interpolation.

[2] See silver coins of Naxus, and pl. xvi. and xxxix. of Vol. i. of the Select Specimens.

[3] See coins of Camarina, &c.

[4] See gold coins of Lampsacus in Mus. Hunter., and silver of Maronea.

[5] See gold medals of Lampsacus, brass ditto of Rhodes, and pl. xxxix. of Vol. i. of the Select Specimens.

[6] Αμφοτεροι γαρ οἱ θεοι (Ποσειδων και Διονυσος) της ύγρας και γονιμου κυριοι δοκουσιν αρχης ειναι. Plutarch. Symposiac. lib. v. qu. 3.
Ποσειδων δε εστιν ἡ απεργαστικη εν τη γη και περι την γην ύγρου δυναμις. Phurnut. de Nat. Deor. c. iv.

[7] Ὁτι δ' ου μονον του οινου Διονυσον, αλλα και πασης ύγρας φυσεως Ἑλληνες ἡγουνται κυριον και αρχηγον, αρκει Πιδαρος μαρτυς ειναι, κ. τ. λ. Plutarch. de Is. et Osir.

inhabitants of some of the smaller British islands; [1] where the *women, crowned with ivy, celebrated his clamorous nocturnal rites upon the shores of the Northern Ocean, in the same manner as the Thracians did upon the banks of the Apsinthus, or the Indians upon those of the Ganges.* [2] In Stukeley's Itinerary is the ground plan of an ancient Celtic or Scandinavian temple, found in Zealand, consisting of a circle of rude stones within a square : and it is probable that many others of these circles were originally enclosed in square areas. Stonehenge is the most important monument of this kind now extant ; and from a passage of Hecatæus, preserved by Diodorus Siculus, it seems to have been not wholly unknown to that ancient historian ; who might have collected some vague accounts of the British islands from the Phœnician and Carthaginian merchants, who traded there for tin. " *The Hyperboreans,*" said he, " *inhabit an island beyond Gaul, in which Apollo is worshipped in a circular temple considerable for its size and riches.*" This island can be no other than Britain ; in which we know of no traces of any other circular temple, which could have appeared considerable to a Greek or Phœnician of that age. That the account should be imperfect and obscure is not surprising ; since even the most inquisitive and credulous travellers among the Greeks could scarcely obtain sufficient information concerning the British islands to satisfy them of their existence. [3] A temple of the same form was situated upon Mount Zilmissus in Thrace, and dedicated to the

---

[1] Αγχι δε νησιαδων ἑτερος πορος, ενθα γυναικες
Ανδρων αντιπαρηθεν αγαυων αμνιταων
Ορνυμεναι τελεουσι κατα νομον ἱερα Βακχῳ,
Στεψαμεναι κισσοιο μελαμφυλλοιο κορυμβοις,
Εννυχιαι· παταγης δε λιγυθροος ορνυται ηχη. κ. τ. λ.

V. 570.

What islands are meant is uncertain ; but probably the Hebrides or Orcades.

[2] Ἑκαταιος και τινες ἑτεροι φασιν, εν τοις αντιπεραν της Κελτικης τοποις κατα τον Ωκεανον ειναι νησον ουκ ελαττω της Σικελιας——ὑπαρχειν δε κατα την νησον τεμενος τε Απολλωνος μεγαλοπρεπες, και ναον αξιολογον αναθημασι πολλοις κεκοσμημενον σφαιροειδη τῳ σχηματι. Diodor. Sic. lib. ii. c. xiii. The whole passage is extremely curious.

[3] Ουτε νησους οιδα Κασσιτεριδας εουσας, εκ των ὁ Κασσιτερος ἡμιν φοιτᾳ. Herodot. lib. iii. 115.

Sun under the title of Bacchus Sebazius;[1] and another is mentioned by Apollonius Rhodius, which was dedicated to Mars upon an island in the Euxine Sea near the coast of the Amazons.[2]

102. The large obelisks of stone found in many parts of the North, such as those at Rudstone and near Boroughbridge in Yorkshire, belonged to the same religion : obelisks, as Pliny observes, being sacred to the Sun; whose rays they signified both by their form and name.[3] They were therefore the emblems of light, the primary and essential emanation of the Deity; whence radiating the head, or surrounding it with a diadem of small obelisks, was a mode of consecration or deification, which flattery often employed in the portraits both of the Macedonian kings and Roman emperors.[4] The mystagogues and poets expressed the same meaning by the epithet *ΛΥΚΕΙΟΣ* or *ΛΥΚΑΙΟΣ*; which is occasionally applied to almost every personification of the Deity, and more especially to Apollo; who is likewise called *ΛΥΚΗΓΕΝΕΤΗΣ*, or as contracted *ΛΥΚΗΓΕΝΗΣ*;[5] which mythologists have explained by an absurd fable of his having been born in Lycia ; whereas it signifies the *Author* or *Generator of Light ;* being derived from *ΛΥΚΗ* otherwise *ΛΥΚΟΣ*, of which the Latin word *LUX* is a contraction.

103. The titles LUCETIUS and DIESPITER applied to Jupiter are expressive of the same attribute ; the one signifying *luminous*, and the other the *Father of Day*, which the Cretans called by the name of the Supreme God.[6] In symbolical writing the same meaning was signified by the appropriate emblems in various countries ; whence the *ΖΕΥΣ ΜΕΙΛΙΧΙΟΣ* at Sicyon, and the

---

[1] Macrob. Sat. i. c. 18.

[2] Argonaut. lib. ii. 1169.

[3] Lib. xxxvi. l. 14.
το φως γενεσεως εστι σημειον. Plutarch, Q. R.

[4] See Plin. Panegyr. s. lii. and the coins of Antiochus IV. and VI. of Syria, Philip IV. of Macedonia, several of the Ptolemies, Augustus, &c.

[5] Il. Δ. 101. Schol. Didym. et Ven. Heraclid. Pant. p. 417. ed. Gale.

[6] Macrob. Sat. i. c. 15.

Apollo Carinas at Megara in Attica were represented by stones of the above-mentioned form;[1] as was also the Apollo Agyieus in various places;[2] and both Apollo and Diana by simple columns pointed at the top; or, as the symbol began to be humanised, with the addition of a head, hands, and feet.[3] On a Lapland drum the goddess Isa or Disa is represented by a pyramid surmounted with the emblem so frequently observed in the hands of the Ægyptian deities;[4] and the pyramid has likewise been observed among the religious symbols of the savages of North America.[5] The most sacred idol, too, of the Hindoos in the great temple of Jaggernaut, in the province of Orissa, is a pyramidal stone;[6] and the altar in the temple of Mexico, upon which human victims were sacrificed to the deity of the Sun, was a pointed pyramid, on which the unhappy captive was extended upon his back, in order to have his heart taken out by the priest.[7]

104. The spires and pinnacles, with which our old churches are decorated, come from these ancient symbols; and the weathercocks, with which they are surmounted, though now only employed to show the direction of the wind, were originally emblems of the Sun: for the cock is the natural herald of the day; and therefore

---

[1] Εστι δε Ζευς Μειλιχιος και Αρτεμις ονομαζομενη Πατρωα συν τεχνη πεποιημενα ουδεμια· πυραμιδι δ' ὁ Μειλιχιος, ἡ δε κιονι εστιν εικασμενη. Pausan. in Cor. c. 9. s. 6.

Λιθος παρεχομενος πυραμιδος σχημα ου μεγαλης· τουτον Απολλωνα ονομαζουσι Καριναν. Id. in Att. c. 44. s. 3.

[2] Αγυιευς δε εστι κιων εις οξυ ληγων, ὁν ιστασι προ των θυρων· ιδιους δε φασιν αυτους ειναι Απολλωνος· οἱ δε Διονυσου· οἱ δε αμφοιν.

Αγυιευς, ὁ προ των αυλιων θυρων κωνοειδης κιων, ἱερος Απολλωνος, και αυτος θεος. Suidas in voce Αγυιας. Vide et Schol. in Aristoph. Vesp. et Schol. in Eurip. Phœniss. 684. et Eustath. in Hom. p. 166.

[3] 'Οτι μη προσωπον αυτῳ και ποδες εισιν ακροι και χειρες, το λοιπον χαλκῳ κιονι εστιν εικασμενον εχει δε επι τῃ κεφαλῃ κρανος, λογχην δε εν ταις χερσι και τοξον. Pausan. in Lacon. c. 19. s. 2.

[4] Ol. Rudbeck. Atlant. p. 11. c. v. p. 277. and c. xi. p. 261.

[5] Lafitan Mœurs des Sauvages. t. 1. p. 146 and 8.

[6] Hamilton's Travels in India.

[7] Acosta's History of the Indies. p. 382.

sacred to the fountain of light.¹ In the symbolical writing of the Chinese, the Sun is still represented by a cock in a circle;² and a modern Parsee would suffer death rather than be guilty of the crime of killing one.³ It appears on many ancient coins, with some symbol of the passive productive power on the reverse ;⁴ and in other instances it is united with priapic and other emblems and devices, signifying different attributes combined.⁵

105. The Ægyptians, among whom the obelisk and pyramid were most frequently employed, held that there were two opposite powers in the world perpetually acting against each other; the one generating and the other destroying ; the former of whom they called Osiris, and the latter Typhon. By the contention of these two, that mixture of good and evil, of procreation and dissolution, which was thought to constitute the harmony of the world, was supposed to be produced ;⁶ and the notion of such a necessary mixture, or reciprocal operation, was, according to Plutarch, *of immemorial antiquity, derived from the earliest theologists and legislators, not only in traditions and reports, but also in mysteries and sacred*

---

¹ 'Ηλιου δε ιερον φασιν ειναι τον ορνιθα, και αγγελειν ανιεναι μελλοντος του ἡλιου. Pausan. lib. v. p. 444.

² Pour peindre le Soleil, ils (les Chinois) mettent un Coq dans un Cercle. Du Halde vol. ii. p. 252.

³ Hyde de Relig. vet. Persarum.

⁴ See coins of Himera, Samothrace, Suessa, &c.

⁵ Ib. and Selinus.

⁶ Ουκ αν γενοιτο χωρις εσθλα και κακα,
αλλ' εστι τις συγκρασις, ὡστ' εχειν καλως.
Eurip. apud Plutarch. de Is. et Osir.

Γαια μεγιστη κα Διος αιθηρ,
ὁ μεν ανθρωπων και θεων γενετωρ,
ἡ δ' ὑγροβολους σταγονας νοτιους
παραδεξαμένη τικτει θνατους,
τικτει δε βοραν, φυλα τε θηρων·
χωρει δ' οπισω τα μεν εκ γαιας
φυντ' εις γαιαν· τα δ' απ' αιθεριου
βλαστοντα γονης εις ουρανιον
πολον ηλθε παλιν. κ. τ. λ.
Ejusd. in Grotii excerpt. p. 417.

rites both Greek and Barbarian.[1] Fire was held to be the efficient principle of both; and, according to some of the later Ægyptians, that ætherial fire supposed to be concentred in the Sun: but Plutarch controverts this opinion, and asserts that Typhon, the evil or destroying power, was a terrestrial or material fire, essentially different from the ætherial; although he, as well as other Greek writers, admits him to have been the brother of Osiris, equally sprung from *KPONOΣ* and *PEA*, or Time and Matter.[2] In this however, as in other instances, he was seduced, partly by his own prejudices, and partly by the new system of the Ægyptian Platonics; according to which there was an original evil principle in nature, co-eternal with the good, and acting in perpetual opposition to it.

106. This opinion owes its origin to a false notion, which we are apt to form, of good and evil, by considering them as self-existing inherent properties, instead of relative modifications dependent upon circumstances, causes, and events: but, though patronised by very learned and distinguished individuals, it does not appear ever to have formed a part of the religious system of any people or established sect. The beautiful allegory of the two casks in the Iliad, makes Jupiter the distributor of both good and evil;[3] which Hesiod also deduces from the same gods.[4] The statue of Olympian Jupiter at Megara, begun by Phidias and Theocosmus, but never finished, the work having been interrupted by the Peloponnesian war, had the Seasons and Fates over his head, to show, as Pausanias says, that the former were regulated by him, and the latter obedient to his will.[5] In the citadel of Argos was preserved an ancient statue of

---

[1] Διο και παμπαλαιος αυτη κατεισιν εκ θεολογων και νομοθετων εις ποιητας και φιλοσοφους δοξα, την αρχην αδεσποτον εχουσα, την δε πιστιν ισχυραν και δυσεξαλειπτον, ουκ εν λογοις μονον, ουδε εν φημαις, αλλα εν τε τελεταις, εν τε θυσιαις και Βαρβαροις και Ἑλλησι πολλακου περιφερομενην, κ. τ. λ.   de Is. et Osir. p. 369.

γενεσθαι, συμμιγηναι, τὠυτο. απολεσθαι, μειωθηναι, διακριθηναι, τὠυτο.   Hippocrat. Διαιτ. l. 6.

[2] Ibid. p. 355. Diodor. Sic. lib. i. p. 13.

[3] Ω. 527.   [4] Εργ. 60.

[5] Pausan. in Attic. c. 40.

him in wood, said to have belonged to king Priam, which had three eyes (as the Scandinavian deity Thor sometimes had),[1] to shew the triple extent of his power and providence, over Heaven, Earth, and Hell ;[2] and, in the Orphic hymns or mystic invocations, he is addressed as the giver of life, and the destroyer.[3]

107. The third eye of this ancient statue was in the forehead ; and it seems that the Hindoos have a symbolical figure of the same kind :[4] whence we may venture to infer that the Cyclops, concerning whom there are so many inconsistent fables, owed their fictitious being to some such aenigmatical compositions. According to the ancient theogony attributed to Hesiod, they were the sons of Heaven and Earth, and brothers of Saturn or Time ;[5] signifying, according to the Scholiast, the circular or central powers,[6] the principles of the general motion of the universe above noticed. The Cyclops of the Odyssey is a totally different personage : but as he is said to be the son of Neptune or the Sea, it is probable that he equally sprang from some emblematical figure, or allegorical tale. Whether the poet meant him to be a giant of a one-eyed race, or to have lost his other eye by accident, is uncertain ; but the former is most probable, or he would have told what the accident was.— In an ancient piece of sculpture, however, found in Sicily, the artist has supposed the latter, as have also some learned moderns.[7]

108. The Ægyptians represented Typhon by the Hippopotamos, the most fierce and savage animal known to them ; and, upon his

---

[1] Ol. Rudbeck. Atlant. p. ii. c. v. p. 518.

[2] Ζευς ξοανον, δυο μεν, ᾗ πεφυκεν, εχον οφθαλμους, τριτον δε επι του μετωπου· τουτον τον Δια Πριαμῳ φασιν ειναι τῳ Λαοδαμαντος πατρῳον. Pausan. Cor. c. 24. s. 5.

[3] Hymn. lxxii. ed. Gesner.

[4] Asiatic Researches, vol. i. p. 248.

[5] V. 139, &c.

[6] Κυκλωπας τας εγκυκλιους δυναμεις. Schol. vet. in vers. 139.
The two lines 144-5 in the text, containing the etymology of the name, appear to be spurious; the licentious extended form ἑεις being incompatible with the language of the old poets.

[7] See Houel Voyage en Sicile, pl. cxxxvii., et Damm. Lex.

F

back they put a hawk fighting with a serpent, to signify the direction of his power ; for the hawk was the emblem of power,[1] as the
serpent was of life ; whence it was employed as the symbol of
Osiris, as well as of Typhon.[2] Among the Greeks it was sacred to
Apollo ;[3] but we do not recollect to have seen it on any monuments
of their art, though other birds of prey, such as the eagle and cor-
morant, frequently occur.[4] The eagle is sometimes represented
fighting with a serpent, and sometimes destroying a hare ;[5] which,
being the most prolific of all quadrupeds, was probably the emblem
of fertility.[6] In these compositions the eagle must have represented
the destroying attribute ; but, when alone, it probably meant the
same as the Ægyptian hawk : whence it was the usual symbol of
the supreme God, in whom the Greeks united the three great attributes of creation, preservation, and destruction. The ancient
Scandinavians placed it upon the head of their god Thor, as they
did the bull upon his breast,[7] to signify the same union of attributes ; which we sometimes find in subordinate personifications
among the Greeks. On the ancient Phœnician coins above cited, an
eagle perches on the sceptre, and the head of a bull projects from
the chair of a sitting figure of Jupiter, similar in all respects to that
on the coins of the Macedonian kings supposed to be copied from
the statue by Phidias at Olympia, the composition of which
appears to be of earlier date.

109. In the Bacchæ of Euripides, the chorus invoke their inspiring god *to appear under the form of a bull, a many-headed serpent,*

---

[1] Εν Ἑρμοπολει δε Τυφωνος αγαλμα δεικνυουσι ἱππον ποταμιον· εφ' οὑ βεβηκε ἱεραξ
οφει μαχομενος· τῳ μεν ἱππῳ τον Τυφωνα δεικνυντες, τῳ δε ἱερακι δυναμιν και αρχην,
Plutarch. de Is. et Osir. p. 371. fol.

[2] Γραφουσι και ἱερακι τον θεον τουτον (Οσιριν) πολλακις. Ibid.

[3] Aristoph. Ορνιθ. v. 514.

[4] The latter on the coins of Agrigentum, as the symbol of Hercules : the
former, as the symbol of Jupiter, is the most common of all devices.

[5] See coins of Chalcis in Eubœa, of Elis, Agrigentum, Croto, &c.

[6] See coins of Messena, Rhegium, &c. It was also deemed aphrodisiac
and androgynous. See Philostrat. Imag.

[7] Ol. Rudbeck. Atlantic. p. ii. c. v. p. 300. and 321.

or a flaming lion;[1] and we sometimes find the lion among the accessary symbols of Bacchus; though it is most commonly the emblem of Hercules or Apollo; it being the natural representative of the destroying attribute. Hence it is found upon the sepulchral monuments of almost all nations both of Europe and Asia; even in the coldest regions, at a vast distance from the countries in which the animal is capable of existing in its wild state.[2] Not only the tombs but likewise the other sacred edifices and utensils of the Greeks, Romans, Chinese and Tartars, are adorned with it; and in Tibet there is no religious structure without a lion's head at every angle having bells pendent from the lower jaw, though there is no contiguous country that can supply the living model.[3]

110. Sometimes the lion is represented killing some other symbolical animal such as the bull, the horse, or the deer; and these compositions occur not only upon the coins and other sacred monuments of the Greeks and Phœnicians;[4] but upon those of the Persians,[5] and the Tartar tribes of Upper Asia;[6] in all which they express different modifications of the ancient mystic dogma above mentioned concerning the adverse efforts of the two great attributes of procreation and destruction.

---

[1] Φανηθι, ταυρος, η πολυκρανος γ' ιδειν
δρακων, η πυριφλεγων
ορασθαι λεων.
V. 1015.
κριας, ταυρεους, χαραποντε λεοντος
(κεφαλας fert ὁ φανης Ορφικος).
Procl. apud Eschenb. Epig. p. 77.

[2] Hist. gén. des Voyages. t. v. p. 458. Embassy to Tibet. p. 262. Houel Voyage en Sicile.

[3] Embassy to Tibet. p. 288.

[4] See the coins of Acanthus and Velia; and also those of some unknown city of Phœnicia. Houel Voyage en Sicile, pl. xxxv. and vi.

[5] Ruins of Persepolis by Le Bruyn.

[6] On old brass coins in the cabinet of Mr. Payne Knight. On a small silver coin of Acanthus in the same cabinet, where there was not room for the lion on the back of the bull, as in the larger, the bull has the face of a lion.

111. The horse was sacred to Neptune and the Rivers;[1] and employed as a general symbol of the waters, on account of a supposed affinity, which we do not find that modern naturalists have observed.[2] Hence came the composition, so frequent upon the Carthaginian coins, of the horse with the asterisk of the Sun, or the winged disc and hooded snakes, over his back ;[3] and also the use made of him as an emblematical device on the medals of many Greek cities.[4] In some instances the body of the animal terminates in plumes ;[5] and in others has only wings, so as to form the Pegasus, fabled by the later Greek poets to have been ridden by Bellerophon, but only known to the ancient theogonists as the bearer of Aurora and of the thunder and lightning to Jupiter;[6] an allegory of which the meaning is obvious. The Centaur appears to have been the same symbol partly humanised ; whence the fable of these fictitious beings having been begotten upon a cloud appears to be an allegory of the same kind.[7] In the ancient bronze engraved in plate lxxv. of volume i. of the Select Specimens, a figure of one is represented bearing the Cornucopiæ between Hercules and Æsculapius, the powers of destruction and preservation ; so that it here manifestly represents the generative or productive attribute. A symbolical figure similar to that of the Centaur occurs among the hieroglyphical sculptures of the magnificent temple of Isis at Ten-

---

[1] Virgil Georg. i. 12. and iii. 122. Iliad. Φ. 132.

[2] Φιλολουτρον ζωον, ὁ ἱππος, και φιλυδρον, και χαιρει λειμωσι και ἑλεσι. Aristot. apud Eustath. in Hom. p. 658. l. 59.

[3] See Mus. Hunter. Gesner. &c.; the coins being extremely common.

[4] Cyrenè, Syracuse, Maronea, Erythræ in Bœotia, &c. &c. .

[5] As on those of Lampsacus.

[6] Lycophr. Alexandr. 17.

Ζηνος δ᾽ εν δωμασι ναιει
Βροντην τε Στεροπην τε φερων Διι μητιοεντι.

Hesiod. Theogon. v. 285.

The history of Bellerophon is fully related in the Iliad (Z. 155. &c.); but of his riding a flying horse, the old poet knew nothing.

[7] According to another fable preserved by Nonnus, they were begotten by Jupiter on the Earth, in an unsuccessful attempt upon the chastity of Venus.

Ου Παφιης τοσον ηλθον ες ἱμερον, ἡς χαριν ευνης
Κενταυρους εφυτευσα, βαλων σπορον αυλικι γαιης.

Dionysiac. lib. xxxii.

tyris in Ægypt;[1] and also one of the Pegasus or the winged horse:[2] nor does the winged bull, the cherub of the Hebrews, appear to be any other than an Ægyptian symbol, of which a prototype is preserved in the ruins of Hermontis.[3] The disguised indications, too, of wings and horns on each side of the conic or pyramidal cap of Osiris are evident traces of the animal symbol of the winged bull.

112. On the very ancient coins found near the banks of the Strymon in Thrace, and falsely attributed to the island of Lesbos, the equine symbol appears entirely humanised, except the feet, which are terminated in the hoofs of a horse: but on others, apparently of the same date and country, the Centaur is represented in the same action; namely, that of embracing a large and comely woman. In a small bronze of very ancient sculpture, the same priapic personage appears, differing a little in his composition; he having the tail and ears, as well as the feet of a horse, joined to a human body, together with a goat's beard;[5] and in the Dionysiacs of Nonnus we find such figures described under the title of Satyrs; which all other writers speak of as a mixture of the goat and man. These, he says, were of the race of the Centaurs; with whom they made a part of the retinue of Bacchus in his Indian expedition;[6] and they were probably the original Satyrs derived from Saturn, who is fabled to have appeared under the form of a horse in his addresses to Philyra the daughter of the Ocean;[7] and who, having been the chief deity of the Carthaginians, is probably the personage

---

[1] Denon. pl. cxxxii. n. 2.   [2] Ib. pl. cxxxi. n. 3.   [3] Ib. pl. cxxix. n. 2.

[4] See pl. ii. vol. i. of the Select Specimens.

[5] Inaccurately published in the Recherches sur les Arts de la Grèce. pl. xiii. vol. i.; M. D'Hancarville having been misled by his system into a supposition that the animal parts are those of a bull. The figure is now in the cabinet of Mr. Knight.

[6] Lib. xiii. and xiv.

[7] Talis et ipse jubam cervice effundit equina
Conjugis adventu pernix Saturnus, et altum
Pelion hinnitu fugiens implevit acuto.
Virg. Georg. iii. 92.

represented by that animal on their coins.[1] That these equine
Satyrs should have been introduced among the attendants of Bacchus, either in poetry or sculpture, is perfectly natural; as they
were personifications of the generative or productive attribute
equally with the Πανισκοι, or those of a caprine form ; wherefore we
find three of them on the handle of the very ancient Dionysiac
patera terminating in his symbol of the Minotaur in the cabinet of
Mr. Payne Knight. In the sculptures, however, they are invariably without horns ; whereas Nonnus calls them κεροεντες and ευκε-
ραεις: but the authority of this turgid and bombastic compiler of
fables and allegories is not great. The Saturn of the Romans, and
probably of the Phœnicians, seems to have been the personification of
an attribute totally different from that of the Κρονος of the Greeks, and
to have derived his Latin name from *Sator*, the *sower* or *planter;*
which accords with the character of Pan, Silenus, or Sylvanus, with
which that of Neptune, or humidity, is combined. Hence, on the
coins of Naxus in Sicily, we find the figure usually called Silenus
with the tail and ears of a horse, sometimes priapic, and sometimes
with the priapic term of the Pelasgian Mercury as an adjunct, and
always with the head of Bacchus on the reverse. Hence the equine
and caprine Satyrs, Fauns, and Πανισκοι, seem to have had nearly the
same meaning, and to have respectively differed in different stages
and styles of allegorical composition only by having more or less
of the animal symbol mixed with the human forms, as the taurine
figures of Bacchus and the Rivers have more or less of the original
bull. Where the legs and horns of the goat are retained, they are
usually called Satyrs; and where only the ears and tail, Fauns;
and, as this distinction appears to have been observed by the best
Latin writers, we see no reason to depart from it, or to suppose,

---

[1] These are probably the personages represented on the Thracian or Macedonian coins above cited ; but the Saturn of both seems to have answered
rather to the Neptune of the Greeks, than to the personification of Time,
commonly called ΚΡΟΝΟΣ or Saturn. The figure represented mounted upon
a winged horse terminating in a fish, and riding upon the waters, with a
bow in his hand, is probably the same personage. See Méd. Phen. de
Dutens pl. 1. f. 1. The coin is better preserved in the cabinet of Mr.
Knight.

with some modern antiquaries, that Lucretius and Horace did not apply properly the terms of their own language to the symbols of their own religion.[1] The baldness always imputed to Silenus is perhaps best explained by the quotation in the margin.[2]

113. In the Orphic hymns we find a goddess 'Ιππα celebrated as the nurse of the generator Bacchus, and the soul of the world;[3] and, in a cave of Phigalè in Arcadia, the daughter of Ceres by Neptune was represented with the head of a horse, having serpents and other animals upon it, and holding upon one hand a dolphin, and upon the other a dove;[4] the meaning of which symbols, Pausanias observes, were evident to every learned and intelligent man; though he does not choose to relate it, any more than the name of this goddess;[5] they being both probably mystic. The title 'ΙΠ-ΠΙΟΣ or 'ΙΠΠΙΑ was applied to several deities;[6] and occasionally

---

[1] Bassirilievi di Roma, vol. ii. p. 149. not. 14.

[2] 'Οκοσοι φαλακροι γινονται, οὗτοι δη φλεγματωδεες εισι· και εν τῃ κεφαλῃ αυτεων ἅμα τῃ λαγνειῃ κλονεομενον και θερμαινομενον το φλεγμα, προσπιπτον προς την επιδερμιδα καιει των τας ριζας, και εκρεουσιν αἱ τριχες. Οἱ δε ευνουχοι δια τουτο ου γινονται φαλακροι, ὅτι σφεων ου γινεται κινησις ισχυρη· κ. τ. λ. Hippocrat. de N. P. s. xviii. xix. Φλεγμα is not to be understood here, as translated, *pituita, phlegm* or *morbid rheum*, but *animal viscus* or *gluten*, the material of organisation.

The bald Jupiter, Ζευς φαλακρος, of the Argives, mentioned by Clemens (Cohort. s. ii.) seems to have signified the same.

[3] Hymn. xlviii., and Fragm. No. xliii.

[4] Τεχθηναι δε ὑπο της Δημητρος (εκ του Ποσειδωνος) οἱ Φιγαλεις φασιν ουκ ἱππον, αλλα την Δεσποιναν ονομαζομενην ὑπο Αρκαδων.——Pausan. Arcad. c. xlii. s. 2.

Το τε σπηλαιον νομισαι τουτο ἱερον Δημητρος, και ες αυτο αγαλμα αναθειναι ξυλου. πεποιησθαι δε οὑτω σφισι το αγαλμα· καθεζεσθαι μεν επι πετρᾳ, γυναικι δε εοικεναι τα αλλα πλην κεφαλην· κεφαλην δε και κομην ειχεν ἱππου, και δρακοντων τε και αλλων θηριων εικονες προσεπεφυκεσαν τῃ κεφαλῃ· χιτων δε ενδεδυτο και ακρους τους ποδας· δελφις δε επι της χειρος ην αυτῃ, περιστερα δε ἡ ορνις επι τῃ ἑτερᾳ. Pausan. Arcad. c. xlii. s. S.

[5] Της δε Δεσποινης το ονυμα εδεισα ες του ατελεστους γραφων. Pausan. in Arcad. c. xxxvii. s. 6.

[5] Near the Academia in Attica was βωμος Ποσειδωνος 'Ιππιου και Αθηνας 'Ιππιας. Pausan. in Attic. c. xxx. s. 4.

Ποσειδωνος 'Ιππιου και 'Ηρως εισιν 'Ιππιας βωμοι——τῃ Αρεως 'Ιππιου, τῃ δε Αθηνας 'Ιππιας βωμος. Pausan. Eliac. 1. c. xv. s. 4.

Και Αθηνας βωμος εστι 'Υγιειας· τηνδ' 'Ιππιαν Αθηναν ονομαζουσι, και Διονυσον Μελ-πομενον. και Κισσον τον αυτον θεον. Pausan. in Attic. c. xxxi. s. 3.

even to living sovereigns, whom flattery had decked out with divine attributes ; as appears in the instance of Arsinoë the wife of Ptolemy Philadelphus, who was honored with it.[1] One of the most solemn forms of adjuration in use among the ancient inhabitants of Sweden and Norway was by the shoulder of the horse ; [2] and when Tyndarus engaged the suitors of Helen to defend and avenge her, he is said to have made them swear upon the testicles of the same animal.[3]

114. In an ancient piece of marble sculpture in relief, Jupiter is represented reposing upon the back of a Centaur, who carries a deer in his hand ; by which singular composition is signified, not Jupiter going to hunt, as antiquaries have supposed ; [4] but the all-pervading Spirit, or supreme active principle incumbent upon the waters, and producing fertility; or whatever property or modification of properties the deer was meant to signify. Diana, of whom it was a symbol, was in the original planetary and elementary worship, the Moon ; but in the mystic religion, she appears to have been a personification of the all-pervading Spirit acting through the Moon upon the Earth and the waters. Hence she comprehended almost every other female personification, and has innumerable titles and symbols expressive of almost every attribute, whether of creation, preservation, or destruction ; as appears from the Pantheic figures of her ; such as she was worshipped in the celebrated temple of Ephesus, of which many are extant. Among the principal of these symbols is the deer, which also appears among the accessary symbols of Bacchus ; and which is sometimes blended into one figure with the goat, so as to form a composite fictitious animal called a Tragelephus ; of which there are several examples now extant.[5] The very ancient colossal statue of

---

[1] Hesych. in v. Ἱππια.

[2] Mallet. Introd. à l'Hist. de Danemarc.

[3] Pausan. lib. iii. c. xx.

[4] Winkelman Monument. Antic. ined. No. ii.

[5] Τραγελαφων προτομαι εκτυπεις were among the ornaments of the magnificent hearse, in which the body of Alexander the Great was conveyed from Babylon to Alexandria (Diodor. Sic. l. xxviii. c. 20.); where it was deposited

the androgynous Apollo near Miletus, of which there is an engraving from an ancient copy in the Select Specimens, pl. xii. carried a deer in the right hand, and on a very early gold coin probably of Ephesus a male beardless head is represented with the horns of the same animal ;[1] whence we suspect that the metamorphose of Actæon, like many other similar fables, arose from some such symbolical composition.

115. It is probable therefore that the lion devouring the horse, represents the diurnal heat of the Sun exhaling the waters ; and devouring the deer, the same heat withering and putrefying the productions of the earth ; both of which, though immediately destructive, are preparatory to reproduction : for the same fervent rays which scorch and wither, clothe the earth with verdure, and mature all its fruits. As they dry up the waters in one season, so they return them in another, causing fermentation and putrefaction, which make one generation of plants and animals the means of producing another in regular and unceasing progression ; and thus constitute that varied yet uniform harmony in the succession of causes and effects, which is the principle of general order and economy in the operations of nature. The same meaning was signified by a composition more celebrated in poetry, though less frequent in art, of Hercules destroying a Centaur; who is sometimes distinguished, as in the ancient coins above cited, by the pointed goat's beard.

116. This universal harmony is represented, on the frieze of the temple of Apollo Didumæus near Miletus, by the lyre supported by two symbolical figures composed of the mixed forms and features of the goat and the lion, each of which rests one of its fore feet upon it.[2] The poets expressed the same meaning in their allegorical tales of the loves of Mars and Venus; from

in a shrine or coffin of solid gold; which having been melted down and carried away during the troubles by which Ptolemy XI. was expelled, a glass one was substituted and exhibited in its place in the time of Strabo. See Geogr. l. xvii.

[1] In the cabinet of Mr. Payne Knight.

[2] See Ionian Antiquities published by the Society of Dilettanti. vol. i. c. iii. pl. ix.

whioh sprang the goddess Harmony,[1] represented by the lyre; which, according to the Egyptians, was strung by Mercury with the sinews of Typhon.[3]

117. The fable of Ceres and Proserpine is the same allegory inverted : for Proserpine or Περσεφονεια, who, as her name indi‑ cates, was the goddess of Destruction, is fabled to have sprung from Jupiter and Ceres, the most general personifications of the creative powers. Hence she is called κορη, *the daughter;* as being the universal daughter, or general secondary principle : for though properly the goddess of Destruction, she is frequently dis‑ tinguished by the title *ΣΩΤΕΙΡΑ,*[4] *Saviour;* and represented with ears of corn upon her head, as the goddess of Fertility. She was, in reality, the personification of the heat or fire supposed to pervade the earth, which was held to be at once the cause and effect of fertility and destruction, as being at once the cause and effect of fermentation ; from which both proceed.[5] The mystic concealment of her operation was expressed by the black veil or bandage upon her head;[6] which was sometimes dotted with

---

[1] Εκ δ' Αφροδιτης και Αρεως 'Αρμονιαν γεγονεναι μυθολογουνται. Plutarch. de Is. et Osir. p. 370.

——— Αρεα τε τον μαλερον
ὃς νυν αχαλκος ασπιδων
φλεγει με περιβοητος αντιαζων. Sophocl. Œd. Tyr. v. 190.

This unarmed Mars is the plague: wherefore that god must have been considered as the Destroyer in general, not as the god of War in particular. —σκοπει δε τον Αρη καθαπερ εν πινακι χαλκῳ την αντικειμενην εκ διαμετρου τῳ Ερωτι χωραν εχοντα. Plutarch. Amator. p. 757.

[2] 'Ην ἁρμοζεται Ζηνος ευειδης Απολλων,
πασαν αρχην και τελος συλλαβων,
εχει δε λαμπρον πληκτρον, ἡλιου φαος.
Scythin. apud Plutarch. de Pyth. Orac.

[3] Και τον 'Ερμην μυθολογουσιν, εξελοντα του Τυφωνος τα νευρα, χορδαις χρησασθαι· διδασκοντες ὡς το παν ὁ λογος διαρμασαμενος, συμφωνον εξ ασυμφωνων μερων εποιησε, και την φθαρτικην ουκ απωλεσεν αλλ' ανεπληρωσε δυναμιν. Plutarch. de Is. et Osir. p. 373.

[4] See coins of Agathocles, &c.

[5] Ζωη και θανατος μουνη θνητοις πολυμοχθοις
Περσεφονεια· φερεις γαρ αει, και παντα φονευεις. Orph. Hymn. xxix.

[6] ——————— και τα κελαινα
ορνυμεν αρρητου δειλια Φερσεφονης.
Meleagr. Epigr. cxix. in Brunck. Anal.

asterisks; whilst the hair, which it enveloped, was made to imitate flames.[1]

118. The Nephthè or Nephthus of the Egyptians, and the Libitina, or goddess of Death of the Romans, were the same personage : and yet, with both these peoples, she was the same as Venus and Libera, the goddess of Generation.[2] Isis was also the same, except that, by the later Ægyptians, the personification was still more generalised, so as to comprehend universal nature; whence Apuleius invokes her by the names of Eleusinian Ceres, Celestial Venus, and Proserpine; and she answers him by a general explanation of these titles. " I am," says she, " Nature, the parent of things, the sovereign of the elements, the primary progeny of time, the most exalted of the deities, the first of the heavenly gods and goddesses, the queen of the shades, the uniform countenance; who dispose with my nod the luminous heights of heaven, the salubrious breezes of the sea, and the mournful silence of the dead; whose single deity the whole world venerates in many forms, with various rites, and many names. The Ægyptians skilled in ancient lore worship me with proper ceremonies; and call me by my true name, Queen Isis."

119. This universal character of the goddess appears, however, to have been subsequent to the Macedonian conquest; when a new modification of the ancient systems of religion and philosophy

---

[1] See silver coins of Syracuse, &c.

[2] Plutarch in Numa.

Νεφθην, ην και Τελευτην και Αφροδιτην, ενιοι δε και Νικην ονομαζουσιν.
Plutarch. de Is. et Osir.
Liberam, quam eandem Proserpinam vocant. Cic. in Verr. A. ii. l. iv. s. xlvii.

[3] Metam. lib. xi. p. 257. " En adsum, tuis commota, Luci, precibus, rerum natura parens, elementorum omnium domina, sæculorum progenies initialis, summa numinum, regina manium, prima cœlitum, deorum, dearumque, facies uniformis: quæ cœli luminosa culmina, maris salubria flamina, inferorum deplorata silentia nutibus meis dispenso, cujus numen unicum, multiformi specie, ritu vario, nomine multijugo totus veneratur orbis.——— priscâ doctrinâ pollentes Ægyptii, cerimoniis me prorsus propriis percolentes, appellant vero nomine reginam Isidem."

took place at Alexandria, and spread itself gradually over the
world. The statues of this Isis are of a composition and form
quite different from those of the ancient Ægyptian goddess; and
all that we have seen are of Greek or Roman sculpture. The
original Ægyptian figure of Isis is merely the animal symbol
of the cow humanised, with the addition of the serpent, disc, or
some other accessary emblem : but the Greek and Roman figures
of her are infinitely varied, to signify by various symbols the various
attributes of universal Nature.[1] In this character she is confounded with the personifications of Fortune and Victory, which
are in reality no other than those of Providence, and therefore
occasionally decked with all the attributes of universal Power.[2]
The figures of Victory have frequently the antenna or sail-yard of a
ship in one hand, and the chaplet or crown of immortality in the
other;[3] and those of Fortune, the rudder of a ship in one hand, and
the cornucopiæ in the other, with the modius or polos on her head;[4]
which ornaments Bupalus of Chios is said to have first given her
in a statue made for the Smyrnæans about the sixtieth Olympiad;[5]
but both have occasionally Isiac and other symbols.[6]

---

[1] See plate lxx. of vol. 1. The Ægyptian figures with the horns of the
cow, wrought under the Roman empire, are common in all collections of
small bronzes.

[2] Ἅπαντα δ' ὅσα νοουμεν, ηγουν πραττομεν,
Τυχη 'στιν, ἡμεις δ' εσμεν επιγεγραμμενοι.
Τυχη κυβερνᾳ παντα· ταυτην και φρενας
Δει, και προνοιαν, την θεον, καλειν μονην,
Ει μη τις αλλως ονομασιν χαιρει κενοις.
Menandr. in Supp. Fragm. 1.

Εγω μεν ουν Πινδαρου τα τε αλλα πειθομαι τη ῳδη, και Μοιρων τε ειναι μιαν την
Τυχην, και ὑπερ τας αδελφας τι ισχυειν. Pausan. in Achaic. c. xxvi. s. 3.

[3] See medals, in gold, of Alexander the Great, &c.

[4] Bronzi d' Ercolano. tom. ii. tav. xxviii.

[5] Πρωτος δε, ὡν οιδα, εποιησατο εν τοις επεσιν 'Ομηρος Τυχης μνημην' εποιησατο δε εν
ὑμνῳ τῳ ες την Δημητρα. (Vide v. 417. et seq.)——και Τυχην ὡς Ωκεανου και ταυτην
παιδα ουσαν (i. e. Νυμφην Ωκεανιτιδα.)——περα δε εδηλωσεν ουδεν ετι, ὡς ἡ θεος εστιν
αὑτη μεγιστη θεων εν τοις ανθρωπινοις πραγμασι, και ισχυν παρεχει πλειστην.——Βου-
παλος δε—Σμυρναιους αγαλμα εργαζομενος Τυχην πρωτος εποιησεν, ὡν ισμεν, πολον τε
εχουσαν επι τη κεφαλη, και τη ετερᾳ χειρι το καλουμενον Αμαλθειας κερας ὑπο Ἑλληνων.——ῃσε δε και ὑστερον Πινδαρος αλλα τε ες την Τυχην, και δη και Φερεπολιν ανε-
καλεσεν αυτην. Pausan. in Messen. c. xxx. s. 3 et 4. Pindar. in Fragm.

Bronzi d' Ercolano. tom. ii. tav. xxvi. Medals of Leucadia.

120. The allegorical tales of the loves and misfortunes of Isis and Osiris are an exact counterpart of those of Venus and Adonis;[1] which signify the alternate exertion of the generative and destructive attributes. Adonis or Adonai was an oriental title of the Sun, signifying Lord ; and the boar, supposed to have killed him, was the emblem of Winter ;[2] during which the productive powers of nature being suspended, Venus was said to lament the loss of Adonis until he was again restored to life : whence both the Syrian and Argive women annually mourned his death, and celebrated his resurrection ;[3] and the mysteries of Venus and Adonis at Byblus in Syria were held in similar estimation with those of Ceres and Bacchus at Eleusis, and Isis and Osiris in Ægypt.[4] Adonis was said to pass six months with Proserpine, and six with Venus ;[5] whence, some learned persons have conjectured that the allegory was invented near the pole : where the sun disappears during so long a time :[6] but it may signify merely the decrease and increase of the productive powers of nature as the sun retires and advances. The Vistnoo or Jaggernaut of the Hindoos is equally said to lie in a dormant state during the four rainy months of that climate:[8] and the Osiris of the Ægyptians was supposed to be dead or absent forty days in each year, during which the people lamented his loss, as the Syrians did that of Adonis,[9] and the Scandinavians that of

---

[1] Οσιριν οντα και Αδωνιν ὁμου κατα μυστικην θεοκρασιαν. Suidas in voce διαγνω-μων.

[2] Hesych. in v. Macrob. Sat. i. c. xx. τον δε Αδωνιν ουχ᾽ έτερον, αλλα Διονυσον ειναι νομιζουσιν. Plutarch. Sympos. lib. iv. qu. v.

[3] Lucian. de Dea Syria. Pausan. Corinth. c. xx. s. 5.

[4] Lucian. ib. s. 6.

[5] Λεγουσι δε περι του Αδωνιδος, ὁτι και αποθανων, ἐξ μηνας εποιησεν εν αγκαλαις Αφροδιτης, ὡσπερ και εν ταις αγκαλαις της Περσεφονης. Schol. in Theocrit. Idyll. 111.

[6] Ol. Rudbeck. Atlantic. No. ii. c. iii. p. 34. Baillie Hist. de l'Astronomie Ancienne.

[7] Φρυγες δε τον θεον οιομενοι χειμωνος καθευδειν, θερους δ᾽ εγρηγορεναι, τοτε μεν κατευνασμους, τοτε δ᾽ ανεγερσεις, βακχευοντες αυτῳ τελουσι. Παφλαγονες δε κατα-δεισθαι, και κατειγνυσθαι χειμωνος, ηρος δε κινεισθαι και αναλυεσθαι, φασκουσι. Plutarch. de Is. et Osir. Ut lacrymare cultrices Veneris sæpe spectantur in sollemnibus Adonidis sacris, quod simulacrum aliquod esse frugum adultarum religiones mysticæ docent. Am. Marcellin. lib. xix. c. 1.

[8] Holwell, Part ii. p. 125.

[9] Theophil. ad Autolyc. lib. i. p. 75.

Frey : though at Upsal, the great metropolis of their worship, the sun never continues any one day entirely below the horizon.[1] The story of the Phœnix ; or, as that fabulous bird was called in the north, of the Fanina, appears to have been an allegory of the same kind, as was also the Phrygian tale concerning Cybelè and Attis ; though variously distinguished by the fictions of poets and mythographers.[2]

121. On some of the very ancient Greek coins of Acanthus in Macedonia we find a lion killing a boar ;[3] and in other monuments a dead boar appears carried in solemn procession ;[4] by both which was probably meant the triumph of Adonis in the destruction of his enemy at the return of spring. A young pig was also the victim offered preparatory to initiation into the Eleusinian mysteries,[5] which seems to have been intended to express a similar compliment to the Sun. The Phrygian Attis, like the Syrian Adonis, was fabled to have been killed by a boar ; or, according to another tradition, by Mars in the shape of that animal ;[6] and his death and resurrection were annually celebrated in the same manner.[7] The beauty of his person, and the style of his dress, caused his statues to be confounded with those of Paris, who appears also to have been canonised ; and it is probable that a symbolical composition representing him in the act of fructifying nature, attended by Power and Wisdom, gave rise to the story of the Trojan prince's adjudging the prize of beauty between the three contending goddesses ; a story, which appears to have been wholly unknown to the ancient poets, who have celebrated the events of the war supposed to have arisen from it. The fable of Ganymede, the cup-bearer of Jupiter, seems to have arisen from some symboli-

---

[1] Ol. Rudbeck. Atlantic. p. ii. c. v. p. 153.

[2] See Ol. Rudbeck, p. ii. c. iii. et v.   Nonni Dionys. M. 396.

[3] Pelerin. vol. i. pl. xxx. No. 17.

[4] On a marble fragment in relief in the Townley collection.

[5] Aristoph. Ειρην 374.

[6] ————·———επει συος εικονι μορφης
   Αρης καρχαροδων θανατηφορον ιον ιαλλων
   Ζηλομανης ημελλεν Αδωνιδι ποτμον υφαινειν.   Nonni Dionys.

[7] Strabo. lib. x. p. 323.   Julian. Orat. v. p. 316.

cal composition of the same kind, at first misunderstood, and afterwards misrepresented in poetical fiction: for the lines in the Iliad alluding to it, are, as before observed, spurious; and according to Pindar, the most orthodox perhaps of all the poets, Ganymede was not the son of Laomedon, but a mighty genius or deity who regulated or caused the overflowings of the Nile by the motion of his feet.' His being, therefore, the cup-bearer of Jupiter means no more than that he was the distributor of the waters between heaven and earth, and consequently a distinct personification of that attribute of the supreme God, which is otherwise signified by the epithet Pluvius. Hence he is only another modification of the same personification, as Attis, Adonis, and Bacchus; who are all occasionally represented holding the cup or patera; which is also given, with the cornucopiæ, to their subordinate emanations, the local genii; of which many small figures in brass are extant.

122. In the poetical tales of the ancient Scandinavians, Frey, the deity of the Sun, was fabled to have been killed by a boar; which was therefore annually offered to him at the great feast of Juul, celebrated during the winter solstice.² Boars of paste were also served on their tables during that feast; which, being kept till the following spring, were then beaten to pieces and mixed with the seeds to be sown, and with the food of the cattle and hinds employed in tilling the ground.³ Among the Ægyptians likewise, those who could not afford to sacrifice real pigs, had images of them in paste served up at the feasts of Bacchus or Osiris; which seem, like the feasts of Adonis in Syria, and the Juul in Sweden, to have been expiatory solemnities meant to honor and conciliate the productive power of the Sun by the symbolical destruction of the adverse or inert power. From an ancient fragment preserved by Plutarch, it seems that Mars, considered as the

---

¹ Τον Γανυμηδην γαρ αυτον εφασαν οἱ περι Πινδαρον ἑκατοντοργυιον ανδριαντα, αφ' οὑ της κινησεως των ποδων τον Νειλον πλημμυρειν. Schol. in Arat. Phænom, v. 282.

² Ol. Rudbeck. part i. c. v. viii. and s. part ii. c. v.

³ Ibid and fig. i. p. 229.

⁴ Herodot. ii. 47. Macrob. Sat. i. c. xx. Of the same kind are the small votive boars in brass; of which several have been found: and one of extreme beauty is in the cabinet of Mr. Payne Knight.

destroyer, was represented by a boar among the Greeks;[1] and on coins we find him wearing the boar's, as Hercules wears the lion's skin;[2] in both of which instances the old animal symbol is humanised, as almost all the animal symbols gradually were by the refinement of Grecian art.

123. From this symbolical use of the boar to represent the destroying, or rather the anti-generative attribute, probably arose the abhorrence of swine's flesh; which prevailed universally among the Ægyptians and Jews; and partially in other countries, particularly in Pontus; where the temple of Venus at Comana was kept so strictly pure from the pollution of such enemies, that a pig was never admitted into the city.[3] The Ægyptians are said also to have signified the inert power of Typhon by an ass;[4] but among the ancient inhabitants of Italy, and probably among the Greeks, this animal appears to have been a symbol of an opposite kind;[5] and is therefore perpetually found in the retinue of Bacchus: the dismemberment of whom by the Titans, was an allegory of the same kind as the death of Adonis and Attis by the boar, and the dismemberment of Osiris by Typhon:[6] whence his festivals were in the spring;[7] and at Athens, as well as in Ægypt, Syria, and Phrygia, the ΑΦΑ-ΝΙΣΜΟΣ και ΕΤΡΕΣΙΣ, or *death* and *resurrection*, were celebrated, the one with lamentation, and the other with rejoicing.[8]

---

[1] Τυφλος γαρ, ω γυναικες, ουδ᾽ ὁρων Αρης
Συος προσωπω παντα τυρβαζει κακα.   Amator. p. 757.

[2] See brass coins of Rome, common in all collections.

[3] Strabo, lib. xii. p. 575.   [4] Ælian. de Anim. lib. x. c. xxviii.

[5] Juvenal. Sat. xi. 96.   Colum. x. 344.

[6] Τα γαρ δη περι τον Διονυσον μεμενθυμενα παθη του διαμελισμου, και τα Τιτανων επ᾽ αυτον τολμηματα, γευσαμενων τε του φονου κολασεις (τε τουτων delend.) και κεραυνο-σεις, ηνιγμενος εστι μυθος εις την παλιγγενεσιαν.   Plutarch. de Carn. Orat. i.

Ουκ απο τροπου μυθολογουσι την Οσιριδος ψυχην αἴδιον ειναι και αφθαρτον, το δε σωμα πολλακις διασπαν και αφανιζειν τον Τυφωνα.   Id. de Is. et Osir.

[7] ηρι τε επερχομενω Βρομιαχαρις.

[8] Demosth. περι Στεφ. p. 568.   Jul. Firmic. p. 14. ed. Ouz.

124. The stories of Prometheus were equally allegorical: for Prometheus was only a title of the Sun expressing providence,[1] or foresight: wherefore his being bound in the extremities of the earth, signified originally no more than the restriction of the power of the sun during the winter months; though it has been variously embellished and corrupted by the poets; partly, perhaps, from symbolical compositions ill understood: for the vulture might have been naturally employed as an emblem of the destroying power. Another emblem of this power, much distinguished in the ancient Scandinavian mythology, was the wolf; who in the last day was expected to devour the sun:[2] and among the symbolical ornaments of a ruined mystic temple at Puzzuoli, we find a wolf devouring grapes; which, being the fruit peculiarly consecrated to Bacchus, are not unfrequently employed to signify that god. Lycopolis in Ægypt[1] takes its name from the sacred wolf kept there;[3] and upon the coins of Cartha in the island of Ceos, the fore part of this animal appears surrounded with diverging rays, as the centre of an asterisk.[4]

125. As putrefaction was the most general means of natural destruction or dissolution, the same spirit of superstition, which turned every other operation of nature into an object of devotion, consecrated it to the personification of the destroying power: whence, in the mysteries and other sacred rites belonging to the generative attributes, every thing putrid, or that had a tendency to putridity, was carefully avoided; and so strict were the Ægyptian priests upon this point, that they wore no garments made of any animal substance ; but circumcised themselves, and shaved their whole bodies even to their eye-brows, lest they should unknowingly harbour any filth, excrement, or vermin supposed to be bred from putrefaction.[5] The common fly being, in its first stage of exist-

---

[1] Pindar. Olymp. Z. 81.

[2] Lupus devorabit
Seculorum patrem.   Edda Sæmondi. liii.
See also Mallet Introd. à l'Hist. de Danemarc. c. vi.

[3] Macrob. Sat. 1. c. xvii.   [4] The wolf is also the device on those of Argos.

[5] Εσθητα δε φορεουσι οἱ ἱερεες λινεην μουνην, και ὑποδηματα βυβλινα. Herodot. lib. ii. s. 37.   Τα τε αιδοια περιταμνονται καθαριοτητος εἱνεκεν. Ibid.

G

ence, a principal agent in dissolving and dissipating all putrescent bodies, it was adopted as an emblem of the Deity to represent the destroying attribute: whence the Baal-Zebub, or Jupiter Fly of the Phœnicians, when admitted into the creed of the Jews, received the rank and office of prince of the devils. The symbol was humanised at an early period, probably by the Phœnicians themselves; and thus formed into one of those fantastic compositions, which ignorant antiquaries have taken for wild efforts of disordered imagination, instead of regular productions of systematic art.[1]

126. Bacchus frequently appears accompanied by leopards;[2] which in some instances are employed in devouring clusters of grapes, and in others drinking the liquor pressed from them; though they are in reality incapable of feeding upon that or any other kind of fruit. On a very ancient coin of Acanthus, too, the leopard is represented, instead of the lion, destroying the bull:[3] wherefore we have no doubt that in the Bacchic processions, it means the destroyer accompanying the generator; and contributing, by different means, to the same end. In some instances his chariot is drawn by two leopards, and in others by a leopard and a goat coupled together:[4] which are all different means of signifying different modes and combinations of the same ideas. In the British Museum is a group in marble of three figures, the middle one a human form growing out of a vine, with leaves and clusters of grapes growing out of its body. On one side is an androgynous figure representing the Mises or Bacchus διφυης; and on the other a leopard, with a garland of ivy round its neck, leaping up and devouring the grapes, which spring from the body of the personified vine; the hands of

---

Οἱ δε ἱερεες ξυρευνται παν το σωμα δια τριτης ἡμερης, ἱνα μητε φθειρ, μητε αλλο μυσαρον εγγιγνηται σφι θεραπευουσι τους θεους. Ibid.

[1] See Winkelman Mon. ant. ined. No. 13; and Hist. des Arts, Liv. iii. c. ii. p. 143.

[2] These are frequently called tigers: but the first tiger seen by the Greeks or Romans was presented by the ambassadors of India to Augustus, while settling the affairs of Asia, in the year of Rome 734. Dion. Cass. Hist. lib. liv. s. 9.

[3] In the cabinet of Mr. Knight.

[4] See medal of Maronea. Gesner. tab. xliii. fig. 26.

which are employed in receiving another cluster from the Bacchus. This composition represents the vine between the creating and destroying attributes of the Deity; the one giving it fruit, and the other devouring it when given. The poets conveyed the same meaning in the allegorical tales of the Loves of Bacchus and Ampelus; who, as the name indicates, was only the vine personified.

127. The Chimera, of which so many whimsical interpretations have been given by the commentators on the Iliad, seems to have been an emblematical composition of the same class, veiled, as usual, under historical fable to conceal its meaning from the vulgar. It was composed of the forms of the goat, the lion, and the serpent; the symbols of the generator, destroyer, and preserver united and animated by fire, the essential principle of all the three. The old poet had probably seen such a figure in Asia; but knowing nothing of mystic lore, which does not appear to have reached Greece or her colonies in his time, received whatever was told him concerning it. In later times, however, it must have been a well-known sacred symbol; or it would not have been employed as a device upon coins.

128. The fable of Apollo destroying the serpent Python, seems equally to have originated from the symbolical language of imitative art; the title Apollo signifying, according to the etymology already given, the destroyer as well as the deliverer: for, as the ancients supposed destruction to be merely dissolution, as creation was merely formation, the power which delivered the particles of matter from the bonds of attraction, and broke the δεσμον περιβριθη ερωτος, was in fact the destroyer. Hence the verb ΛΥΩ or ΛΥΜΙ, from which it is derived, means both to free and to destroy.[1] Pliny mentions a statue of Apollo by Praxiteles, much celebrated in his time, called ΣΑΥΡΟΚΤΟΝΟΣ,[2] the lizard-killer, of which several copies are now extant.[3] The lizard, being supposed to exist upon the dews and moisture of the earth, was employed as the symbol of humidity; so that the god destroying it, signifies the same as

---

[1] See Iliad A. 20, & I. 25.   [2] Lib. xxxiv. c. viii.

[3] See Winkelman Mon. ant. ined. pl. xl.

the lion devouring the horse, and Hercules killing the centaur; that is, the sun exhaling the waters. When destroying the serpent, he only signifies a different application of the same power to the extinction of life; whence he is called *ΠΤΘΙΟΣ*,[1] or the putrefier, from the verb *ΠΤΘΩ*. The title *ΣΜΙΝΘΕΤΣ* too, supposing it to mean, according to the generally received interpretation, mouse-killer, was expressive of another application of the same attribute: for the mouse was a priapic animal;[2] and is frequently employed as such in monuments of ancient art.[3] The statue, likewise, which Pausanias mentions of Apollo with his foot upon the head of a bull, is an emblem of similar meaning.[4]

129. The offensive weapons of this deity, which are the symbols of the means by which he exerted his characteristic attribute, are the bow and arrows, signifying the emission of his rays; of which the arrow or dart, the *βελος* or *οβελος*, was, as before observed, the appropriate emblem. Hence he is called *ΑΦΗΤΩΡ*, *ΕΚΑΤΟΣ* and *ΕΚΑΤΗΒΟΛΟΣ*; and also, *ΧΡΤΣΑΩΡ* and *ΧΡΤ- ΣΑΟΡΟΣ*; which have a similar signification; the first syllable expressing the golden colour of rays, and the others their erect position: for *αορ* does not signify merely a sword, as a certain writer, upon the authority of common Latin versions and school Lexicons, has supposed; but any thing that is held up; it being the substantive of the verb *αειρω*.

130. Hercules destroying the hydra, signifies exactly the same as Apollo destroying the serpent and the lizard;[5] the water-snake

---

[1] Πυθιος απο του πυθειν, id est σηπειν. Macrob. Sat. 1. c. xvii.

[2] Ælian. Hist. Anim. lib. xii. c. 10.

[3] It was the device upon the coins of Argos, (Jul. Poll. onom. ix. vi. 86.) probably before the adoption of the wolf, which is on most of those now extant. A small one, however, in gold, with the mouse, is in the cabinet of Mr. P. Knight.

[4] Και Απολλων χαλκους γυμνος εσθητος· ——— και ετερω ποδι επι κρανιου βεβηκε βοος. Pausan. Achaic. c. xx. s. 2.

[5] Τῳ μεν 'Ηλιῳ τον 'Ηρακλεα μυθολογουσιν ενιδρυμενον συμπεριπολειν. Plutarch. de Is. et Osir.

comprehending both symbols; and the ancient Phœnician Hercules being merely the lion humanised. The knowledge of him
appears to have come into Europe by the way of Thrace; he having been worshipped in the island of Thasus, by the Phœnician colony settled there, five generations before the birth of the Theban
hero;[1] who was distinguished by the same title that he obtained in
Greece; and whose romantic adventures have been confounded
with the allegorical fables related of him. In the Homeric times,
he appears to have been utterly unknown to the Greeks, the Hercules of the Iliad and Odyssey being a mere man, pre-eminently
distinguished indeed for strength and valour, but exempt from
none of the laws of mortality.[2] His original symbolical arms,
with which he appears on the most ancient medals of Thasus, were
the same as those of Apollo;[3] and his Greek name, which, according to the most probable etymology, signifies the *glorifier of
the earth*, is peculiarly applicable to the Sun. The Romans held
him to be the same as Mars;[4] who was sometimes represented
under the same form, and considered as the same deity as Apollo;[5]
and in some instances we find him destroying the vine instead of the
serpent,[6] the deer, the centaur, or the bull; by all which the same
meaning, a little differently modified, is conveyed : but the more
common representation of him destroying the lion is not so easily
explained; and it is probable that the traditional history of the
deified hero has, in this instance as well as some others, been
blended with the allegorical fables of the personified attribute : for

[1] Herodot. lib. ii. c. 44.

[2] Iliad Ξ. 117. Odyss. Λ. 600. The three following lines, alluding to his
deification, have long been discovered to be interpolated.

[3] Strabo, lib. xv. p. 688. Athenæ, lib. xii. p. 512. The club was given
him by the Epic poets, who made the mixed fables of the Theban hero and
personified attribute the subjects of their poems.

[4] Varro apud Macrob. Sat. 1. c. xx.

[5] Εκ μεν Λητους ὁ Απολλων· εκ δε ‘Ηρας ὁ Αρης γεγονε· μια δε εστιν αμφοτερων ἡ
δυναμις. ———— ουκουν ἡ τε ‘Ηρα και ἡ Λητω δυο εισι μιας θεου προσηγοριαη Plutarch. apud Euseb. Præp. Evang. lib. iii. c. 1.

[6] Mus. Florent. in gemm. T. 1. pl. xcii. 9.

we have never seen any composition of this kind upon any monument of remote antiquity.[1]

131. Upon the pillars which existed in the time of Herodotus in different parts of Asia, and which were attributed by the Ægyptians to Sesostris, and by others to Memnon, was engraved the figure of a man holding a spear in his right hand and a bow in his left; to which was added, upon some of them, γυναικος αιδοια, said by the Ægyptians to have been meant as a memorial of the cowardice and effeminacy of the inhabitants, whom their monarch had subdued.[2] The whole composition was however, probably, symbolical; signifying the active power of destruction, and passive power of generation ; whose co-operation and conjunction are signified in so many various ways in the emblematical monuments of ancient art. The figure holding the spear and the bow is evidently the same as appears upon the ancient Persian coins called Darics, and upon those of some Asiatic cities, in the Persian dress ; but which, upon those of others, appears with the same arms, and in the same attitude, with the lion's skin upon its head.[3] This attitude is that of kneeling upon one knee ; which is that of the Phœnician Hercules upon the coins of Thasus above cited : wherefore we have no doubt that he was the personage meant to be represented ; as he continued to be afterwards upon the Bactrian and Parthian coins. The Hindoos have still a corresponding deity, whom they call Ram ; and the modern Persians a fabulous hero called Rustam, whose exploits are in many respects similar to those of Hercules, and to whom they attribute all the stupendous remains of ancient art found in their country.

---

[1] The earliest coins which we have seen with this device are of Syracuse, Tarentum, and Heraclea in Italy; all of the finest time of the art, and little anterior to the Macedonian conquest. On the more ancient medals of Selinus, Hercules is destroying the bull, as the lion or leopard is on those of Acanthus; and his destroying a centaur signifies exactly the same as a lion destroying a horse ; the symbols being merely humanised.

[2] Herodot. lib. ii. 102 and 106.

[3] See coins of Mallus in Cilicia, and Soli in Cyprus in the Hunter Collection.

132. It was observed, by the founders of the mystic system, that the destructive power of the Sun was exerted most by day, and the generative by night : for it was by day that it dried up the waters and produced disease and putrefaction; and by night that it returned the exhalations in dews tempered with the genial heat that had been transfused into the atmosphere. Hence, when they personified the attributes, they worshipped the one as the *diurnal* and the other as the *nocturnal* sun ; calling the one Apollo, and the other Dionysus or Bacchus ;[1] both of whom were anciently observed to be the same god ; whence, in a verse of Euripides, they are addressed as one, the names being used as epithets.[2] The oracle at Delphi was also supposed to belong to both equally ;[3] or, according to the expression of a Latin poet, to the united and mixed deity of both.[4]

133. This mixed deity appears to have been represented in the person of the Apollo Didymæus ; who was worshipped in another celebrated oracular temple near Miletus ; and whose symbolical image seems to be exhibited in plates xii. xliii. and iv. of volume I. of the Select Specimens ; and in different compositions on different

---

[1] In sacris enim hæc religiosi arcani observantia tenetur, ut Sol, cum in supero, id est in diurno Hemisphærio est, Apollo vocitetur; cum in infero, id est nocturno, Dionysus, qui et Liber pater habeatur. Macrob. Sat. i. c. 18. Hence Sophocles calls Bacchus

Πυρπνεοντων χορηγον αστερων. apud Eustath. p. 514.

and he had temples dedicated to him under correspondent titles. Εστι μεν Διονυσου ναος Νυκτελιου. Pausan. in Att. c. 40. s. 5. Ἱερον——Διονυσου Λαμπτηρος εστιν επικλησιν. Paus. Act. c. 27. s. 2. Hence too the corresponding deity among the Ægyptians was lord of the Inferi. Αρχηγετευειν δε των κατω Αιγυπτιοι λεγουσι Δημητρα και Διονυσον. Herodot. lib. ii. 123. Aristoteles, qui theologumena scripsit, Apollinem et Liberum patrem unum eundemque deum esse, cum multis argumentis, asserit. Macrob. Sat. i. c. 17.

[2] Δεσποτα φιλοδαφνε, Βακχε, Παιαν, Απολλον ευλυρε. Apud eund.

[3] ——Τον Διονυσον, ᾧ των Δελφων ουδεν ἡττον η τῳ Απολλωνι μετεστιν. Plutarch. ei apud Delph. p. 388.

[4] Mons Phœbo Bromioque sacer; cui numine mixto
Delphica Thebanæ referunt tricterica Bacchæ.
Lucan. Phars. v. 73.

coins of the Macedonian kings; sometimes sitting on the prow of a ship, as lord of the waters, or Bacchus Hyes;[1] sometimes on the cortina, the veiled cone or egg; and sometimes leaning upon a tripod; but always in an androgynous form, with the limbs, tresses, and features of a woman; and holding the bow or arrow, or both, in his hands.[2] The double attribute, though not the double sex, is also frequently signified in figures of Hercules; either by the cup or cornucopiæ held in his hand, or by the chaplet of poplar or some other symbolical plant, worn upon his head; whilst the club or lion's skin indicates the adverse power.

134. In the refinement of art, the forms of the lion and goat were blended into one fictitious animal to represent the same meaning, instances of which occur upon the medals of Capua, Panticapæum, and Antiochus VI. king of Syria, as well as in the frieze of the temple of Apollo Didymæus before mentioned. In the former, too, the destroying attribute is further signified by the point of a spear held in the mouth of the monster; and the productive, by the ear of corn under its feet.[3] In the latter, the result of both is shown by the lyre, the symbol of universal harmony, which is supported between them; and which is occasionally given to Hercules, as well as to Apollo. The two-faced figure of Janus seems to have been a composite symbol of the same kind, and to have derived the name from Ιαο or Ιαων, an ancient mystic title of Bacchus. The earliest specimens of it extant are on the coins of Lampsacus and Tenedos, some of which cannot be later than the sixth century before the Christian æra; and in later coins of the former city, heads of Bacchus of the usual form and character occupy its place.

---

[1] ('Ελληνες) και τον Διονυσον, 'Υην, ὡς κυριον της ὑγρας φυσεως, ουχ' ἑτερον οντα του Οσιριδος (καλουσι). Plutarch. de Is. et Osir.

[2] See medals of Antigonus, Antiochus I., Seleucus II. and III., and other kings of Syria; and also of Magnesia ad Mæandrum, and ad Sipylum.

The beautiful figure engraved on plates xliii. and iv. of vol. i. of the Select Specimens is the most exquisite example of this androgynous Apollo.

[3] Numm. Pembrok. tab. v. fig. 12.

135. The mythological personages Castor and Pollux, who lived and died alternately, were the same as Bacchus and Apollo: whence they were pre-eminently distinguished by the title of the *great gods* in some places ; though, in others, confounded with the canonised or deified mortals, the brothers of Helen.' Their fabulous birth from the egg, the form of which is retained in the caps usually worn by them, is a remnant of the ancient mystic allegory, upon which the more recent poetical tales have been engrafted; whilst the two asterisks, and the two human heads, one going upwards and the other downwards, by which they are occasionally represented, more distinctly point out their symbolical meaning,ª which was the alternate appearance of the sun in the upper and lower hemispheres. This meaning, being a part of what was revealed in the mysteries, is probably the reason why Apuleius mentions the *seeing the sun at midnight* among the circumstances of initiation, which he has obscurely and ænigmatically related.³

136. As the appearance of the one necessarily implied the cessation of the other, the tomb of Bacchus was shown at Delos near to the statue of Apollo ; and one of these mystic tombs, in the form of a large chest of porphyry, adorned with goats, leopards, and other symbolical figures, is still extant in a church at Rome. The mystic cistæ, which were carried in procession occasionally ; and in which some emblem of the generative or preserving atrribute was generally kept, appear to have been merely models or portable representations of these tombs, and to have had exactly the same signification. By the mythologists, Bacchus is said to have terminated his expedition in the extremities of the East ; and Hercules, in the extremities of the West ; which means no more than that the nocturnal sun finishes its progress, when it mounts above the surrounding ocean in the East ; and the diurnal,

---

¹ Pausan. lib. i. p. 77. ; and lib. iii. p. 242. They were also called ANAKEΣ or Kings, and more commonly ΔIOΣKOΥPOI or Sons of Jupiter, as being pre-eminently such. To των Διοσκουρων ἱερον Ανακειον εκαλειτο· Ανακες γαρ αυτοι παρ' Ελληνων εκαλουντο. Schol. in Lucian. Timon.

ª See medals of Istrus, which are very common.

³ Metamorph. lib. xi.

when it passes the same boundary of the two hemispheres in the West.

137. The latter's being represented by the lion, explains the reason why the spouts of fountains were always made to imitate lions' heads; which Plutarch supposes to have been, because the Nile overflowed when the sun was in the sign of the Lion:[1] but the same fashion prevails as universally in Tibet as ever it did in Ægypt, Greece, or Italy; though neither the Grand Lama nor any of his subjects know any thing of the Nile or its overflowings; and the signs of the zodiac were taken from the mystic symbols; and not, as some learned authors have supposed, the mystic symbols from the signs of the zodiac. The emblematical meaning, which certain animals were employed to signify, was only some particular property generalised; and, therefore, might easily be invented or discovered by the natural operation of the mind : but the collections of stars, named after certain animals, have no resemblance whatever to those animals ; which are therefore merely signs of convention adopted to distinguish certain portions of the heavens, which were probably consecrated to those particular personified attributes, which they respectively represented. That they had only begun to be so named in the time of Homer, and that not on account of any real or supposed resemblance, we have the testimony of a passage in the description of the shield of Achilles, in which the polar constellation is said to be called *the Bear or otherwise the Waggon ;*[2] objects so different that it is impossible that one and the same thing should be even imagined to resemble both. We may therefore rank Plutarch's explanation with other tales of the later Ægyptian priests ; and conclude that the real intention of these symbols was to signify that the water, which they conveyed, was the gift of the diurnal sun, because separated from the salt of the sea, and distri-

---

[1] Κρηναι δε και καταχασματα των λεοντων εξιασι κρουνους, ὅτι Νειλος επαγει νεον ὕδωρ ταις Αιγυπτιων αρουραις, ἡλιου τον λεοντα παροδευοντος. Symposiac. lib. iv. p. 670.

[2] Il. ℥. 487.

buted over the earth by exhalation. Perhaps Hercules being crowned with the foliage of the white poplar, an aquatic tree, may have had a similar meaning : which is at least more probable than that assigned by Servius and Macrobius.[1]

138. Humidity in general, and particularly the Nile, was called by the Ægyptians the *defluxion of Osiris*;[2] who was with them the God of the Waters, in the same sense as Bacchus was among the Greeks :[3] whence all rivers, when personified, were represented under the form of the bull ; or at least with some of the characteristic features of that animal.[4] In the religion of the Hindoos this article of ancient faith, like most others, is still retained ; as appears from the title, *Daughter of the Sun*, given to the sacred river Yamuna.[5] The God of Destruction is also mounted on a white bull, the sacred symbol of the opposite attribute, to show the union and co-operation of both.[6] The same meaning is more distinctly represented in an ancient Greek fragment of bronze, by a lion trampling upon the head of a bull, while a double phallus appears behind them, and shows the result.[7] The title *ΣΩΤΗΡ ΚΟΣΜΟΥ* upon the composite priapic figure published by La Chausse is well known ;[8] and it is probable that the ithyphallic ceremonies, which the gross flattery of the dege-

---

[1] In Æn. viii. 276. Saturn. lib. iii. c. 12.

[2] Ου μονον τον Νειλον, αλλα παν ὑγρον ἁπλως Οσιριδος απορροην καλοισιν (οἱ Αιγυπτιοι). Plutarch. de Is. et Osir.

[3] Οἱ δε σοφωτεροι των ἱερεων, ου μονον τον Νειλον Οσιριν καλουσιν, ουδε Τυφωνα την θαλασσαν· αλλα Οσιριν μεν ἁπλως ἁπασαν την ὑγροποιον αρχην και δυναμιν, αιτιαν γενεσεως και σπερματος ουσιαν νομιζοντες. Τυφωνα δε παν το αυχμηρον και πυρωδες και ξηραντικον, ὁλως και πολεμιον τῃ ὑγροτητι. Ibid. p. 363.
——Ου μονον δε του οινου Διονυσον, αλλα και πασης ὑγρας φυσεως ῾Ελληνες ἡγουνται κυριον και αρχηγον. Ibid. p. 364.

[4] Horat. lib. iv. od. xiv. 25. et Schol. Vet. in loc. Rivers appear thus personified on the coins of many Greek cities of Sicily and Italy.

[5] Sir W. Jones in the Asiatic Researches, vol. i. p. 29.

[6] Maurice's Indian Antiquities, vol. i. pt. 1. p. 261.

[7] On a handle of a vase in the cabinet of Mr. Knight.

[8] Mus. Rom. s. vii. pl. 1. vol. ii.

nerate Greeks sometimes employed to honor the Macedoman princes,[1] had the same meaning as this title of *Saviour*, which was frequently conferred upon, or assumed by them.[2] It was also occasionally applied to most of the deities who had double attributes, or were personifications of both powers; as to Hercules, Bacchus, Diana, &c.[3]

139. Diana was, as before observed, originally and properly the Moon; by means of which the Sun was supposed to impregnate the air, and scatter the principles of generation both active and passive over the earth : whence, like the Bacchus διφυης and Apollo διδυμαιος, she was both male and female,[4] both heat and humidity ; for the warmth of the Moon was supposed to be moistening, as that of the Sun was drying.[5] She was called the Mother of the World;[6] and the Daughter, as well as the Sister of the Sun ;[7] because the productive powers with which she impregnated the former, together with the light by which she was illumined, were supposed to be derived from the latter. By attracting or heaving the waters

---

[1] Οἱ Αθηναιοι εδεχοντο (τον Δημητριον) ου μονον θυμιωντες, και στεφανουντες, και οινοχοουντες, αλλα και προσοδια και χοροι και ιθυφαλλοι μετ᾽ ορχησεως της φδης απην· των αυτφ. Athen. lib. vi. c. 15.

[2] Ibid. c. 16.

[3] Ετι δε Ἡλιος επωνυμιαν εχων Σωτηρ δε ειναι και Ἡρακλης. Pausan. in Arcad. c. xxxi. s. 4. See also coins of Thasus, Maronea, Agathocles, &c.

[4] Οὑτω την Οσιριδος δυναμιν εν τη Σεληνη τιθενται (lege τιθεμενοι) την Ισιν αυτφ γενεσιν ουσαν συνειναι λεγουσι. διο και μητερα την σεληνην του κοσμου καλουσι, και φυσιν εχειν αρσενοθηλυν οιονται, πληρουμενην ὑπο ἡλιου, και κυισκομενην, αυτην δε παλιν εις τον αερα προιεμενην γεννητικας αρχας, και κατασπειρουσαν. Plutarch. de Is. et Osir. p. 368.

[5] Calor solis arefacit, lunaris humectat.
Macrob. sat. vii. c. x.

Την μεν γαρ σεληνην γονιμον το φως και ὑγροποιον εχουσαν, ευμενη και γοναις ζωων, και φυτων ειναι βλαστησεσι. Plutarch. de Is. et Osir.

[6] Plutarch. in l. c.

[7] Ω λιπαροξωνου θυγατερ
Αελιου Σεληναια. Eurip. Phœn. 178.
Οὑτως Αισχυλος και οἱ φυσικωτεροι. Ἡσιοδος δε φησιν αδελφην ἡλιου ειναι την σεληνην. Schol. in loc.

of the ocean, she naturally appeared to be the sovereign of humidity; and by seeming to operate so powerfully upon the constitutions of women, she equally appeared to be the patroness and regulatress of nutrition and passive generation: whence she is said to have received her nymphs, or subordinate personifications, from the ocean ;[1] and is often represented by the symbol of the sea-crab ;[2] an animal that has the property of spontaneously detaching from its own body any limb, that has been hurt or mutilated, and re-producing another in its place. As the heat of the Sun animated the seminal particles of terrestrial matter, so was the humidity of the Moon supposed to nourish and mature them ;[3] and as her orbit was held to be the boundary that separated the celestial from the terrestrial world,[4] she was the mediatress between both ; the primary subject of the one, and sovereign of the other, who tempered the subtility of ætherial spirit to the grossness of earthly matter, so as to make them harmonise and unite.[5]

---

[1] Æschyl. Prometh. Vinct. 138. Callimach. Hymn. in Dian. 13. Catullus in Gell. 84.

[2] See coins of the Brettii in Italy, Himera in Sicily, &c.

[3] Duobus his reguntur omnia terrena, calore quidem solis per diem, humore vero lunæ per noctem.———Nam ut calore solis animantur semina, ita lunæ humore nutriuntur, penes ipsam enim et corporum omnium ratio esse dicitur et potestas. Schol. Vet. in Horat. Carm. Sec.

> Luna alit ostrea; et implet echinas, et muribus fibras,
> Et pecui addit.   Lucil. apud Aul. Gell. l. xx. c. 8.

[4] Ισθμος γαρ εστιν αθανασιας και γενεσεως ὁ περι την σεληνην δρομος. Ocell. Lucan. de Universo, p. 516. ed. Gale.

Απο γαρ της σεληνιακης σφαιρας, ἡν ἑσχατην μεν των κατ' ουρανον κυκλων, πρωτην δε των προς ἡμας, αναγραφουσιν οἱ φροντισται των μετεωρων, αχρι γης ἑσχατης ὁ αηρ παντη ταθεις εφθασεν. Philon. de Somn. vol. i. p. 641. Oper.

[5] 'Ηλιος δε καρδιας εχων δυναμιν, ὡσπερ αἱμα και πνευμα, διαπεμπει και διασκεδαγγυσιν εξ ἑαυτου θερμοτητα και φως· γῃ δε και θαλασσῃ χρηται κατα φυσιν ὁ κοσμος, ὁσα κοιλια και κυστει ζωον· σεληνη, ἡλιου μεταξυ και γης, ὡσπερ καρδιας και κοιλιας ἡπαρ, η τι μαλθακον αλλο σπλαγχνον, εγκειμενη, την τ' ανωθεν αλεαν ενταυθα διαπεμπει, και τας εντευθεν αναθυμιασεις πεψει τινι και καθαρσει λεπτυνουσα περι ἑαυτην αναδιδωσιν. Plutarch. de Facie in Orbe Lunæ, p. 928.

140. The Greeks attributed to her the powers of destruction as well as nutrition; humidity, as well as heat, contributing to putrefaction : whence sudden death was supposed to proceed from Diana as well as from Apollo ; who was both the sender of disease, and the inventor of cure : for disease is the father of medicine, as Apollo was fabled to be of Æsculapius. The rays of the Moon were thought relaxing, even to inanimate bodies, by means of their humidity: whence wood cut at the full of the moon was rejected by builders as improper for use.[1] The Ilithyiæ, supposed to preside over child-birth, were only personifications of this property,[2] which seemed to facilitate delivery by slackening the powers of resistance and obstruction; and hence the crescent was universally worn as an amulet by women ; as it still continues to be in the southern parts of Italy; and Juno Lucina, and Diana, were the same goddess, equally personifications of the Moon.[3]

141. The Ægyptians represented the Moon under the symbol of a cat ; probably on account of that animal's power of seeing in the night ; and also, perhaps, on account of its fecundity ; which seems to have induced the Hindoos to adopt the rabbit as the symbol of the same deified planet.[4] As the arch or bend of the mystical instrument, borne by Isis and called a sistrum, represented the lunar orbit, the cat occupied the centre of it ; while the rattles below represented the terrestrial elements ;[5] of which there are

---

[1] Γινεται δε και περι τα αψυχα των σωματων επιδηλος ἡ της σεληνης δυναμις· των τε γαρ ξυλων τα τεμνομενα ταις πανσελπναις αποβαλλουσιν οἱ τεκτονες, ὡς ἁπαλα και μυδοντα ταχεως δι' ὑγροτητα. Plutarch. Sympos. lib. iii. qu. 10.

[2] —'Οθεν οιμαι και την Αρτεμιν, Λοχειαν και Ειλειθυιαν, ουκ ουσαν ἑτεραν η την σεληνην, ωνομασθαι. Ibid.

[3] Tu Lucina dolentibus
Juno dicta puerperis
Tu potens Trivia, et notho es
Dicta lumine Luna.   Catull. xxxiv. 13.

[4] Maurice's Indian Antiquities, vol. i. p. 513. See fabulous reasons assigned for the Ægyptian symbol. Demetr. Phaler. s. 159.

[5] Plutarch. de Is. et Osir. p. 376.

sometimes four, but more frequently only three in the instances now extant : for the ancient Ægyptians, or at least some of them, appear to have known that water and air are but one substance.[1]

142. The statues of Diana are always clothed, and she had the attribute of perpetual virginity; to which her common Greek name *APTEMIΣ* seems to allude : but the Latin name appears to be a contraction of DIVIANA, the feminine, according to the old Etruscan idiom, of DIVUS, or *ΔIFOΣ* ;[2] and therefore signifying the Goddess, or general female personification of the Divine nature, which the Moon was probably held to be in the ancient planetary worship, which preceded the symbolical. As her titles and attributes were innumerable, she was represented under an infinite variety of forms, and with an infinite variety of symbols ; sometimes with three bodies, each holding appropriate emblems,[3] to signify the triple extension of her power, in heaven, on earth, and under the earth; and sometimes with phallic radii enveloping a female form, to show the universal generative attribute both active and passive.[4] The figures of her, as she was worshipped at Ephesus, seem to have consisted of an assemblage of almost every symbol, attached to the old humanised column, so as to form a composition purely emblematical ;[5] and it seems that the ancient inhabitants of the north of Europe represented their goddess Isa as nearly in the same manner as their rude and feeble efforts in art could accomplish; she having the many breasts to signify the nutritive attribute ; and being surrounded by deer's horns instead of the animals themselves, which accompany

---

[1] Ἡ γαρ ὑγρα φυσις, αρχη και γενεσις ουσα παντων εξ αρχης, τα πρωτα τρια σωματα, γην, αερα, και πυρ εποιησε. Plutarch. de Is. et Osir.

[2] Varr. lib. iv. c. 10. Lanzi sopra le lingue morte d'Italia, vol. ii. p. 194.

[3] See La Chausse Mus. Rom. vol. i. s. ii. tab. 20, &c. These figures are said to have been first made by Alcamenes, about the lxxxiv. Olympiad.

Αλκαμενης δε (εμοι δοκειν) πρωτος αγαλματα Ἑκατης τρια εποιησε προσεχομενα αλληλοις, ἡν Αθηναιοι καλουσιν επιπυργιδιαν. Pausan. in Corinth. c. xxx. s. 2.

[4] See Duane's coins of the Seleucidæ, tab. xiv. fig. 1 and 2.

[5] See De la Chausse Mus. Rom. vol. i. s. ii. tab. xviii.

the Ephesian statues.[1] In sacrificing, too, the reindeer to her, it was their custom to hang the testicles round the neck of the figure,[2] probably for the same purpose as the phallic radii, above mentioned, were employed to serve.

143. Brimo, the Tauric and Scythic Diana, was the destroyer:[3] whence she was appeased with human victims and other bloody rites ;[4] as was also *Bacchus the devourer* ;[5] who seems to have been a male personification of the same attribute, called by a general title which confounds him with another personification of a directly opposite kind. It was at the altar of Brimo, called at Sparta *Αρτεμις ορθια* or *ορθωσια*, that the Lacedæmonian boys voluntarily stood to be whipped until their lives were sometimes endangered;[5] and it was during the festival of Bacchus at Alea, that the Arcadian women annually underwent a similar penance, first imposed by the Delphic oracle ; but probably less rigidly inforced.[7] Both appear to have been substitutions for human sacrifices ;[8] which the stern hierarchies of the North frequently performed ; and to which the Greeks and Romans resorted upon great and awful occasions ; when real danger had excited imaginary fear.[9] It is probable, therefore, that drawing blood, though in ever so small a quantity, was necessary to complete the rite : for blood being thought to contain

---

[1] Ol. Rudbeck. Atlant. vol. ii. pp. 212 and 291. fig. 30 and 31. and p. 277. fig. G.

[2] Ibid. p. 212. fig. 31. and p. 292.

[3] Βριμω τριμορφος.   Lycophr. Cassandra, v. 1176.

Βριμω ἡ αυτη ἡ Εκατη·————και ἡ Περσεφονη Βριμω λεγεται· δοκει δε ἡ αυτη ειναι 'Εκατη και Περσεφονη.   Tzetz. Schol. in eund.

[4] See Johan. Meurs. Græc. Feriata. διαμαστιγωσις.

[5] Διονυσῳ ωμαδιῳ et ωμηστῃ. See Porphyr. περι αποχης, l. ii. p. 224. Plutarch. in Themistoc.

[6] Plutarch. in Lycurg. et Lacon. Institut.

[7] Και εν Διονυσου τη ἑορτῃ, κατα μαντευμα εκ Δελφων, μαστιγουνται γυναικες, καθα και οἱ Σπαρτιατων εφηβοι παρα τη Ορθιᾳ. Pausan. in Arcad. c. 23.

[8] ————Θυομενου δε, ὁντινα ὁ κληρος απελαμβανε, Λυκουργος μετεβαλεν ες τας επι τοις εφηβοις μαστιγας. Pausan. in Lacon.

[9] Plutarch. in Themistocl. Liv. Hist.

the principles of life, the smallest effusion of it at the altar might seem a complete sacrifice, by being a libation of the soul; the only part of the victim which the purest believers of antiquity supposed the Deity to require.[1] In other respects, the form and nature of these rites prove them to have been expiatory; which scarcely any of the religious ceremonies of the Greeks or Romans were.

144. It is in the character of the destroying attribute, that Diana is called *ΤΑΥΡΟΠΟΛΑ*, and *ΒΟΩΝ ΕΛΑΤΕΙΑ*, in allusion to her being borne or drawn by bulls, like the Destroyer among the Hindoos before mentioned ; and it is probable that some such symbolical composition gave rise to the fable of Jupiter and Europa ; for it appears that in Phœnicia, Europa and Astarte were only different titles for the same personage, who was the deity of the Moon;[2] comprehending both the Diana and celestial Venus of the Greeks : whence the latter was occasionally represented armed like the former ;[3] and also distinguished by epithets, which can be properly applied only to the planet, and which are certainly derived from the primitive planetary worship.[4] Upon the celebrated ark or box of Cypselus, Diana was represented winged, and holding a lion in one hand and a leopard in the other ;[5] to signify the destroying attribute, instead of the usual symbols of the bow and arrow ; and in an ancient temple near the mouth of the Alpheus she was repre-

---

[1] Strabo. lib. xv. p. 732.

[2] Ενι δε και αλλο ίρον εν Φοινικη μεγα, το Σιδονιοι εχουσι, ὡs μεν αυτοι λεγουσι, Ασταρτηs εστι· Ασταρτην δε εγω δοκεω Σεληναιην εμμεναι· ὡs δε μοι τις των ίρεων απηγεετο, Ευρωπηs εστι της Καδμου αδελφεηs. Lucian. de Syra Dea. s. 4.

[3] Ανελθουσι δε εs τον Ακροκορινθον, ναος εστιν Αφροδιτηs· αγαλματα δε, αυτη τε ὡπλισμενη, και Ἡλιος, και Ερως εχων τοξον. Pausan. in Corinth. c. 4. s. 7.
Also at Cythera, in the most ancient temple of Urania in all Greece, was ξοανον ὡπλισμενον of the goddess. Id. in Lacon. c. 23. s. 1.

[4] Noctivigila, noctiluca, &c. Plaut. Cureul. act. 1. sc. iii. v. 4. Horat. lib. iv. od. 6.

[5] Αρτεμις δε, ουκ οιδα εφ' ὁτῳ λογῳ, πτερυγας εχουσα εστιν επι των ωμων, και τῃ μεν δεξιᾳ κατεχει παρδαλιν, τῃ δε ἑτεοα των χειρων λεοντα. Pausan. in Eliac. i. c. 19. s. 1.

H

sented riding upon a gryphon;[1] an emblematical monster composed
of the united forms of the lion and eagle, the symbols of destruction and dominion.[2] As acting under the earth, she was the same
as Proserpine ; except that the latter has no reference to the Moon ;
but was a personification of the same attributes operating in the
terrestrial elements only.

145. In the simplicity of the primitive religion, Pluto and
Proserpine were considered merely as the deities of death presiding over the infernal regions; and, being thought wholly inflexible
and inexorable, were neither honored with any rites of worship,
nor addressed in any forms of supplication :[3] but in the mystic system they acquired a more general character ; and became personifications of the active and passive modifications of the pervading
Spirit concentrated in the earth.   Pluto was represented with the
πολος or modius on his head, like Venus and Isis ; and, in the character of Serapis, with the patera of libation, as distributor of the
waters, in one hand, and the cornucopiæ, signifying its result, in the
other.[4] His name Pluto or Plutus signifies the same as this latter
symbol ; and appears to have arisen from the mystic worship ; his
ancient title having been ΑΙΔΗΣ or ΑΓΙΔΗΣ, signifying the Invisible, which the Attics corrupted to Hades.   Whether the title
Serapis, which appears to be Ægyptian, meant a more general
personification, or precisely the same, is difficult to ascertain ;
ancient authority rather favoring the latter supposition ;[5] at the same
time that there appears to be some difference in the figures of them
now extant ; those of Pluto having the hair hanging down in large
masses over the neck and forehead, and differing only in the front

---

[1] Strabo. lib. viii. p. 343. Αρτεμις αναφερομενη επι γρυπος, a very celebrated
picture of Aregon of Corinth.

[2] See coins of Teïos, &c. in the Hunter collection.

[3] Iliad I. 158. They are invoked indeed Il. I. 565. and Od. K. 535.; but
only as the deities of Death.

[4] In a small silver figure belonging to Mr. P. Knight.

[5] Ου γαρ αλλον ειναι Σεραπιν η τον Πλουτωνα φασι. Plutarch. de Is. et Osir.

curls from that of the celestial Jupiter; while Serapis has, in some instances, long hair formally turned back and disposed in ringlets hanging down upon his breast and shoulders like that of women. His whole person too is always enveloped in drapery reaching to his feet; wherefore he is probably meant to comprehend the attributes of both sexes; and to be a general personification, not unlike that of the Paphian Venus with the beard, before mentioned; from which it was perhaps partly taken;[1] there being no mention made of any such deity in Ægypt prior to the Macedonian conquest; and his worship having been communicated to the Greeks by the Ptolemies; whose magnificence in constructing and adorning his temple at Alexandria was only surpassed by that of the Roman emperors in the temple of Jupiter Capitolinus.[2]

146. The mystic symbol called a modius or πολος, which is upon the heads of Pluto, Serapis, Venus, and Fortune or Isis, appears to be no other than the bell or seed-vessel of the lotus or water-lily, the nymphæa nelumbo of Linnæus. This plant, which appears to be a native of the eastern parts of Asia, and is not now found in Ægypt,[3] grows in the water; and amidst its broad leaves, which float upon the surface, puts forth a large white flower; the base and centre of which is shaped like a bell or inverted cone, and punctuated on the top with little cells or cavities, in which the seeds grow. The orifices of these cells being too small to let them drop out when ripe, they shoot forth into new plants in the places where they were formed; the bulb of the vessel serving as a matrice to nourish them until they acquire a degree of magnitude sufficient to burst it open and release themselves; when they sink to the bottom, or take root wherever the current happens to deposit them.

---

[1] Πλαττουσι δε αυτην (Αφροδιτην) και γενειον εχουσαν· διοτι και αρρενα και θηλεα εχει οργανα. ταυτην γαρ λεγουσιν εφορον πασης γενεσεως, και απο της οσφυος και ανω λεγουσιν αυτην αρρενα· τα δε κατω, θηλειαν. πλαττουσι δε αυτην και εφιππον. Suidas in Αφροδ.

Σεραπιδος εστιν ιερον, ὁν Αθηναιοι παρα Πτολεμαιου θεον εσηγαγοντο Αιγυπτιοις δε ιερα Σεραπιδος, επιφανεστατον μεν εστιν Αλεξανδρευσιν, αρχαιοτατον δε εν Μεμφει. Pausan. in Att. ç. 18. s. 4.

[2] Ammian. Marcellin. lib. xxii.   [3] Embassy to China, vol. ii. p. 391.

Being, therefore, of a nature thus reproductive in itself, and, as it were, of a viviparous species among plants, the nelumbo was naturally adopted as the symbol of the productive power of the waters, upon which the active Spirit of the Creator operated in spreading life and vegetation over the earth. It also appeared to have a peculiar sympathy with the Sun, the great fountain of life and motion, by rising above the waters as it rose above the horizon, and sinking under them as it retired below.[1] Accordingly we find it employed in every part of the Northern hemisphere, where symbolical worship either does or ever did prevail. The sacred images of the Tartars, Japanese, and Indians, are almost all placed upon it;[2] and it is still sacred both in Tibet and China.[3] The upper part of the base of the lingam also consists of the flower of it blended with the more distinctive characteristic of the female sex; in which that of the male is placed, in order to complete this mystic symbol of the ancient religion of the Bramins;[4] who, in their sacred writings speak of the Creator Brama *sitting upon his lotus throne.*

147. On the Isiac table, the figures of Isis are represented holding the stem of this plant, surmounted by the seed-vessel, in one hand, and the circle and cross, before explained, in the other; and in a temple, delineated upon the same mystic table, are columns exactly resembling the plant, which Isis holds in her hand, except that the stem is made proportionately large, to give that stability, which is requisite to support a roof and entablature. Columns and capitals of the same kind are still existing in great numbers among the ruins of Thebes in Ægypt; and more particularly among those on the island of Philæ on the borders of Æthiopia; which was anciently held so sacred that none but priests

---

[1] Theophrast. Hist. Plant. lib. iv. c. 10.

[2] See Kæmpfer, D'Auteroche, Sonnerat, and the Asiatic Researches.

[3] Embassy to Tibet, p. 143. Sir G. Staunton's Embassy to China, p. 391. vol. ii.

[4] Sonnerat Voyage aux Indes, &c.

[5] Bagvat Geeta, p. 91. See also the figure of him by Sir William Jones, in the Asiatic Researches, vol. i. p. 243.

were permitted to go upon it.¹ These are probably the most ancient monuments of art now extant; at least, if we except some of the neighbouring temples of Thebes; both having been certainly erected when that city was the seat of wealth and empire; as it seems to have been, even proverbially, in the time of the Trojan war.² How long it had then been so, we can form no conjecture; but that it soon after declined, there can be little doubt; for, when the Greeks, in the reign of Psammetichus (generally computed to have been about 530 years after, but probably more) became personally acquainted with Ægypt,³ Memphis had been for many ages its capital, and Thebes was in a manner deserted.

148. We may therefore reasonably infer that the greatest part of the superb edifices now remaining were executed or at least begun before the Homeric or even Trojan times, many of them being such as could not have been finished but in a long course of years, even supposing the wealth and resources of the ancient kings of Ægypt to have equalled that of the greatest of the Roman emperors. The completion of Trajan's column in three years has been justly deemed a very extraordinary effort; as there could not have been less than three hundred sculptors employed: and yet at Thebes the ruins of which, according to Strabo, extended ten miles on both sides of the Nile,⁴ we find whole temples and obelisks of enormous magnitude covered with figures carved out of the hard and brittle granite of the Libyan mountains, instead of the soft and yielding marbles of Paros and Carara. To judge, too, of the mode and degree of their finish by those on the obelisk of Rameses, once a part of them, but now lying in

---

¹ Diodor. Sic. lib. i. p. 25. ed. Wess.   ² See Il. I. v. 381.

³ Πρωτος (ὁ Ψαμμητικος) των κατ' Αιγυπτον βασιλεων ανεωξε τοις αλλοις εθνεσι τα κατα την αλλην χωραν εμπορια. This prince was the fifth before Amasis who died in the 2nd year of the lxiiird. Olympiad, in which Cambyses invaded Ægypt. Diodor. Sic. lib. i. p. 78 and 9.

⁴ Και νυν δεικνυται δ' ιχνη του μεγεθους αυτης επι ογδοηκοντα σταδιους το μηκος. lib. xvii. p. 816.

fragments at Rome, they are far more elaborately wrought than those of Trajan's pillar.[1]

149. The age of Rameses is as uncertain as all other very ancient dates: but he has been generally supposed by modern chronologers to be the same person as Sesostris, and to have reigned at Thebes about fifteen hundred years before the Christian æra, or about three hundred before the siege of Troy. They are, however, too apt to confound personages for the purpose of contracting dates ; which being merely conjectural in events of this remote antiquity, every new system-builder endeavours to adapt them to his own prejudices; and, as it has been the fashion, in modern times, to reduce as much as possible the limits of ancient history, whole reigns and even dynasties have been annihilated with the dash of a pen, notwithstanding the obstinate evidence of those stupendous monuments of art and labor, which still stand up in their defence.[2]

150. From the state in which the inhabitants have been found in most newly-discovered countries, we know how slow and difficult the invention of even the commonest implements of art is ; and how reluctantly men are dragged into those habits of industry, which even the first stages of culture require. Ægypt, too, being periodically overflowed, much more art and industry were required even to render it constantly habitable and capable of cultivation, than would be employed in cultivating a country not liable to inundations. Repositories must have been formed, and places of safety built, both for men and cattle; the adjoining deserts of Libya affording neither food nor shelter for either. Before this could have been done, not only the arts and implements necessary to do it must have been invented, but the rights of property in some degree defined and ascertained ; which they could only be in a

---

[1] Figures in relief, finished in the same style, are upon the granite sarcophagus in the British Museum : it is equal to that of the finest gems, and must have been done with similar instruments.

[2] Warburton has humorously introduced one of these chronologers proving that William the Conqueror and William the IIId. were one and the same person. Div. Leg.

regular government, the slow result of the jarring interests and passions of men; who, having long struggled with each other, acquiesce at length in the sacrifice of some part of their natural liberty in order to enjoy the rest with security. Such a government, formed upon a very complicated and artificial plan, does Ægypt appear to have possessed even in the days of Abraham, not five hundred years after the period generally allowed for the universal deluge. Yet Ægypt was a new country, gained gradually from the sea by the accumulation of the mud and sand annually brought down in the waters of the Nile; and slowly transformed, by the regularly progressive operation of time and labor, from an uninhabitable salt-marsh to the most salubrious and fertile spot in the universe.[1]

151. This great transformation took place, in all the lower regions, after the genealogical records of the hereditary priests of Ammon at Thebes had commenced; and, of course, after the civil and religious constitution of the government had been formed. It was the custom for every one of these priests to erect a colossal statue of himself, in wood—of which there were three hundred and forty-five shown to Hecatæus and Herodotus;[2] so that, according to the Ægyptian computation of three generations to a century,[3] which, considering the health and longevity of that people,[4] is by no means unreasonable, this institution must have lasted between eleven and twelve thousand years, from the times of the first king, Menes, under whom all the country below Lake Mœris was a bog,[5] to that of

---

[1] Και γαρ ουτος αει ξηροτερος ὁ τοπος φαινεται γιγνομενος, και πασα ἡ χωρα του ποταμου προσχωσις ουσα του Νειλου· δια δε το κατα μικρον ξηραινομενων των ἑλων, τους πλησιον εισοικιζεσθαι, το του χρονου μηκος αφαιρηται την αρχην. Φαινεται δ' ουν και τα στοματα παντα πλην ἑνος του Κανωβικου, χειροποιητα και ου του ποταμου οντα. Aristot. Meteor. lib. i. c. xiv.

[2] Lib. ii. s. 143.

[3] Γενεαι γαρ τρεις ανδρων εκατον ετεα εστι. Ibid. s. 142.

[4] Εισι μεν γαρ και αλλως Αιγυπτιοι μετα Λιβυας ὑγιηρεστατοι παντων ανθρωπων, των ὡρεων (εμοι δοκεειν) εἱνεκα, ὁτι ου μεταλλασσουσι αἱ ὡραι. Ib. s. 77.

[5] Επι τουτου, πλην του Θηβαϊκου νομου πασαν Αιγυπτον ειναι ἑλος· και αυτης ειναι ουδεν ὑπερεχον των νυν ενερθε λιμνης της Μοιριος εοντων· ες την αναπλους απο θαλασσης ἑπτα ἡμερεων εστι ανα τον ποταμον. Ib. s. 4.

the Persian invasion, when it was the garden of the world. This is a period sufficient, but not more than sufficient, for the accomplishment of such vast revolutions, both natural and artificial; and, as it is supported by such credible testimony, there does not appear to be any solid room for suspecting it to have been less : for, as to the modern systems of chronology, deduced from doubtful passages of Scripture, and genealogies, of which a great part were probably lost during the captivity of the Jews, they bear nothing of the authority of the sacred sources from which they have been drawn. Neither let it be imagined that either Herodotus, or the priest who informed him, could have confounded symbolical figures with portraits : for all the ancient artists, even those of Ægypt, were so accurate in discriminating between ideal and real characters, that the difference is at once discernible by any experienced observer, even in the wrecks and fragments of their works that are now extant.

152. But, remote as the antiquity of these Ægyptian remains seems to be, the symbols which adorn them appear not to have been invented by that, but to have been copied from those of some other people, who dwelt on the other side of the Erythræan Ocean. Both the nelumbo, and the hooded snake, which are among those most frequently repeated, and most accurately represented upon all their sacred monuments, are, as before observed, natives of the East; and upon the very ancient Ægyptian temple, near Girge, figures have been observed exactly resembling those of the Indian deities, Jaggernaut, Gonnes, and Vishnoo. The Ægyptian architecture appears, however, to have been original and indigenous ; and in this art only the Greeks seem to have borrowed from them; the different orders being only different modifications of the symbolical columns which the Ægyptians formed in imitation of the nelumbo plant.

153. The earliest capital seems to have been the bell, or seed-vessel, simply copied, without any alteration except a little expansion at bottom, to give it stability. [1] The leaves of some other

---

[1] Denon. pl. lx. 12.

plant were then added to it, and varied in different capitals, according to the different meanings intended to be signified by these accessary symbols. [1] The Greeks decorated it in the same manner, with the foliage of various plants, sometimes of the acanthus, and sometimes of the aquatic kind; [2] which are, however, generally so transformed by their excessive attention to elegance, that it is difficult to ascertain them. The most usual seems to be the Ægyptian acacia, which was probably adopted as a mystic symbol for the same reasons as the olive; it being equally remarkable for its powers of reproduction. [3] Theophrastus mentions a large wood of it in the Thebais; where the olive will not grow; [4] so that we may reasonably suppose it to have been employed by the Ægyptians in the same symbolical sense. From them the Greeks seem to have borrowed it about the time of the Macedonian conquest; it not occurring in any of their buildings of a much earlier date: and as for the story of the Corinthian architect, who is said to have invented this kind of capital from observing a thorn growing round a basket, it deserves no credit, being fully contradicted by the buildings still remaining in Upper Ægypt. [5]

154. The Doric column, which appears to have been the only one known to the very ancient Greeks, was equally derived from the nelumbo; its capital being the same seed-vessel pressed flat, as it appears when withered and dry; the only state, probably, in which it had been seen in Europe. The flutes in the shaft were

---

[1] Denon, pl. lix. and lx.

[2] See ib. pl. lix. 1. 2. and 3. and lx. 1. 2. 3., &c.; where the originals from which the Greeks took their Corinthian capitals plainly appear. It might have been more properly called the Ægyptian order, as far at least as relates to the form and decoration of the capitals.

[3] Martin in Virg. Georg. ii. 119.

[4] Περι φυτων.

[5] If the choragic monument of Lysicrates was really erected in the time of the Lysicrates to whom it is attributed, it must be of about the hundred and eleventh Olympiad, or three hundred and thirty years before the Christian æra; which is earlier than any other specimen of Corinthian architecture known.

made to hold spears and staves ; whence a spear-holder is spoken of, in the Odyssey, as part of a column :[1] the triglyphs and blocks of the cornice were also derived from utility; they having been intended to represent the projecting ends of the beams and rafters which formed the roof.

155. The Ionic capital has no bell, but volutes formed in imitation of sea-shells, which have the same symbolical meaning. To them is frequently added the ornament which architects call a honeysuckle ; but which seems to be meant for the young petals of the same flower viewed horizontally, before they are opened or expanded. Another ornament is also introduced in this capital, which they call eggs and anchors ; but which is, in fact, composed of eggs and spear-heads, the symbols of passive generative, and active destructive power; or, in the language of mythology, of Venus and Mars.

156. These are, in reality, all the Greek orders, which are respectively distinguished by the symbolical ornaments being placed *upwards, downwards,* or *sideways :* wherefore, to invent a new order is as much impossible as to invent an attitude or position, which shall incline to neither of the three. As for the orders called Tuscan and Composite, the one is that in which there is no ornament whatsoever, and the other that in which various ornaments are placed in different directions; so that the one is in reality no order, and the other a combination of several.

157. The columns being thus sacred symbols, the temples themselves, of which they always formed the principal part, were emblems of the Deity, signifying generally the passive productive power; whence ΠΕΡΙΚΙΟΝΙΟΣ, *surrounded with columns,* is among the Orphic or mystic epithets of Bacchus, in his character of god of the waters;[2] and his statue in that situation had the same meaning as the Indian lingam, the bull in the labyrinth, and other symbolical compositions of the same kind before cited. A variety of accessary symbols were almost always added, to enrich the sacred edifices ;

[1] Od. A. 127.   [2] Orph. Hymn. xlvi.

the Ægyptians covering the walls of the cells and the shafts of the columns with them ; while the Greeks, always studious of elegance, employed them to decorate their entablatures, pediments, doors, and pavements. The extremities of the roofs were almost always adorned with a sort of scroll of raised curves,[1] the meaning of which would not be easily discovered, were it not employed on coins evidently to represent water; not as a symbol, but as the rude effort of infant art, feebly attempting to imitate waves.[2]

158. The most obvious, and consequently the most ancient symbol of the productive power of the waters, was a fish; which we accordingly find the universal symbol upon many of the earliest coins ; almost every symbol of the male or active power, both of generation and destruction, being occasionally placed upon it ; and Dirceto, the goddess of the Phœnicians, being represented by the head and body of a woman, terminating below in a fish :[3] but on the Phœnician as well as Greek coins now extant, the personage is of the other sex ; and in plate L. of vol. 1. of the Select Specimens, is engraved a beautiful figure of the mystic Cupid, or first-begotten Love, terminating in an aquatic plant ; which, affording more elegance and variety of form, was employed to signify the same meaning ; that is, the Spirit upon the waters; which is otherwise expressed by a similar and more common mixed figure, called a Triton, terminating in a fish, instead of an aquatic plant. The head of Proserpine appears, in numberless instances, surrounded by dolphins ;[4] and upon the very ancient medals of Sidè in Pamphylia, the pomegranate, the fruit peculiarly consecrated to her, is borne upon the back of one.[5] By prevailing upon her to eat of it, Pluto is said to have procured her stay during half the year in the infernal regions ; and a part of the Greek ceremony of marriage still consists, in many places, in the bride's tread-

---

[1] See Stuart's Athens, vol. 1. c. iv. pl. iii.

[2] See coins of Tarentum, Camerina, &c.

[3] Δερκετους δε ειδος εν Φοινικη εθηησαμην, θεαμα ξενον· ἡμισεη μεν γυνη· το δε ὁκοσόν εκ μηρων ες ακρους ποδας ιχθυος ουρη αποτεινεται· ἡ δε εν τῃ ἱρῃ πολει πασα γυνη εστι. Lucian. de Syr. Dea. s. 14.

[4] See coins of Syracuse, Motya, &c.

[5] Mus. Hunter. tab. 49. fig. iii. &c.

ing upon a pomegranate. The flower of it is also occasionally employed as an ornament upon the diadems of both Hercules and Bacchus; and likewise forms the device of the Rhodian medals ; on some of which we have seen distinctly represented an ear of barley springing from one side of it, and the bulb of the lotus, or nelumbo, from the other. It therefore holds the place of the male, or active generative attribute ; and accordingly we find it on a bronze fragment published by Caylus, as the result of the union of the bull and lion, exactly as the more distinct symbol of the phallus is in a similar fragment above cited. [1] The pomegranate, therefore, in the hand of Porserpine or Juno, signifies the same as the circle and cross, before explained, in the hand of Isis; which is the reason why Pausanias declines giving any explanation of it, lest it should lead him to divulge any of the mystic secrets of his religion. [2] The cone of the pine, with which the thyrsus of Bacchus is always surmounted, and which is employed in various compositions, is probably a symbol of similar import, and meaning the same, in the hand of Ariadne and her attendants, as the above-mentioned emblems do in those of Juno, Porserpine, and Isis.

159. Upon coins, Diana is often accompanied by a dog,[3] esteemed to be the most sagacious and vigilant of animals ;[4] and therefore employed by the Ægyptians as the symbol of Hermes, Mercury, or Anubis ; who was the conductor of the soul from one habitation to another ; and consequently the same, in some respects, as Brimo,

---

[1] Recueil d'Antiquités, &c. vol. vii. pl. lxiii. fig. 1. 2. and 3.

The bull's head is, indeed, here half humanised, having only the horns and ears of the animal; while in the more ancient fragment above cited both symbols are unmetamorphosed.

[2] Το δε αγαλμα της 'Ηρας επι θρονου καθηται, μεγεθει μεγα χρυσου μεν και ελεφαντος, Πολυκλειτου δε εργον· επεστι δε οἱ στεφανος χαριτας εχων και 'Ωρας επειργασμενας· και των χειρων, τη μεν καρπον φερει ροιας, τη δε σκηπτρον· τα μεν ουν εις την ροιαν (απορρητερος γαρ εστιν ὁ λογος) αφεισθω μοι. Corinth. c. xvii. s. 4.

[3] See coins of Syracuse, &c.

[4] Ου γαρ τον κυνα κυριως 'Ερμην λεγουσιν (οἱ Αιγυπτιοι) αλλα του ξωου το φυλακτικον, και το αγρυπνον, και το φιλοσοφον. Plutarch. de Is. et Osir.

Hecatè, or Diana, the destroyer. [1] In monuments of Grecian art, the cock is his most frequent symbol; and in a small figure of brass, we have observed him sitting on a rock, with a cock on his right side, the goat on his left, and the tortoise at his feet. The ram, however, is more commonly employed to accompany him, and in some instances he appears sitting upon it: [2] wherefore it is probable that both these animals signified nearly the same ; or, at most, only different modifications of the influence of the nocturnal sun, as the cock did that of the diurnal. Hence Mercury appears to have been a personification of the power arising from both; and we accordingly find that the old Pelasgian Mercury, so generally worshipped at Athens, [3] was a priapic figure, [4] and probably the same personage as the Celtic Mercury, who was the principal deity of the ancient Gauls; [5] who do not, however, appear to have had any statues of him till they received them from the Greeks and Romans.

160. In these, one hand always holds a purse, to signify that productive attribute, which is peculiarly the result of mental skill and sagacity, [6] while the other holds the caduceus ; a symbol composed of the staff or sceptre of dominion between two serpents, the emblems of life or preservation, and therefore signifying his power over it. Hence it was always borne by heralds; of whom Mercury, as the messenger of the gods, was the patron, and whose office was to proclaim peace, and denounce war ; of both which it might be con-

---

[1] Ταύτην εχειν δοκει παρ' Αιγυπτιοις την δυναμιν ὁ Ανουβις οίαν ἡ Ἑκατη παρ' Ἑλλησι χθονιος ων ὁμου και Ὀλυμπιος. Ibid.

[2] Particularly in an intaglio of exquisite work, in the collection of the Earl of Carlisle.

[3] Αθηναιων δε εστι το σχημα το τετραγωνον επι ταις Ἑρμαις, και παρα τουτων μεμαθηκασιν οἱ αλλοι. Paus. in Mess. c. xxxiii.

[4] Του δε Ἑρμεω τα αγαλματα ορθα εχειν τα αιδοια ποιευντες, ουκ απ' Αιγυπτων μεμαθηκασι, αλλ' απο Πελασγων. Herodot. ii. 51.

Του Ἑρμου δε το αγαλμα, ὁν οἱ ταυτη (Κυλληνη) περισσως σεβουσιν, ορθον εστιν αιδοιον επι του βαθρου. Pausan. in Eliac. ii. c. xxvi. s. 3.

[5] Cæsar. de B. G. lib. vi.

[6] Occultè Mercurio supplicabat (Julianus) quem mundi velociorem sensum esse, motum mentium suscitantem, theologiæ prodidere doctrinæ. Ammian. Marcellin. lib. xvi. c. 5.

sidered as the symbol : for the staff or spear, signifying power in general, [1] was employed by the Greeks and Romans to represent Juno [2] and Mars ; [3] and received divine honors all over the North, as well as the battle-axe and sword ; by the latter of which the God of War, the supreme deity of those fierce nations, was signified : [4] whence, to swear by the shoulder of the horse and the edge of the sword, was the most solemn and inviolable of oaths ; [5] and deciding civil dissensions or personal disputes by duel, was considered as appealing directly and immediately to the Deity. The ordeal, or trial by fire and water, which seems once to have prevailed in Greece and Italy, [6] as well as Germany and the North, is derived from the same source ; it being only an appeal to the essence, instead of the symbol, of the Divine nature. The custom of swearing by the implements of war as divine emblems, appears likewise to have prevailed among the Greeks ; whence Æschylus introduces the heroes of the Thebaïd taking their military oath of fidelity to each other upon the point of a spear or sword. [7]

161. The dog represented Mercury as the keeper of the boundary between life and death, or the guardian of the passage from the upper to the lower hemisphere ; to signify the former of which, the

---

[1] Hence the expressions, ευθυνειν δορι, to govern, and venire sub hasta, to be sold as a slave.

[2] Ἡρας δε ίερον το δορυ νενομισται, και των αγαλματων αυτης στηριζεται τα πλειστα, και Κυριτις ή θεος επωνομασται· το γαρ δορυ κουριν εκαλουν οἱ παλαιοι. Plutarch. Quæst. Rom. p. 149.

[3] Εν δε Ρηγια δορυ καθιδρυμενον Αρεα προσαγορευειν. Plutarch. in Romulo.

[4] Ab origine rerum pro diis immortalibus veteres hastas coluere: ad cujus religionis memoriam adhuc deorum simulachris hastæ adduntur. Justin. Hist. lib. xliii. c. 3. See also Herodot. lib. iv. c. 62. : Ammian. Marcellin. lib. xvii. c. 12. and lib. xxxi. : Lucian. Scyth. p. 864. : Prisci Frag. in excerp. Legat.

[5] Mallet Introd. à l'Hist. de Danemarc, c. ix.

[6] Ημεν δ' ετοιμοι και μυδρους αιρειν χεροιν
Και πυρ διερπειν.   Sophocl. Antig. 270.

Summe Deûm, sancti custos Soractis Apollo,
Quem primi colimus, cui pineus ardor acervo
Pascitur; et medium freti pietate per ignem
Cultores multa premimus vestigia pruna,   Æn. xi. 785.

[7] Ομνυσι δ' αιχμην.   V. 535.

face of Anubis was gilded, and to signify the latter, black.[1] In the Greek and Roman statues of him, the wings and petasus, or cap, which he occasionally wears upon his head, seem to indicate the same difference of character;[2] similar caps being frequently upon the heads of figures of Vulcan, who was the personification of terrestrial fire:[3] whence he was fabled to have been thrown from heaven into the volcanic island of Lemnos, and to have been saved by the sea;[4] volcanos being supported by water. These caps, the form of which is derived from the egg,[5] and which are worn by the Dioscuri, as before observed, surmounted with asterisks, signify the hemispheres of the earth;[6] and it is possible that the asterisks may, in this case, mean the morning and evening stars; but whence the cap became a distinction of rank, as it was among the Scythians,[7] or a symbol of freedom and emancipation, as it was among the Greeks and Romans, is not easily ascertained.[8]

162. The dog was the emblem of destruction as well as vigilance, and sacred to Mars as well as Mercury:[9] whence the ancient northern deity, Gamr, the devourer or engulpher, was represented under the form of this animal; which sometimes appears in the same character on monuments of Grecian art.[10] Both destruction and creation were, according to the religious philosophy of the ancients, merely dissolution and renovation; to which all sublunary bodies, even that of the Earth itself, were supposed to be periodi-

---

[1] Hic horrendum attollens canis cervices arduas, ille superum commeator et inferum nunc atrâ nunc aureâ facie sublimis. Apul. Metam. lib. xi.

[2] See small brass coins of Metapontum, silver tetradrachms of Ænos, &c.

[3] See coins of Lipari, Æsernia, &c.: also plate xlvii. of Vol. 1.

[4] Iliad A. 593. and Σ. 395.

[5] Του ωου το ἡμιτονον και αστηρ ὑπερανω. Lucian. Dial. Deor. xxvi.

[6] Πιλους τ' επιτιθεασιν αυτοις, και επι τουτοις αστερας, αινισσομενοι την ἡμισφαιρεων κατασκευην. Sext. Empiric. xi. 37.; see also Achill. Tat. Isagog. p. 127 b. and 130 c.
This cap was first given to Ulysses by Nicomachus, a painter of the age of Alexander the Great. Plin. xxxv. c. x.

[7] Πιλοφορικοι. Scythians of rank. Lucian. Scyth.

[8] See Tib. Hemsterhuis. Not. in Lucian. Dialog. Deor. xxvi.

[9] Phurnut. de Nat. Deor. c. xxi.   [10] See coins of Phocœa, &c.

cally liable.[1]   Fire and water were held to be the great efficient principles of both ; and as the spirit or vital principle of thought and mental perception was alone supposed to be immortal and unchanged, the complete dissolution of the body, which it animated, was conceived to be the only means of its complete emancipation. Hence the Greeks, and all the Scythic and Celtic nations, burned the bodies of their dead, as the Hindoos do at this day ; whilst the Ægyptians, among whom fuel was extremely scarce, embalmed them, in order that they might be preserved entire to the universal conflagration ; till when the soul was supposed to migrate from one body to another.[2]   In this state those of the vulgar were deposited in subterraneous caverns, excavated with vast labor for the purpose ; while their kings erected, for their own bodies, those vast pyramidal monuments,

---

[1] Αφθαρτους δε λεγουσι ουτοι και οἱ αλλοι (Κελται) τας ψυχας και τον κοσμον επικρατησειν δε ποτε και πυρ και ὑδωρ.   Strabo lib. iv. p. 197.   See also Justin lib. ii. and Edda Myth. iv. and xlviii.   Voluspa stroph. xlix.   Vafthrud. xlvii. et seqq.   The same opinion prevailed almost universally ; see Plutarch. de Placit. Philos. lib. ii. c. xviii.   Lucret. lib. v. ver. 92.   Cic. de Nat. Deor. lib. ii.   Bagvat Geeta Lect. ix.   And Brucker Hist. Crit. Philos. vol. i. p. 11. lib. i.   Some indeed supposed the world to be eternal in its present state. Diodor. Sic. lib. i. p. 10.

Θεοπομπος δε φησι κατα τους μαγους, ανα μερος τρισχιλια ετη τον μεν κρατειν, τον δε κρατεισθαι των θεων, αλλα δε τρισχιλια μαχεσθαι και πολεμειν και αναλυειν τα του ἑτερου τον ἑτερον· τελος δ' απολειπεσθαι (lege απολεισθαι) τον ἀδην, και τους μεν ανθρωπους ευδαιμονας εσεσθαι, μητε τροφης δεομενους, μητε σκιαν ποιουντας.   Plutarch. de Is. et Osir. p. 370.   Hence the period of 6,000 years so important in ecclesiastical history.

Ισασι δε και Ἑλληνες κατακλυσμῳ η πυρι την γην κατα περιοδους καθαιρομενην.   Origen. contra Cels. lib. iv. s. 20.

Εσται γαρ εσται κεινος αιωνων χρονος
ὁταν πυρος γεμοντα θησαυρον σχασῃ
χρυσωπος αιθηρ· ἡ δε βοσκηθεισα φλοξ
ἁπαντα τ'απιγεια και μεταρσια
φλεξει μανεισ'· επαν δ' αρ ελλιπῃ το παν,
φρουδος μεν εσται κυματων ἁπας βυθος,
γη δενδρεων ερημος· ουδ' αηρ ετι
πτερωτα φυλα βλαστανει πυρουμενος·
καπειτα σωσει πανθ' ἁ προσθ' απωλεσε.

Sophocl. in Grotii excerpt. p. 115.

[2] Herodot. lib. ii. 123.

(the symbols of that fire to which they were consigned) whose excessive strength and solidity were well calculated to secure them as long as the earth, upon which they stood, should be able to support them. The great pyramid, the only one that has been opened, was closed up with such extreme care and ingenuity, that it required years of labor and enormous expense to gratify the curiosity or disappoint the avarice of the Mohammedan prince who first laid open the central chamber where the body lay.[1] The rest are still impenetrable, and will probably remain so, according to the intention of the builders, *to the last syllable of recorded time.*

163. The soul, that was to be finally emancipated by fire, was the divine emanation, the vital spark of heavenly flame, the principle of reason and perception, which was personified into the familiar dæmon or genius, supposed to have the direction of each individual, and to dispose him to good or evil, wisdom or folly, with all their respective consequences of prosperity or adversity.[2] Hence proceeded the notion, that all human actions depended immediately upon the gods ; which forms the fundamental principle of morality both in the elegant and finished compositions of the most ancient Greek poets,[3] and in the rude strains of the northern

---

[1] Savary sur l'Egypte.

[2] Ὁ νους γαρ ἡμων ὁ θεος. Menand. apud Plutarch. Qu. Platon.

Ἁπαντι δαιμων ανδρι συμπαρισταται,
ευθυς γενομενῳ μυσταγωγος του βιου·
αγαθος· κακον γαρ δαιμον' ου νομιστεον
ειναι, τον βιον βλαπτοντα χρηστον· παντα γαρ
δει αγαθον ειναι τον θεον. Menandr. Fragm. incerta. No. 205.

Plutarch, according to his own system, gives two genii to each individual, and quotes the authority of Empedocles against this passage of Menander; which seems, however, to contain the most ancient and orthodox opinion.

Αυτη τον αὑτης δαιμον' ανακαλουμενη. Sophocl. Trachin. 910.

Est deus in nobis ; agitante calescimus illo:
Impetus hic sacræ semina mentis habet. Ovid. Fast. lib. vi. 5.

Scit genius, natale comes qui temperat astrum,
Naturæ deus humanæ, mortalis in unum-
Quodque caput ; vultu mutabilis, albus et ater.
Horat. lib. ii. ep. ii. 187.

[3] Ουτι μοι αιτιη εσσι, θεοι νυ μοι αιτιοι εισιν
Οἱ μοι εφωρμησαν πολεμον πολυδακρυν Αχαιων—

I

Scalds :¹ for as the soul was supposed to be a part of the ætherial
substance of the Deity detached from the rest ; and doomed, for
some unknown causes, to remain during certain periods imprisoned
in matter; all its impulses, not immediately derived from the material organs, were of course impulses of the Deity.² As the
principles of this system were explained in the mysteries, persons
initiated were said to pass the rest of their time with the gods ;³

---

says the polite old Priam to the blushing and beautiful Helen. Agamemnon excuses himself for having injured and insulted Achilles, by saying,

――――― Εγω δ' ουκ αιτιος ειμι,
αλλα Ζευς και Μοιρα, και ηεροφοιτις Εριννυς.

Pindar continually inculcates this doctrine.

Διος τοι νοος μεγας κυβερνᾳ
Δαιμον' ανδρων φιλων. Pyth. ε. v. 164.
Ξενοφωντος ευθυνε Δαιμονος ουρον. Olymp. ιγ. v. 38.
Εκ θεου δ' ανηρ σοφαις ανθει εσαει πραπιδεσσι. Olymp. ια. v. 10.

――――― Αγαθοι δε
και σοφοι κατα Δαιμον' ανδρες
εγενοντο. Olymp. θ. v. 41.
Εκ θεων γαρ μαχαναι πα-
σαι βροτεαις αρεταις·
και σοφοι, και χερσι βια-
ται, περιγλωσσοι τ' εφυν. Pyth. α. v. 79.

¹ See Eddas, and Bartholinus.

² Μαρτυρεονται δε οἱ παλαιοι θεολογοι τε και μαντεις, ὡς δια τινας τιμωριας ἁ ψυχα
τῳ σωματι συνεζευκται, και καθαπερ εν σωματι τουτῳ τεθαπται. Philolaus Pythagoric. apud Clem. Alex. Strom. iii.
Αἱ δ' απηλλαγμεναι γενεσεως ψυχαι, και σχολαζουσαι το λοιπον απο σωματος, οἱον ελευ-
θεραι παμπαν αφιεμεναι, δαιμονες εισιν ανθρωπων επιμελεις, καθ' Ἡσιοδον. ὡς γαρ αθλη-
τας καταλυσαντας ασκησιν ὑπο γηρως, ου τελεως απολειπει το φιλοτιμον και φιλοσωματον,
αλλ' ἑτερους ασκουντας ὁρωντες ἡδονται, και παρακαλουσι και συμπαραθεουσι· οὑτως οἱ
πεπαυμενοι των περι τον βιον αγωνων, δι' αρετην ψυχης γενομενοι δαιμονες, ου παντελως
ατιμαζουσι τα ενταυθα, και λογους και σπουδας, αλλα τοις επι ταυτο γυμναζομενοις
τελος ευμενεις οντες, και συμφιλοτιμουμενοι προς την αρετην εγκελευονται και συνεξορ-
μωσιν, ὁταν εγγυς ηδη της ελπιδος αμιλλωμενους και ψαυοντας ὁρωσιν. Interloc.
Pythagoric. in Plutarch. Dialog. de Socrat. Dæmon.
Και μην ἁ των αλλων ακουεις, οἱ πειθουσι πολλους, λεγοντες ὡς ουδεν ουδαμη τῳ διαλυθεντι κακον ουδε λυπηρον εστιν, οιδα ὁτι κωλυει σε πιστευειν ὁ πατριος λογος, και τα
μυστικα συμβολα των περι τον Διονυσον οργιασμων, ἁ συνισμεν αλληλοις οἱ κοινωνουντες.
Plutarch. ad Uxor. Consol.

³ Ὡσπερ δε λεγεται κατα των μεμνημενων, ὡς αληθως τον λοιπον χρονον μετα θεων
διαγουσα (ἡ ψυχη). Platon. Phæd. p. 61.

it being by initiation that they acquired a knowledge of their affinity with the Deity; and learned to class themselves with the more exalted emanations, that flowed from the same source.

164. The corporeal residence of this divine particle or emanation, as well as of the grosser principle of vital heat and animal motion, was supposed to be the blood:[1] whence, in Ulysses's evocation of the Dead, the shades are spoken of as void of all perception of corporeal objects until they had tasted the blood of the victims[2] which he had offered; by means of which their faculties were replenished by a re-union with that principle of vitality from which they had been separated: for, according to this ancient system, there were two souls, the one the principle of thought and perception, called *NOOΣ*, and *ΦPHN*; and the other the mere power of animal motion and sensation, called *ΨΤΧΗ*;[3] both of which were allowed to remain entire, in the shades, in the person of Tiresias only.[4] The prophetess of Argos, in like manner, became possessed of the knowledge of futurity by

---

[2] Το αίμα τω ανθρωπω πλειστον συμβαλλεται μερος συνεσιος· ενιοι δε λεγουσι, το παν. Hippocrat. de Morbis, lib. i. s. xxviii.

Γνωμη γαρ η του ανθρωπου πεφυκεν εν τη λαιη κοιλιη (της καρδιης,) και αρχει της αλλης ψυχης. τρεφεται δε ουτε σιτιοισιν, ουτε ποτοισιν απο της νηδυος, αλλα καθαρη και φωτοειδεει περιουση, γεγονυη εκ της διακρισιος του αίματος. Hippocrat. de Corde, s. viii.

Το μεν αίμα κυριωτατην των εν ημιν εχον δυναμιν, άμα και θερμον εστι και υγρον. Plutarch. Sympos. lib. viii. c. 10.

Nullius carnis sanguinem comedetis, nam anima omnis carnis est sanguis ejus. Levit. c. xvii. v. 14. ed. Cleric.

[2] Od. Λ. 152 et seq.

[3] Νουν μεν εν ψυχη, ψυχην δ' εν σωματι αργω,
'Ημας εγκατεθηκε πατηρ ανδρων τε θεων τε.
Orphic. Αποσπ. No. xxiv. ed. Gesner.

Secundum hanc philosophiam, ψυχη anima est, quâ vivunt, spirant, aluntur τα εμψυχια. νους mens est, divinius quiddam, quibusdam animabus superadditum, sive inditum, a Deo. Gesner. Not. in eund.

[4] ――――― Θηβαιου Τειρεσιαο
Μαντιος αλαου, του τε φρενες εμπεδοι εισι·
Τω και τεθνειωτι νοον πορε Περσεφονεια,
Οιω πεπνυσθαι. Odyss. Κ. v. 492.

tasting the blood of a lamb offered in sacrifice ;[1] and it seems probable that the sanctity anciently attributed to red or purple color, arose from its similitude to that of blood; it having been customary, in early times, not only to paint the faces of the statues of the deities with vermilion; but also the bodies of the Roman Consuls and Dictators,[2] during the sacred ceremony of the triumph; from which ancient custom the imperial purple of later ages is derived.

165. It was, perhaps, in allusion to the emancipation and purification of the soul, that Bacchus is called *ΔΙΚΝΙΤΗΣ* ;[3] a metaphorical title taken from the winnow, which purified the corn from the dust and chaff, as fire was supposed to purify the ætherial soul from all gross and terrestrial matter. Hence this instrument is called by Virgil *the mystic winnow of Bacchus* ;[4] and hence we find the symbols both of the destroying and generative attributes upon tombs, signifying the separation and regeneration of the soul performed by the same power. Those of the latter are, in many instances, represented by very obscene and licentious actions, even upon sepulchral monuments; as appears from many now extant,

---

[1] Pausan. lib. ii. c. iii. and iv.

[2] Ταχυ γαρ εξανθει το μιλθινον, ᾧ τα παλαια των αγαλματων εχριζον. Plutarch. εν Ρωμαικ. See also Plin. Hist. Nat. lib. xxxiii. c. vii. ; and Winkelman. Hist. des Arts, Liv. i. c. ii.
Enumerat auctores Verrius, quibus credere sit necesse, Jovis ipsius simulachri faciem diebus festis minio illini solitam, triumphantumque corpora: sic Camillum triumphasse. Plin. ibid.

[3] Orph. Hymn. xlv. The λικνον, however, was the mystic sieve in which Bacchus was cradled; from which the title may have been derived, though the form of it implies an active rather than a passive sense. See Hesych. in voc.

[4] Mystica vannus Iacchi. Georg. 1. 166. Osiris has the winnow in one hand, and the hook of attraction in the other; which are more distinctly expressed in the large bronze figure of him engraved in pl. ii. of vol. i. of the Select Specimens, than in any other that we know. Even in the common small figures it is strange that it should ever have been taken for a whip; though it might reasonably have been taken for a flail, had the ancients used such an instrument in thrashing corn.

particularly one lately in the Farnese palace at Rome. The Canobus of the Ægyptians appears to have been a personification of the same attribute as the Bacchus *ΔΙΚΝΙΤΗΣ* of the Greeks : for he was represented by the filtering-vase, which is still employed to purify and render potable the waters of the Nile; and these waters, as before observed, were called *the defluxion of Osiris*, of whom the soul was supposed to be an emanation. The means, therefore, by which they were purified from all grosser matter, might properly be employed as the symbol of that power, which separated the ætherial from the terrestrial soul, and purified it from all the pollutions and incumbrances of corporeal substance. The absurd tale of Canobus being the deified Pilate of Menelaus is an invention of the later Greeks, unworthy of any serious notice.

166. The rite of Baptism in fire and water, so generally practised among almost all nations of antiquity, seems to have been a mystic representation of this purification and regeneration of the soul after death. It was performed by jumping three times through the flame of a sacred fire, and being sprinkled with water from a branch of laurel;[1] or else by being bedewed with the vapor from a sacred brand, taken flaming from the altar and dipped in water.[2] The exile at his return, and the bride at her marriage, went through ceremonies of this kind to signify their purification and regeneration for a new life;[3] and they appear to have been commonly practised as modes of expiation or extenuation for private or secret offences.[4]

---

[1] Certè ego transilui positas ter in ordine flammas,
Virgaque roratas laurea misit aquas. Ovid. Fast. lib. iv. ver. 727.

[2] Εστι δε χερνιψ ὑδωρ εις ὁ απεβαπτον δαλον εκ του βωμου λαμβανοντες, εφ' οὑ την θυσιαν επετελουν· και τουτῳ περιραινοντες τους παροντας ἡγνιζον. Athæn. lib. ix. p. 409.

[3] Ovid. ibid. v. 792. et Cnippin. Not. in eund. Το πυρ καθαιρει και το ὑδωρ ἁγνιζει, δει δε και καθαραν και ἁγνην διαμενειν την γαμηθεισαν. Plutarch. Quæst. Rom. i.
Βουλομενη δε αυτον αθανατον ποιησαι, τας νυκτας εις πυρ κατετιθει το βρεφος, και περιηρει τας θνητας σαρκας αυτου. ApoHodor. Biblioth. lib. i. c. v. s. 2.

[4] Ovid. ib. lib. v. 679.

A solemn ablution, too, always preceded initiation into the Ægyptian and Eleusinian mysteries ;[1] and when a Jewish proselyte was admitted, he was baptised in the presence of three witnesses, after being circumcised, but before he was allowed to make the oblation by which he professed himself a subject of the true God. As this ceremony was supposed to wash off all stains of idolatry, the person baptised was said to be regenerated, and animated with a new soul ; to preserve which in purity, he abandoned every former connexion of country, relation, or friend.[2]

167. Baptism or purification by fire, is still in use among the Hindoos, as it was among the earliest Romans ;[3] and also among the native Irish; men, women, and children, and even cattle, in Ireland, leaping over, or passing through the sacred bonfires annually kindled in honour of Baal ;[4] an ancient title of the Sun, which seems to have prevailed in the Northern as well as Eastern dialects : whence arose the compound titles of the Scandinavian deities, Baldur, Habaldur, &c. expressing different personified attributes.[5] This rite was probably the abomination, so severely reprobated by the sacred historians of the Jews, *of parents making their sons and daughters pass through the fire :* for, in India, it is still performed by mothers passing through the flames with their children in their arms ;[6] and though commentators have construed the expression in the Bible to mean the burning them alive, as offerings to Baal Moloch, it is more consonant to reason, as well as to history, to suppose that it alluded to this more innocent mode of purification and consecration to the Deity, which continued in use among the ancient inhabitants of Italy to the later periods of Heathenism ; when it was performed exactly as it

---

[1] Apuleii Metamorph. lib. ix.   Diodor. Sic. lib. i.

[2] Marsham Canon Chronic. s. ix. p. 192.

[3] Πυρκαιας προ των σκηνων γενεσθαι κελευσας (ὁ Ρωμυλος), εξαγει τον λεων τας φλογας ὑπερθρωσκοντα της ὁσιωσεως των σωματων ἑνεκα. Dionys. Hal. A. R. 1. lxxxviii.

[4] Collectan. de reb. Hibernic. No. v. p. 64.

[5] Ol. Rudbeck. Atlant. P. ii. c. v. p. 140.

[6] Ayeen Akbery, and Maurice's Antiquities of India, vol. v. p. 1075.

is now in Ireland, and held to be a holy and mystic means of communion with the great active principle of the universe.[1]

168. It must, however, be admitted that the Carthaginians and other nations of antiquity did occasionally sacrifice their children to their gods, in the most cruel and barbarous manner; and, indeed, there is scarcely any people whose history does not afford some instances of such abominable rites. Even the patriarch Abraham, when ordered to sacrifice his only son, does not appear to have been surprised or startled at it, or to have conceived the slightest suspicion that it might have been the contrivance of an evil being to seduce him: neither could Jephtha have had any notion that such sacrifices were odious or even unacceptable to the Deity, or he would not have considered his daughter as included in his general vow, or imagined that a breach of it in such an instance could be a greater crime than fulfilling it. Another mode of mystic purification by baptism was the Taurobolium, Ægobolium, or Criobolium of the Mithriac rites; which preceded Christianity but a short time in the Roman empire, and spread and flourished with it. The catechumen was placed in a pit covered with perforated boards; upon which the victim, whether a bull, a goat, or a ram, was sacrificed so as to bathe him in the blood which flowed from it. To this the compositions, so frequent in the sculptures of the third and fourth centuries, of Mithras the Persian Mediator, or

---

[1] Moxque per ardentes stipulæ crepitantis acervos
   Trajicias celeri strenua membra pede.
Expositus mos est : moris mihi restat origo.
   Turba facit dubium ; cœptaque nostra tenet.
Omnia purgat edax ignis, vitiumque metallis
   Excoquit : idcirco cum duce purgat oves.
An, quia cunctarum contraria semina rerum
   Sunt duo, discordes ignis et unda dei ;
Junxerunt elementa patres : aptumque putarunt
   Ignibus, et sparsâ tangere corpus aquâ ?
An, quod in his vitæ caussa est ; hæc perdidit exul :
   IIis nova fit conjux : hæc duo magna putant?
               Ovid. Fast. lib. iv. 781.

his female personification a winged Victory, sacrificing a bull, seem to allude :[1] but all that we have seen are of late date, except a single instance of the Criobolium or Victory sacrificing a ram, on a gold coin of Abydos, in the cabinet of Mr. Payne Knight, which appears anterior to the Macedonian conquest.

169. The celestial or ætherial soul was represented in symbolical writing by the butterfly ; an insect which first appears from the egg in the shape of a grub, crawling upon the earth, and feeding upon the leaves of plants. In this state it was aptly made an emblem of man in his earthly form ; when the ætherial vigor and activity of the celestial soul, the *divinæ particula mentis*, was clogged and encumbered with the material body. In its next state, the grub becoming a chrysalis appeared, by its stillness, torpor, and insensibility, a natural image of death, or the intermediate state between the cessation of the vital functions of the body, and the emancipation of the soul in the funeral pile : and the butterfly breaking from this torpid chrysalis, and mounting in the air, afforded a no less natural image of the celestial soul bursting from the restraints of matter, and mixing again with its native æther. Like other animal symbols, it was by degrees melted into the human form ; the original wings only being retained, to mark its meaning. So elegant an allegory would naturally be a favorite subject of art among a refined and ingenious people ; and it accordingly appears to have been more diversified and repeated by the Greek sculptors, than almost any other, which the system of emanations, so favorable to art, could afford. Being, however, a subject more applicable and interesting to individuals than communities, there is no trace of it upon any coin, though it so constantly occurs upon gems.

170. The fate of the terrestrial soul, the regions to which it retired at the dissolution of the body, and the degree of sensibility which it continued to enjoy, are subjects of much obscurity, and

[1] See Bassirel. di Roma, tav. lviii.-lx. &c.

seem to have belonged to the poetry, rather than to the religion, of the ancients. In the Odyssey it is allowed a mere miserable existence in the darkness of the polar regions, without any reward for virtue or punishment for vice; the punishments described being evidently allegorical, and perhaps of a different, though not inferior author. The mystic system does not appear to have been then known to the Greeks, who catched glimmering lights and made up incoherent fables from various sources. Pindar, who is more systematic and consistent in his mythology than any other poet, speaks distinctly of rewards and punishments; the latter of which he places in the central cavities of the earth, and the former in the remote islands of the ocean, on the other side of the globe; to which none were admitted, but souls that had transmigrated three times into different bodies, and lived piously in each ; after which they were to enjoy undisturbed happiness in this state of ultimate bliss, under the mild rule of Rhadamanthus, the associate of *ΚΡΟΝΟΣ* or Time.[1] A similar region of bliss in the extremities of the earth is spoken of in the Odyssey; but not as the retreat of the dead, but a country which Menelaus was to visit while living.[2] Virgil has made up an incoherent mixture of fable and allegory, by bringing the regions of recompense, as well as those of punishment, into the centre of the earth; and then giving them the ætherial light of the celestial luminaries,[3] without which even his powers of description could not have embellished them to suit their purpose. He has, also, after Plato,[4] joined Tartarus to them, though it was not part of the regions regularly allotted to the dead by the ancient Greek mythologists; but a distinct and separate world beyond chaos, as far from earth, as earth from heaven.[5] According to another poetical fiction, the higher parts of the sublunary regions were appropriated to the future residence of the

---

[1] Olymp. ii. 108—123. &c.

Τοισι δε λαμπει μεν μενος αελιου ταν ενθαδε νυκτα κατω. Id. apud Plutarch. de Cons. ad Apoll. in ed. Heyn. Pind. inter fragm. e threnis. i.

[2] Odyss. Δ. 561. [3] Solemque suum, sua sidera norunt. Æn. vi. 641.
[4] Phæd. p. 83.

[5] —————— Περην χαεος ζοφεροιο. Hesiod. Theog. v. 700.

Τοσσον ενερθ' αϊδεω, ὁσον ουρανος εστ' απο γαιης. Homer. Il. Θ. v.

souls of the great and good, who alone seemed deserving of immortality.[1]

171. Opinions so vague and fluctuating had of course but little energy ; and accordingly we never find either the hope of reward, or the fear of punishment after death, seriously employed by the Greek and Roman moralists as reasonable motives for human actions; or considered any otherwise than as matters of pleasing speculation or flattering error.[2] Among the barbarians of the North, however, the case was very different. They all implicitly believed that their valor in this life was to be rewarded in the next, with what they conceived to be the most exquisite of all possible enjoyments. Every morning they were to fight a great and promiscuous battle ; after which Odin was to restore the killed and wounded to their former strength and vigor, and provide a sumptuous entertainment for them in his hall, where they were to feed upon the flesh of a wild boar, and drink mead and ale out of the skulls of their enemies till night, when they were to go to bed with beautiful women.[3] Mankind in general in all stages of society are apt to fashion their belief to their dispositions, and thus to make their religion a stimulus instead of a curb to their passions.

172. As fire was supposed to be the medium through which the soul passed from one state to another, Mercury the conductor was nearly related to Vulcan, the general personification of that element. The Ægyptians called him his son ;[4] and the Greeks,

---

Milton's Hell is taken from the Tartarus of Hesiod, or whoever was the author of the Theogony which bears his name. His descriptions of Chaos are also drawn from the same source.

[1] Quæ niger astriferis connectitur axibus aër,
Quodque patet terras interlunæque meatus,
Semidei manes habitant, quos ignea virtus
Innocuos vitæ patientes ætheris imi
Fecit, et æternos animam collegit in orbes.

Lucan. Pharsal. ix. 5.

[2] Juvenal. Sat. ii. 149. Lucan. Phars. i. 458.
[3] Mallet Introd. à l'Hist. de Danemarc.   [4] Syncell. Chron. p. 124.

in some instances, represented him not only with the same cap, but also with the same features ; so that they are only to be distinguished by the adscititious symbols.[1] He has also, for the same reason, a near affinity with Hercules considered as the personification of the diurnal sun : wherefore they were not only worshipped together in the same temple,[2] but blended into the same figure, called a Hermheracles from its having the characteristic forms or symbols of both mixed.[3]

173. As the operations of both art and nature were supposed to be equally carried on by means of fire, Vulcan is spoken of by the poets, sometimes as the husband of Grace or Elegance,[4] and sometimes of Venus or Nature ;[5] the first of which appears to have been his character in the primary, and the second in the mystic or philosophical religion of the Greeks : for the whole of the song of Demodacus in the Odyssey, here alluded to, is an interpolation of a much later date ;[6] and the story, which it contains, of Vulcan detecting Mars and Venus, and confining them in invisible chains, evidently a mystic allegory, signifying the active and passive powers of destruction and generation fixed in their mutual operation by the invisible exertions of the universal agent, fire. It was probably composed as a hymn to Vulcan, and inserted by some rhapsodist, who did not understand the character of the Homeric language, with which the Attic contraction 'Ηλιος for Ηελιος is utterly incompatible.

174. The Ægyptian worship, being under the direction of a permanent Hierarchy, was more fixed and systematic than that of the Greeks ; though, owing to its early subversion, we have less knowledge of it. Hence the different personifications of fire were by them more accurately discriminated ; Phthas, whom the Greeks call Hephaistus, and the Latins Vulcan, being the primitive uni-

---

[1] See coins of Æsernia, Lipara, &c.

[2] Ηρακλεους δε κοινος και Ερμου προς τῳ σταδιῳ ναος. Paus.

[3] Cicer. ad Attic. lib. i. ep. x.   [4] Iliad Σ. 382.

[5] Odyss. Θ. 266.   [6] Odyss. Θ. 266-369.

versal element, or principle of life and motion in matter; Anubis, whom they called Hermes and Mercury, the Minister of Fate; and Thoth, whom they called by the same titles, the parent of Arts and Sciences. Phthas was said to be the father of all their Cabiri or chief gods;[1] and his name signified the *Ordinator* or *Regulator,* as it does still in the modern Coptic. His statues were represented lame, to signify that fire acts not alone, but requires the sustenance of some extraneous matter;[2] and he was fabled by the Greek mythologists to have delivered Minerva from the head of Jupiter; that is, to have been the means by which the wisdom of the omnipotent Father, the pure emanation of the Divine Mind, was brought into action.

175. This pure emanation, which the Ægyptians called Neith,[3] was considered as the goddess both of Force and Wisdom, the first in rank of the secondary deities,[4] and the only one endowed with all the attributes of the supreme Father:[5] for as wisdom is the most exalted quality of the mind, and the Divine Mind the perfection of wisdom, all its attributes are the attributes of wisdom; under whose direction its power is always exerted. Force and wisdom, therefore, when considered as attributes of the Deity, are the same; and Bellona and Minerva are but different titles for one personification. Both the Greeks and Ægyptians considered her as male and female;[6] and upon monuments of art still extant, or accurately recorded, she is represented with almost every symbol

---

[1] Herodot. lib. iii. 37.

[2] Jablonski Panth. Ægypt. lib. i. c. ii. s. 11 et 13.

[3] Ἡ της πολεως αρχηγος εστιν Αιγυπτιστι μεν τουνομα Νηιθ, Ἑλληνιστι δε, ὡς εκεινων λογος, Αθηνα. Platon. Tim. p. 474.

[4] Proximos illi tamen occupavit
Pallas honores.   Horat. lib. i. Ode xii.

[5] ——— Επει μωνα Ζευς τογε θυγατερων
Δωκεν Αθαναια, πατρωια παντα φερεσθαι.
Callimach. εις λουτ. της Παλλ. v. 132.

[6] Αρσην και θηλυς εφυς. Orph. Hymn. εις Αθην. Jablonsk. Panth. Ægypt. lib. i. c. iii. s. 6.

of almost every attribute, whether of creation, preservation, or destruction.[1]

176. Before the human form was adopted, her proper symbol was the owl; a bird which seems to surpass all other creatures in acuteness and refinement of organic perception; its eye being calculated to discern objects, which to all others are enveloped in darkness; its ear to hear sounds distinctly, when no other can perceive them at all; and its nostrils to discriminate effluvia with such nicety, that it has been deemed prophetic from discovering the putridity of death, even in the first stages of disease.[2] On some very ancient Phœnician coins, we find the owl with the hook of attraction and winnow of separation under its wing to show the dominion of Divine Wisdom over both; while on the reverse is represented the result of this dominion, in the symbolical composition of a male figure holding a bow in his hand, sitting upon the back of a winged horse terminating in the tail of a dolphin; beneath which are waves and another fish.[3] A similar meaning was veiled under the fable of Minerva's putting the bridle into the mouth of Pegasus,[4] or Divine Wisdom controlling and regulating the waters when endued with motion,

177. The Ægyptians are said to have represented the pervading Spirit or ruling providence of the Deity by the black beetle, which frequents the shores of the Mediterranean sea,[5] and which some have supposed to be an emblem of the Sun.[6] It occurs very frequently upon Phœnician, Greek, and Etruscan, as well as Ægyp-

---

[1] The celebrated statue of her at Athens by Phidias held a spear, near which was a serpent. Pausan. lib. i. c. xxiv. A sacred serpent was also kept in her great temple in the Acropolis. Aristoph. Lysistrat. v. 758.

Και Αθηνας (αγαλμα) επικλησιν και ταυτης Ὑγιειας. Pausan. in Attic. c. xxiii. s. 5. See also medals of Athens, in which almost every symbol occasionally accompanies the owl.

[2] Of this we have known instances, in which the nocturnal clamors of the screech-owl have really foretold death, according to the vulgar notion.

[3] See Dutens Médailles Phénic. pl. i. v. i.   [4] Pausan. lib. ii. c. iv.

[5] Horapoll. l. i. c. x.   [6] Plutarch. de Is. et Osir. p. 380.

tian sculptures; and is sometimes with the owl, and sometimes
with the head of Minerva, upon the small brass coins of Athens.
It is of the androgynous class, and lays its eggs in a ball of dung
or other fermentable matter, which it had previously collected, and
rolled backwards and forwards upon the sand of the sea, until it
acquired the proper form and consistency; after which it buries it
in the sand, where the joint operation of heat and moisture matures
and vivifies the germs into new insects.[1] As a symbol, therefore,
of the Deity, it might naturally have been employed to signify the
attribute of Divine Wisdom, or ruling Providence, which directs,
regulates, and employs the productive powers of nature.

178. When the animal symbols were changed for the human,
Minerva was represented under the form of a robust female figure,
with a severe, but elegant and intelligent countenance, and armed
with a helmet, shield, and breast-plate, the emblems of preservation;
and most frequently with a spear, the emblem, as well as the instrument of destruction. The helmet is usually decorated with some animal symbol; such as the owl, the serpent, the ram, the gryphon, or
the sphinx; which is a species of gryphon, having the head of the
female personification, instead of that of the eagle, upon the body
of the lion. Another kind of gryphon, not unfrequent upon the
helmets of Minerva, is composed of the eagle and horse,[2] signifying
the dominion of water instead of fire: whence came the symbol
of the flying horse, already noticed. In other instances the female
head and breast of the sphinx are joined to the body of a horse;
which, in these compositions is always male, as well as that of the
lion in the sphinx; so as to comprehend the attributes of both
sexes.[3] In the stand of a mirror of very ancient sculpture belonging

---

[1] Το δε κανθαρον γενος ουκ εχειν θηλειαν, αρρενας δε παντας αφιεναι τον γονον εις την
σφαιροποιουμενην ύλην, ήν κυλινδουσιν αντιβαδην ωθουντες, ώσπερ δοκει τον ουρανον ό
ήλιος εις τουναντιον περιστρεφειν, αυτος απο δυσμων επι τας ανατολας φερομενος. Plutarch de Is. et Osir.

Τον δε ήλιον τω κανθαρω (απεικαζον οἱ Αιγυπτιοι)· επειδη κυκλοτερες εκ της βοειας
ονθου σχημα πλασαμενος, αντιπροσωπος κυλινδει· φασι και ἐξαμηνον μεν ὑπο γης θατερον
δε του ετους τμημα το ζωον τουτο ὑπερ γης διαιτασθαι, σπερμαινειν τε εις την σφαιραν
και γεννην, και θηλυν κανθαρον μη γινεσθαι. Clem. Alex. Strom. lib. v. c. iv.

[2] See Medals of Velia, &c.   [3] Hence the ανδροσφιγγες of Herodotus, lib. ii.

to Mr. Payne Knight is a figure of Isis upon the back of a monkey with a sphinx on each side of her head, and another in her hand, the tail of which terminates in a phallus; so that it is a compound symbol of the same kind as the chimæra and others before noticed. The monkey very rarely occurs in Greek sculptures, but was a sacred animal among the Ægyptians, as it still continues to be in some parts of Tartary and India; but on account of what real or imaginary property is now uncertain.

179. The ægis or breast-plate of Minerva is, as the name indicates, the goat-skin, the symbol of the productive power, fabled to have been taken from the goat which suckled Jupiter; that is, from the great nutritive principle of nature. It is always surrounded with serpents, and generally covered with plumage; and in the centre of it is the Gorgo or Medusa, which appears to have been a symbol of the Moon,[1] exhibited sometimes with the character and expression of the destroying, and sometimes with those of the generative or preserving attribute; the former of which is expressed by the title of Gorgo, and the latter by that of Medusa.[2] It is sometimes represented with serpents, and sometimes with fish, in the hair; and occasionally with almost every symbol of the passive generative or productive power; it being the female personification of the Disk, by which almost all the nations of antiquity represented the Sun;[3] and this female personification was the symbol of the Moon. Among the Romans, the golden bulla or disk was worn by the young men, and the crescent by the women, as it

---

[1] Γοργονιον την σεληνην δια το εν αυτη προσωπον. Orph. in Clem. Alex. Strom. lib. v. p. 675.

[2] ΓΟΡΓΩ is said to have been a barbarian title of Minerva, as ΒΕΝΔΕΙΑ and ΔΙΚΤΥΝΝΑ were of Diana. Palæphat. fab. xxxii. ΜΕΔΟΥΣΑ is the participle of the verb ΜΕΔΩ to govern or take care of. In a beautiful intaglio, the work of Anteros, belonging to Mr. Payne Knight, Perseus sustains the Medusa in his hand, while the Gorgo occupies the centre of a shield, on which he rests his harpè.

[3] See authorities before cited.

Παιονες σεβουσι τον Ἡλιον αγαλμα δε Ἡλιου Παιονικον δισκος βραχυς ὑπερ μακρου ξυλον. Max. Tyr. Dissert. viii.

still is in the South of Italy; and it seems that the same symbolical amulets were in use among the ancient inhabitants of the British islands; several of both having been found made of thin beaten gold both in England and Ireland; which were evidently intended to be hung round the neck.[1] Each symbol, too, occasionally appears worn in like manner upon the figures of Juno or Ceres, which cannot always be discriminated; and the Disk between horns, which seem to form a crescent, is likewise upon the heads of Isis and Osiris, as well as upon those of their animal symbols, the cow and bull.[2]

180. The ægis employed occasionally by Jupiter, Minerva, and Apollo, in the Iliad, seems to have been something very different from the symbolical breast-plate or thorax, which appears in monuments of art now extant; it being borne and not worn; and used to excite courage or instil fear, and not for defence.[3] The name Ægis, however, still seems to imply that it is derived from the same source and composed of the same material; though instead of serpents, or other symbolical ornaments, it appears to have been decorated with golden tassels or knobs hanging loosely from it; the shaking and rattling of which produced the effects above mentioned.[4] Vulcan is said to have made it for Jupi-

---

[1] One three inches in diameter, found in the Isle of Man, is in the collection of Mr. Payne Knight, and another, found in Lancashire, in that of the late C. Townley, esq.

[2] Μεταξυ δε των κερεων, ὁ του ἡλιου κυκλος μιμημενος επεστι χρυσεος· εστι δε ἡ βους ορθη, αλλ' εν γουνασι κειμενη.   Herodot. lib. ii. 132.

[3] ——— ——— Μετα δε γλαυκωπις Αθηνη,
Αιγιδ' εχουσ' εριτιμον
*   *   *   *   *   *
Συν τη παιφασσουσα διεσσυτο λαον Αχαιων,
Οτρυνουσ' ιεναι· εν δε σθενος ωρσεν ἑκαστου
Καρδιη, αλληκτον πολεμιζειν, ηδε μαχεσθαι.   B. 446.
Ζευς δε σφιν Κρονιδης, υψιζυγος, αιθερι ναιων,
Αυτος εισσειησιν ερεμνην Αιγιδα πασι
Της δ' απατης κοτεων.   Δ. 166.
See also O. 308 and 318.

[4] Αιγιδ' εχουσ' εριτιμον, αγηραον, αθανατην τε
Της ἑκατον θυσανοι παγχρυσεοι ηερεθοντο,
Παντες ευπλεκεες· εκατομβοιος δε ἑκαστος.   B. 447.

ter ;¹ and to have furnished it with all those terrific attributes, which became so splendid and magnificent when personified in poetry.

181. Stripped, however, of all this splendor and magnificence, it was probably nothing more than a symbolical instrument, signifying originally the motion of the elements, like the sistrum of Isis, the cymbals of Cybele,² the bells of Bacchus, &c.; whence Jupiter is said to have overcome the Titans with his ægis, as Isis drove away Typhon with her sistrum ;³ and the ringing of bells and clatter of metals were almost universally employed as a mean of consecration, and a charm against the destroying and inert powers.⁴ Even the Jews welcomed the new Moon with such noises ;⁵ which the simplicity of the early ages employed almost everywhere to relieve her during eclipses, supposed then to be morbid affections brought on by the influence of an adverse power. The title Priapus, by which the generative attribute is distinguished, seems to be merely a corruption of ΒΡΙΑΠΤΟΣ, clamorous ; the Β and Π being commutable letters, and epithets of similar meaning being continually applied both to Jupiter and Bacchus by the poets.⁶ Many priapic figures, too, still extant, have bells attached to

---

¹ —————————————- Εχε δ' αιγιδα θουριν
Δεινην, αμφιδασειαν, αριπρεπε', ην αρα χαλκευς
'Ηφαιστος Διι δωκε φορημεναι ες φοβον ανδρων. O. 308.
Αμφι δ' αρ' ωμοισιν βαλετ' αιγιδα θυσσανοεσσαν
Δεινην, ην περι μεν παντη φοβος εστεφανωται·
Εν δ' Ερις, εν δ' Αλκη, εν δε κρυοεσσα Ιωκη·
Εν δε τε Γοργειη κεφαλη δεινοιο πελωρου,
Δεινη τε σμερδνη τε, Διος τερας αιγιοχοιο. E. 738.

² Σοι μεν καταρχαι, Ματερ, παρα
Μεγαλοι ρομβοι κυμβαλων, Pindar. ap. Strab. lib. x. p. 719.

³ Τον γαρ Τυφωνα φασι τοις σειστροις αποτρεπειν και ανακρουεσθαι, δηλουντες, ὀτι της φθορας συνδεουσης και ιστασης, αυθις αναλυει την φυσιν, και ανιστησι δια της κινησεως ἡ γενεσις. Plutarch. de Is. et Osir.

⁴ Schol. in Theocrit. Idyl. ii. 36.
——————— Temesæaque concrepat æra,
Et rogat ut tectis exeat umbra suis. Ovid. Fast. v. 441.

⁵ Numer. c. x. v. 10.
⁶ Such as εριβρεμιτης, εριγδουπος, βρομιος, &c.

K

them ;¹ as the symbolical statues and temples of the Hindoos have;
and to wear them was a part of the worship of Bacchus among the
Greeks ;² whence we sometimes find them of extremely small
size, evidently meant to be worn as amulets with the phalli, lunulæ,
&c. The chief priests of the Ægyptians, and also the high priest
of the Jews, hung them, as sacred emblems, to their sacerdotal
garments ;³ and the Bramins still continue to ring a small bell at
the intervals of their prayers, ablutions, and other acts of mystic
devotion. The Lacedæmonians beat upon a brass vessel or pan,
on the death of their kings ;⁴ and we still retain the custom of
tolling a bell on such occasions ; though the reason of it is not
generally known, any more than that of other remnants of ancient
superstitions still existing.⁵

182. An opinion very generally prevailed among the ancients,
that all the constituent parts of the great machine of the universe
were mutually dependent upon each other; and that the luminaries
of heaven, while they contributed to fecundate and organise terrestrial matter, were in their turn nourished and sustained by exhalations drawn from the humidity of the earth and its atmosphere.
Hence the Ægyptians placed the personifications of the Sun and
Moon in boats ;⁶ while the Greeks, among whom the horse was a
symbol of humidity, placed them in chariots, drawn sometimes by

Bronzi d'Ercolano, t. vi. tav. xcviii.

² Διονυσιακον δε————τους βασιλεας κωδωνοφορεισθαι, και τυμπανιζεσθαι κατα τας
διεξοδους. - Megasthen. apud Strab. lib. xv. p. 712.

³ Plutarch. Symposiac. lib. iv. qu. v.   Exod. c. xxviii.

⁴ Schol. in Theocrit. l. c.

⁵ " It is said," says the Golden Legend by Wynkyn de Worde, " the evil
spirytes that ben in the regyon of th' ayre doubte moche when they here
the belles rongen: and this is the cause why the belles ben rongen when it
thondreth, and when grete tempeste and outrages of wether happen, to the
end that the feindes and wycked spirytes shold be abashed and flee, and
cease of the movying of the tempeste." p. 90.

Εκεινα μεν γαρ (τα φασματα) ην ψοφον ακουση χαλκου η σιδηρου πεφευγε. Lucian.
Philops. 15.

⁶ Ἡλιον δε και σεληνην ουχ ἁρμασιν αλλα πλειοις οχημασι χρωμενους περιπλειν αει,
αινιττομενοι την αφ' ὑγρου τροφην αυτων και γενεσιν. Plutarch. de Is. et Osir.

two, sometimes by three, and sometimes by four of these animals; which is the reason of the number of Bigæ, Trigæ, and Quadrigæ, which we find upon coins: for they could not have had any reference to the public games, as has been supposed; a great part of them having been struck by states, which, not being of Hellenic origin, had never the privilege of entering the lists on those occasions. The vehicle itself appears likewise to have been a symbol of the passive generative power, or the means by which the emanations of the Sun acted; whence the Delphians called Venus by the singular title of The Chariot;[1] but the same meaning is more frequently expressed by the figure called a Victory accompanying; and by the fish, or some other symbol of the waters under it. In some instances we have observed composite symbols signifying both attributes in this situation; such as the lion destroying the bull, or the Scylla;[2] which is a combination of emblems of the same kind as those which compose the sphinx and chimæra, and has no resemblance whatever to the fabulous monster described in the Odyssey.

183. Almost every other symbol is occasionally employed as an accessary to the chariot, and among them the thunderbolt; which is sometimes borne by Minerva and other deities, as well as by Jupiter; and is still oftener represented alone upon coins; it having been an emblem, not merely of the destroying attribute, but of the Divine nature in general: whence the Arcadians sacrificed to thunder, lightning, and tempest;[3] and the incarnate Deity, in an ancient Indian poem, says, " I am the thunderbolt."——" I am the fire residing in the bodies of all things which have life."[4] In the South-Eastern parts of Europe, which frequently suffer from drought, thunder is esteemed a grateful rather than terrific sound,

---

[1] ———Ουτε Δελφους ελεγχει ληρουντας, ὁτι την Αφροδιτην ἁρμα καλουσιν. Plutarch. Amator. p. 769.

[2] See coins of Agrigentum, Heraclea in Italy, Allifa, &c.

[3] Και θυουσι αυτοθι αστραπαις, και θυελλαις, και βρονταις. Pausan. lib. vii. c. 29.

[4] Bagvat Geeta, p. 86 and 113.

Αἱ ἡμετεραι ψυχαι πυρ εισι. Phurnut. de Nat. Deor. c. ii.

because it is almost always accompanied with rain ; which scarcely ever falls there without it.[1]   This rain, descending from ignited clouds, was supposed to be impregnated with electric or ætherial fire, and therefore to be more nutritive and prolific than any other water :[2] whence the thunderbolt was employed as the emblem of fecundation and nutrition, as well as of destruction. The coruscations which accompany its explosions being thought to resemble the glimmering flashes which proceed from burning sulphur ; and the smell of the fixed air arising from objects stricken by it being the same as that which arises from the mineral, men were led to believe that its fires were of a sulphurous nature :[3] wherefore the flames of sulphur were employed in all lustrations, purifications, &c.,[4] as having an affinity with divine or ætherial fire ; to which its name in the Greek language has been supposed to refer.[5]   To represent the thunderbolt, the ancient artists joined two obelisks pointing contrary ways from one centre, with spikes or arrows diverging from them ; thus signifying its luminous essence and destructive power. Wings were sometimes added, to signify its swiftness and activity ; and the obelisks were twisted into spiral forms, to show the whirl in the air caused by the vacuum proceeding from the explosion ; the origin of which, as well as the productive attribute, was signified by the aquatic plants, from which they sprang.[6]

Grateful as thunder in summer, is a simile of Tasso's; who, notwithstanding his frequent and close imitations of the ancients, has copied nature more accurately than any Epic poet except Homer.

[2] Τα δ' αστραπαια των ὑδατων εναλδη καλουσιν οἱ γεωργοι, και νομιζουσι.——ταις βρονταις πολλακις ὑδωρ συνεκπιπτει γονιμον· αιτια δε ἡ της θερμοτητος αναμιξις.—— το κεραυνιον πυρ ακριβεια και λεπτοτητι θαυμαστον εστι. Plutarch. Symposiac. lib. iv. qu. 2.

[3] Αφηκ' αργητα κεραυνον
Δεινη δε-φλοξ ωρτο θειοιο καιομενοιο. Iliad Θ.

[4] —————— Cuperent lustrari, si qua darentur
Sulphura cum tædis, et si foret humida laurus.
Juvenal. Sat. ii. v. 157.

[5] Οιμαι κοι το θειον ωνομασθαι τη ὁμοιοτητι της οσμης, ἡν τα παιομενα τοις κεραυνοις αφιησιν. Plutarch. Symposiac. lib. iv. qu. 2.

[6] See coins of Syracuse, Seleucia, Alexander I. king of Epirus, Elis, &c. Upon some of the most ancient of the latter, however, it is more simply composed of flames only, diverging both ways.

184. After the conquests of Alexander had opened a communication with India, Minerva was frequently represented with the elephant's skin upon her head instead of the helmet ;[1] the elephant having been, from time immemorial, the symbol of divine wisdom among the Gentoos; whose god Gonnis or Pollear is represented by a figure of this animal half humanised ; which the Macha Alla, or god of destruction of the Tartars, is usually seen trampling upon.[2] On some of the coins of the Seleucidæ, the elephant is represented with the horns of the bull; sometimes drawing the chariot of Minerva, in her character of Bellona; and at others bearing a torch, the emblem of the universal agent fire, in his proboscis, and the cornucopiæ, the result of its exertion under the direction of divine wisdom, in his tail.[2]

185. The ram has been already noticed as the symbol of Mercury ; but at Sais in Ægypt, it seems to have represented some attribute of Minerva;[3] upon a small bust of whom, belonging to Mr. Payne Knight, it supplies the ornament for the visor of the helmet, as the sphinx does that of the crest; the whole composition showing the passive and active powers of generation and destruction, as attributes to Divine Wisdom. In another small bronze of very ancient workmanship, which has been the handle of a vase, rams are placed at the feet, and lions at the head, of an androgynous figure of Bacchus, which still more distinctly shows their meaning ; and in the ancient metropolitan temple of the North, at Upsal in Sweden, the great Scandinavian goddess Isa was represented riding upon a ram, with an owl in her hand.[4] Among the Ægyptians, however, Ammon was the deity most commonly represented under this symbol ; which was usually half humanised, as it appears in pl. i. vol. i. of the Select Specimens ; in which form he was worshipped in the cele-

---

[1] See coins of Alexander II. king of Epirus, and some of the Ptolemies.

[2] See those of Seleucus I. Antiochus VI. &c.

[3] Τουτου του νομου μεγιστη πολις Σαις————————της πολεως θεος αρχηγος εστιν, Αιγυπτιστι μεν τουνομα Νηιθ, Ἑλληνιστι δε, ὡς εκεινων λαγος, Αθηνα. Platon. Timæ. p. 474. Serr. 104S. Fic.
Τιμωσι Σαιται προβατον και Θηβαιται. Strabon. lib. xvii. p. 559.

[4] Ol. Rudbeck. Atlant. vol. ii. p. 209. fig. B.

brated oracular temple in Libya, as well as that of Thebes ; [1] and was the father of that Bacchus who is equally represented with the ram's horns, but young and beardless.

186. Ammon, according to some accounts, corresponded with the Jupiter, [2] and according to others, with the Pan [3] of the Greeks; and probably he was something between both, like the Lycæan Pan, the most ancient and revered deity of the Arcadians, the most ancient people of Greece. [4] His title was employed by the Ægyptians as a common form of appellation towards each other, as well as of solemn invocation to the Deity, in the same manner as we employ the title of Lord, and the French that of Seigneur ; and it appears to have been occasionally compounded with other words, and applied to other deities. [5] According to Jablonski, who explains it from the modern Coptic, it signified precisely the same as the epi-

---

[1] Απο τουτου κριοπροσωπον τωγαλμα του Διος ποιευσι Αιγυπτιοι· απο δε Αιγυπτιων Αμμονιοι, εοντες Αιγυπτιων τε και Αιθιοπων αποικοι, και φωνην μεταξυ αμφοτερων νομιζοντες. Herodot. lib. ii. c. 42.

[2] Αμμουν γαρ Αιγυπτιοι καλουσι τον Δια. Lib. ii. s. 42. Herodot.

[3] Τον πρωτον θεον (Αμουν) τῳ παντι τον αυτον νομιζουσι. Plutarch. de Is. et Osir. p. 354.

[4] Ante Jovem genitum terras habuisse feruntur
Arcades, et Lunâ gens prior illa fuit.
Ovid. Fast. lib. ii. v. 289.

They were of the Pelasgian race, and being in possession of a poor and mountainous country, they kept it, whilst the more fertile parts of Greece were continually changing inhabitants. Thucyd. lib. i.; Herodot. lib. i. s. 146.; Pausan. lib. viii. s. 1. Their being anterior to Jupiter and the Moon, means no more than that they were anterior to the established religion, by which the divine personifications were ascertained, and made distinct objects of worship.

[5] Σπενδουσι και Ἡρᾳ τε Αμμωνιᾳ, και Παραμμωνι. Ἑρμου δε επικλησις εστιν ὁ Παραμμων. Pausan. in Eliac. 1. c. xv. s. 7.

Ἑκαταιος ὁ Αβδηριτης φησι τουτῳ και προς αλληλους τῳ ῥηματι χρησθαι τους Αιγυπτιους, ὁταν τινα προσκαλωνται· προσκλητικην γαρ ειναι την φωνην. Plutarch. de Is. et Osir. p. 354.

Mr. Bryant says, that this was calling each other Ammonians, Pref. p. 7. Some future antiquary of this school will probably discover that the English, when they use the word Sir, mean to call each other Sirites; and thence sagaciously infer that Britain was first peopled from Siris in Italy ; an inference quite as probable as most of this learned gentleman's.

thet Lycæan, that is *lucid,* or productive of light.¹ It may therefore have been applied with equal propriety to either Jupiter or Pan ; the one being the luminous ætherial spirit considered abstractedly, and the other, as diffused through the mass of universal matter. Hence Pan is called, in the Orphic Hymns, *Jupiter the mover of all things,* and described as harmonising them by the music of his pipe. ² He is also called the *pervader of the sky* ³ and of *the sea,* ⁴ to signify the principle of order diffused through heaven and earth ; and the Arcadians called him the *Lord of matter,* ⁵ which title is expressed in the Latin name Sylvanus ; SYLVA, 'ΤΑΦΑ, and 'ΤΑΗ, being the same word written according to the different modes of pronouncing of different dialects. In a choral ode of Sophocles, he is addressed by the title of *Author and director of the dances of the gods ;* ⁶ as being the author and disposer of the regular motions of the universe, of which these divine dances were symbols. ⁷ According to Pindar, this Arcadian Pan was the associate or husband of Rhea, ⁸ and consequently the same as Saturn, with whom he seems to be confounded in the ancient coins above cited (s. 112.); some of them having the half-humanised horse, and others the figure commonly called Silenus, which is no other than Pan, in the same attitudes with the same female.

---

¹ Panth. Ægypt. lib. ii. c. ii. s. 12.

² ──────── ──── Ζευς ὁ κεραστης. Hymn. x. ver. 12.
   Ζευς δε τε παντων εστι θεος, παντων τε κεραστης
   Πνευμασι συριζων, φωναισι τε αερομικτοις.
                                    Fragm. No. xxviii. ver. 13. ed. Gesn.

³ ΑΙΘΕΡΟΠΛΑΓΚΤΟΣ. Orph. Hymn. v.

⁴ 'ΑΛΙΠΛΑΓΚΤΟΣ. Sophocl. Aj. 703.

⁵ Τον της λης κυριον. Macrob. Sat. 1. c. 22.

⁶   Παν, Παν ἁλιπλαγκτε
    Κυλλανιας χιονοκτυπου
    Πετραιας αποδειραδος, φανηθ', ω
    Θεων χοροποι' αναξ, ὁππως μοι
    Νυσσια Κνωσσια
    Ορχηματα αυτοδαη
    Ξυνων ιαψης. Ajac.

⁷ 'Η γουν χορεια των αστερων, και ἡ προς τους απλανεις των πλανητων συμπλοκη, και ευρυθμος αυτων κοινωνια, και ευτακτος ἁρμονια, της πρωτογονου ορχησεως δειγματα εστι. Lucian. de Saltatione.

⁸ Schol. in Pind. Pyth. iii. 138.

187. Among the Greeks all dancing was of the mimetic kind: wherefore Aristotle classes it with poetry, music, and painting, as bemg equally an imitative art:[1] and Lucian calls it a science of imitation *and exhibition, which explained the conceptions of the mind, and certified to the organs of sense things naturally beyond their reach.*[2] To such a degree of refinement was it carried, that Athenæus speaks of a Pythagorean, who could display the whole system of his sect in such gesticulations, more clearly and strongly than a professed rhetorician could in words;[3] for the truth of which, however, we do not vouch, the attempt being sufficient. Dancing was also a part of the ceremonial in all mystic rites:[4] whence it was held in such high esteem, that the philosopher Socrates, and the poet Sophocles, both persons of exemplary gravity, and the latter of high political rank and dignity, condescended to cultivate it as an useful and respectable accomplishment.[5] The author of the Homeric Hymn to Apollo, describes that God accompanying his lyre with the dance, joined by other deities ;[6] and a Corinthian poet, cited by Athenæus, introduces the Father of gods and men employed in the same exercise.[7] The ancient Indians, too, paid their devotions to the Sun by a dance imitative of his motions, which they performed every morning and evening, and which was their only act of worship.[8] Among the Greeks the Cnosian dances were peculiarly sacred to Jupiter, as the Nyssian were to Bacchus, both of which were under the direction of Pan ;[9] who, being the principle of universal order, partook of the nature of all the other gods; they being personifications of particular modes of acting of the great all-ruling principle, and he of his general law of pre-established harmony; whence, upon an ancient earthen vase of Greek workmanship, he is represented playing upon a pipe, between two figures, the one male and the other female; over the

---

[1] Poetic. c. i.

[2] Μιμητικη τις εστιν επιστημη, και δεικτικη, και των εννοηθεντων εξαγορευτικη, και των αφανων σαφηνιστικη. Lucian. ib. s. 43.

[3] Deipnos. lib. i. c. xvii.   [4] Ibid.

Τελετην αρχαιαν ουδεμιαν, εστιν ευρειν, ανευ ορχησεως. Lucian. ibid.

[5] Athenæ. ib.   [6] Ver. 194—206.

[7] Ib. c. xix.   [8] Lucian. ibid.   [9] Sophocl. in l. c.

latter of which is written *ΝΟΟΣΣ*, and over the former *ΑΛΚΟΣ*; whilst he himself is distinguished by the title *ΜΟΛΚΟΣ*: so that this composition explicitly shows him in the character of universal harmony, resulting from mind and strength ; these titles being, in the ancient dialect of Magna Græcia, where the vase was found, the same as *ΝΟΤΣ*, *ΑΛΚΗ*, and *ΜΟΛΠΗ*, in ordinary Greek. The ancient dancing, however, which held so high a rank among liberal and sacred arts, was entirely imitative ; and esteemed honorable or otherwise, in proportion to the dignity or indignity of what it was meant to express. The highest was that which exhibited military exercises and exploits with the most perfect skill, grace, and agility; excellence in which was often honored by a statue in some dis tinguished attitude ; [1] and we strongly suspect, that the figure commonly called " The fighting Gladiator," is one of them ; there being a very decided character of individuality both in the form and features ; and it would scarcely have been quite naked, had it represented any event of history.

188. Pan, like other mystic deities, was wholly unknown to the first race of poets; there being no mention of him in either the Iliad, the Odyssey, or in the genuine poem of Hesiod ; and the mythologists of later times having made him a son of Mercury by Penelope, the wife of Ulysses; a fiction, perhaps, best accounted for by the conjecture of Herodotus, that the terrestrial genealogies of the mystic deities, Pan, Bacchus, and Hercules, are mere fables, bearing date from the supposed time of their becoming objects of public worship. [2] Both in Greece and Ægypt, Pan was commonly represented under the symbolical form of the goat half humanised; [3] from which are derived his subordinate ministers or personified emanations, called Satyrs, Fauns, Tituri, *ΠΑΝΙΣΚΟΙ*, &c. ; who,

---

[1] Athen. Deipnos. lib. xiv. c. xxvi. ed. Schweig.

[2] Δηλα μοι ων γεγονε οτι υστερον επυθοντο οἱ Ελληνες τουτων τα ουνοματα, η τα των αλλων θεων· απ' οὗ δε επυθοντο χρονου, απο τουτου γενεηλογεουσι αντεων την γενεσιν. Herodot. lib. ii. s. 146.

[3] Γραφουσι τε δη και γλυφουσι οἱ ζωγραφοι και οἱ αγαλματοποιοι του Πανος τωγαλμα, καταπερ Ελληνες, αιγοπροσωπον και τραγοσκελεα· οντι τοιουτον νομιζοντες ειναι μιν, αλλ' ὁμοιον τοισι αλλοισι θεοισι· ὁτευ δε εἱνεκα τοιουτον γραφουσι αυτον, ου μοι ἡδιον εστι λεγειν. Herodot. ii. 46.

as well as their parent, were wholly unknown to the ancient poets. Neither do they appear to have been known in Ægypt, though "a late traveller was so singularly fortunate as to find a mask of a Caprine Satyr upon an ancient Ægyptian lyre represented in the ancient paintings of the Thebaid ; in a form, indeed, so unlike that of any ancient people, and so like to a Welsh or Irish harp, that we cannot but suspect it to be merely an embellishment of an idea that he carried out with him. [1] M. Denon, in his more accurate and extensive survey of the same ruins, found nothing of the kind.

189. The Nymphs, however, the corresponding emanations of the passive productive power of the universe, had been long known : for whether considered as the daughters of the Ocean or of Jupiter,[2] their parent had long been enrolled among the personages of the vulgar mythology. Upon monuments of ancient art, they are usually represented with the Fauns and Satyrs, frequently in attitudes very licentious and indecent : but in the Homeric times, they seem to have been considered as guardian spirits or local deities of the springs, the vallies, and the mountains ;[3] the companions of the river gods, who were the male progeny of the Ocean ; [4] though the mystic system, as before observed, allowed them a more exalted genealogy.

190. Pan is sometimes represented ready to execute his characteristic office, and sometimes exhibiting the result of it ; in the former of which, all the muscles of his face and body appear strained and contracted; and in the latter, fallen and dilated; while in both the phallus is of disproportionate magnitude, to signify that it represented the predominant attribute. [5] In one instance, he appears

---

[1] See print from Mr. Bruce's drawing, in Dr. Burney's History of Music.

[2] ―――― Genitor Nympharum Oceanus. Catull. in Gell. v. 84. See also Callimach. Hymn. ad Dian. v. 13., and Æschyl. Prometh. Desmot.

[3] Νυμφαι ορεστιαδες, κουραι Διος αιγιοχοιο. Il. Z. 420.
Νυμφαων, αἱ εχουσ' ορεων αιπεινα καρηνα,
Και πηγας ποταμων, και πεισεα ποιηεντα.   Il. Φ. 195.

[4] Ουδε βαθυρρειταο μεγα σθενος Ωκεανοιο
Εξ οὑ περ παντες ποταμοι, και πασα θαλασσα,
Και πασαι κρηναι, και φρειατα μακρα ναουσιν.   Odyss. Z. 123.

[5] The figures are frequent in collections of small bronzes.

pouring water upon it, [1] but more commonly standing near water, and accompanied by aquatic fowls; in which character he is confounded with Priapus, to whom geese were particularly sacred. [2] Swans, too, frequently occur as emblems of the waters upon coins; and sometimes with the head of Apollo on the reverse ;[3] when there may be some allusion to the ancient notion of their singing; a notion which seems to have arisen from the noises which they make in the high latitudes of the North, prior to their departure at the approach of winter. [4] The pedum, or pastoral hook, the symbol of attraction, and the pipe, the symbol of harmony, are frequently placed near him, to signify the means and effect of his operation.

191. Though the Greek writers call the deity who was represented by the sacred goat at Mendes, Pan, he more exactly answers to Priapus, or the generative attribute considered abstractedly ;[5] which was usually represented in Ægypt, as well as in Greece, by the phallus only. [6] This deity was honored with a place in most of their temples, [7] as the lingam is in those of the Hindoos; and all the hereditary priests were initiated or consecrated to him, before they assumed the sacerdotal office : [8] for he was considered as a sort of accessary attribute to all the other divine personifications, the great end and purpose of whose existence was generation or production. A part of the worship offered both to the goat Mendes, and the bull Apis, consisted in the women tendering their persons to him, which it seems the former often accepted, though the taste of the latter was too correct. [9] An attempt seems

---

[1] Bronzi d'Ercolano, tav. xciii.

[2] Petronii Satyric. cxxxvi—vii.

[3] See coins of Clazomenæ in Pellerin, and Mus. Hunter.

[4] Ol. Rudbeck. Atlant. p. ii. c. v. p. 249. Ol. Magn. lib. ix. c. xv.

[5] Τον δε τραγον απεθεωσαν (Αιγυπτιοι) καθαπερ και παρα τοις Ελλησι τετιμησθαι λεγουσι τον Πριαπον, δια το γεννητικον μοριον. Diodor. Sic. lib. i. p. 78.

[6] Ibid. p. 16. [7] Ibid.

[8] Τους τε ιερεις τους παραλαβοντας πατρικας ιερωσυνας κατ' Αιγυπτον, τουτῳ τῳ θεῳ πρωτον μυεισθαι. Ibid. p. 78.

[9] Μενδητα παρα κρημνον, θαλασσης εσχατον,
Νειλου κερας, αιγιβοται οθι τραγοι γυναιξι μισγονται.
Pindar. apud Strabon. xvii. p. 802.

to have been made, in early times, to introduce similar acts of devotion in Italy; for when the oracle of Juno was consulted upon the long-continued barrenness of the Roman matrons, its answer was, " Iliadas matres caper hirtus inito :" but these mystic refinements not being understood by that rude people, they could think of no other way of fulfilling the mandate, than sacrificing a goat, and applying the skin, cut into thongs, to the bare backs of the ladies.

> —— —— Jussæ sua terga maritæ
> Pellibus exsectis percutienda dabant;

which, however, had the desired effect :

> Virque pater subito, nuptaque mater erat. [1]

At Mendes female goats were also held sacred, as symbols of the passive generative attribute; [2] and on Grecian monuments of art, we often find caprine satyrs of that sex. The fable of Jupiter having been suckled by a goat, probably arose from some emblematical composition; the true explanation of which was only known to the initiated. Such was the Juno Sospita of Lanuvium, near Rome, whose goat-skin dress signified the same as her title ; and who, on a votive car of very ancient Etruscan work found near Perugia, appears exactly in the form described by Cicero, as the associate of Hercules dressed in the lion's skin, or the Destroyer. [3]

192. The Greeks frequently combined the symbolical animals,

Γυναικι τραγος εμισγετο αναφανδον· τουτο es επιδειξιν ανθρωπων απικετο. Herodot. lib. ii. s. 46.

Εν δε ταις προειρημεναις τεττερακονθ' ημεραις μονον ορωσιν αυτον (τον Απιν) αι γυναικες, κατα προσωπον ισταμεναι, και δεικνυουσι ανασυραμεναι τα εαυτων γεννητικα μορια· τον δ' αλλον χρονον απαντα κεκωλυμενον εστιν εις οψιν αυτας ερχεσθαι τουτῳ τῳ θεῳ. Diodor. Sic. lib. i.

[1] Ovid. Fast. ii. 448.

[2] Αιγα δε και τραγον Μενδησιοι τιμωσιν. Strabon. lib. xvii. p. 812.

Σεβονται δε παντας τους αιγας οι Μενδησιοι, και μαλλον τους αρσενους των θηλεων. Herodot. lib. ii. s. 46.

[3] Cum pelle caprina, cum hasta, cum scutulo, cum calceolis repandis. De N. D. lib. i. s. xxix.

especially in engravings upon gems, where we often find the forms of the ram, goat, horse, cock, and various others, blended into one, so as to form Pantheic compositions, signifying the various attributes and modes of action of the Deity. [1] Cupid is sometimes represented wielding the mask of Pan, and sometimes playing upon a lyre, while sitting upon the back of a lion; [2] devices of which the ænigmatical meaning has been already sufficiently explained in the explanations of the component parts. The Hindoos, and other nations of the eastern parts of Asia, expressed similar combinations of attributes by symbols loosely connected, and figures unskilfully composed of many heads, legs, arms, &c.; which appear from the epithets *hundred-headed, hundred-handed*, &c., so frequent in the old Greek poets, to have been not wholly unknown to them; though the objects to which they are applied prove that their ideas were taken from figures which they did not understand, and which they therefore exaggerated into fabulous monsters, the enemies or arbitrators of their own gods. [3] Such symbolical figures may, perhaps, have been worshipped in the western parts of Asia, when the Greeks first settled there; of which the Diana of Ephesus appears to have been a remain: for both her temple and that of the Apollo Didymæus were long anterior to the Ionic emigration; [4] though the composite images of the latter, which now exist, are, as before observed, among the most refined productions of Grecian taste and elegance. A Pantheic bust of this kind is engraved in plates lv. and lvi. of Vol. i. of the Select Specimens, having the dewlaps of a goat, the ears of a bull, and the claws of a crab placed as horns upon his head. The hair appears wet; and out of the temples spring fish,

---

[1] They are common, and to be found in all collections of gems; but never upon coins.

[2] See Mus. Florent. gemm.

[3] Il. A. 402. Pindar. Pyth. i. 31., viii. 20.
From the publication of Denon of the sculptures remaining in Upper Ægypt, it seems that such figures had a place in the ancient religious mythology of that country.

[4] Το δε ιερον το εν Διδυμοις του Απολλωνος, και το μαντειον εστιν αρχαιοτερον η κατα την Ιωνων εσοικησιν· πολλῳ δη πρεσβυτερα ετι η κατα Ιωνας τα ες την Αρτεμιν την Εφεσιαν. Pausan. Achaic. c. ii. s. iv.

while the whole of the face and breast is covered with foliage that seems to grow from the flesh; signifying the result of this combination of attributes in fertilising and organising matter. The Bacchus *ΔΕΝΔΡΙΤΗΣ*, and Neptune *ΦΥΤΑΛΜΙΟΣ*,[1] the one the principle of vegetation in trees, and the other in plants, were probably represented by composite symbolical images of this kind.

193. A female Pantheic figure in silver, with the borders of the drapery plated with gold, and the whole finished in a manner surpassing almost any thing extant, was among the things found at Macon on the Saone, in the year 1764, and published by Count Caylus.[2] It represents Cybelè, the universal mother, with the mural crown on her head, and the wings of pervasion growing from her shoulders, mixing the productive elements of heat and moisture, by making a libation upon the flames of an altar from a golden patera, with the usual knob in the centre of it, representing, probably, the lingam. On each side of her head is one of the Dioscuri, signifying the alternate influence of the diurnal and nocturnal sun ; and, upon a crescent supported by the tips of her wings, are the seven planets, each signified by a bust of its presiding deity resting upon a globe, and placed in the order of the days of the week named after them. In her left hand she holds two cornucopiæ, to signify the result of her operation on the two hemispheres of the Earth ; and upon them are the busts of Apollo and Diana, the presiding deities of those hemispheres, with a golden disk, intersected by two transverse lines, such as is observable on other pieces of ancient art, and such as the barbarians of the North employed to represent the solar year, divided into four parts,[3] at the back of each.

---

[1] Αμφοτεροι γαρ οἱ θεοι της ὑγρας και γονιμου κυριοι δοκουσιν αρχης ειναι· και Ποσειδωνι γε Φυταλμιῳ Διονυσῳ δε Δενδριτῃ, παντες, ὡς επος ειπειν, ῾Ελληνες θυουσιν. Plutarch. Sympos. lib. v. qu. 111.

[2] T. vii. pl. lxxi.
He says that the figure had been gilt all over: but he is mistaken; no part of it having been gilt, but several plated, all which remain entire, with the gold upon them. It is now, with most of the other small figures in silver, found with it, in the cabinet of Mr. Knight.

[3] Ol. Rudbeck. Atlant. vol. i. p. 90., and vol. ii. p. 212; fig. 1., and p. 161 and 2.

194. How the days of the week came to be called by the names of the planets, or why the planets were thus placed in an order so different from that of nature, and even from that in which any theorist ever has placed them, is difficult to conjecture. The earliest notice of it in any ancient writing now extant, is in the work of an historian of the beginning of the third century of Christianity;[1] who says that it was unknown to the Greeks, and borrowed by the Romans from other nations, who divided the planets on this occasion by a sort of musical scale, beginning with Saturn, the most remote from the centre, and then passing over two to the Sun, and two more to the Moon, and so on, till the arrangement of the week was complete as at present, only beginning with the day which now stands last. Other explanations are given, both by the same and by later writers ; but as they appear to us to be still more remote from probability, it will be sufficient to refer to them, without entering into further details.[2] Perhaps the difficulty has arisen from a confusion between the deities and the planets; the ancient nations of the North having consecrated each day of the week to some principal personage of their mythology, and called it after his name, beginning with Lok or Saturn, and ending with Freia or Venus : whence, when these, or the corresponding names in other languages, were applied both to the planets and to the days of the week consecrated to them, the ancient mythological order of the titles was retained, though the ideas expressed by them were no longer religious, but astronomical. Perhaps, too, it may be accounted for from the Ptolemaic system ; according to which the order of the planets was, Saturn, Jupiter, Mars, the Sun, Venus, Mercury, the Moon : for if the natural day consisted of twenty-four hours, and each hour was under the influence of a planet in succession, and the first hour of Saturday be sacred to Saturn, the eighth, fifteenth, and twenty-second, will be so likewise ; so that the twenty-third will belong to Jupiter, the twenty-fourth to Mars, and the first hour of the next day to the Sun. In the same manner, the first hour of the

---

[1] The part of Plutarch's Symposiacs, in which it was discussed, is unfortunately lost.

[2] Cass. Dion. lib. xxxvi. p. 37. Hyde de Relig. vet. Persar. c. v. ad fin.

ensuing day will belong to the Moon, and so on through the week, according to the seemingly capricious order in which all nations, using the hebdomadal computation of time, have placed them.

195. The Disa or Isa of the North was represented by a conic figure enveloped in a net, similar to the cortina of Apollo on the medals of Cos, Chersonesus in Crete, Naples in Italy, and the Syrian kings; but instead of having the serpent coiled round it, as in the first, or some symbol or figure of Apollo placed upon it, as in the rest, it is terminated in a human head. [1] This goddess is unquestionably the Isis whom the ancient Suevi, according to Tacitus, worshipped; [2] for the initial letter of the first name appears to be an article or prefix joined to it; and the Egyptian Isis was occasionally represented enveloped in a net, exactly as the Scandinavian goddess was at Upsal. [3] This goddess is delineated on the sacred drums of the Laplanders, accompanied by a child, similar to the Horus of the Egyptians, who so often appears in the lap of Isis on the religious monuments of that people. [4] The ancient Muscovites also worshipped a sacred group, composed of an old woman with one male child in her lap and another standing by her, which probably represented Isis and her offspring. They had likewise another idol, called the golden heifer, which seems to have been the animal symbol of the same personage. [5]

196. Common observation would teach the inhabitants of polar climates that the primitive state of water was ice; the name of which, in all the northern dialects, has so near an affinity with that of the goddess, that there can be no doubt of their having been originally the same, though it is equally a title of the corresponding personification in the East Indies. The conic form also unquestionably means the egg; there being in the Albani collection a

---

[1] Ol. Rudbeck. Atlant. vol. ii. c. v. p. 219.
[2] De M. G. c. ix.
[3] Isiac Table, and Ol. Rudbeck. ib. p. 209 and 210.
[4] Ib. p. 280.
[5] Ib. c. vi. p. 512 and 513.

statue of Apollo sitting upon a great number of eggs, with a serpent coiled round them, exactly as he is upon the veiled cone or cortina, round which the serpent is occasionally coiled, upon the coins above cited. A conic pile of eggs is also placed by the statue of him, draped, as he appears on a silver tetradrachm of Lampsacus,[1] engraved in pl. lxii. of vol. i. of the Select Specimens.

197. Stones of a similar conic form are represented upon the colonial medals of Tyre, and called ambrosial stones; from which, probably, came the amberics, so frequent all over the northern hemisphere. These, from the remains still extant, appear to have been composed of one of these cones let into the ground, with another stone placed upon the point of it, and so nicely balanced, that the wind could move it, though so ponderous that no human force, unaided by machinery, can displace it: whence they are now called *logging rocks*, and *pendre stones*,[2] as they were anciently *living stones*, and *stones of God*;[3] titles, which differ but little in meaning from that on the Tyrian coins. Damascius saw several of them in the neighbourhood of Heliopolis or Baalbeck, in Syria; particularly one which was then moved by the wind;[4] and they are equally found in the western extremities of Europe, and the eastern extremities of Asia, in Britain and in China.[5] Probably the stone which the patriarch Jacob anointed with oil, according to a mode of worship once generally practised,[6] as it still is by the Hindoos, was of this kind.[7] Such immense masses being moved by causes seeming so inadequate, must naturally have conveyed the idea of spontaneous motion to ignorant observers, and persuaded them that they were animated by an emanation of the

---

[1] In the cabinet of Mr. Payne Knight.

[2] Norden's Cornwall, p. 79.

[3] Λιθοι εμψυχοι et βαιτυλια. Psendc-Sanchon. Fragm. apud Euseb. The last title seems to be a corruption of the scriptural name Bethel.

[4] Ειδον τον βαιτυλον δια του αερος κινουμενον. In Vita Isidori apud Phot. Biblioth. Cod. 242.

[5] Norden. ib. Kercheri China illustrata. p. 270.

[6] Clem. Alex. Strom. lib. vii. p. 713.: Arnob. lib. i.: Herodian. in Macrino.

[7] Cleric. Comm. in Genes. c. xxviii. v. 22.

L

vital Spirit : whence they were consulted as oracles, the responses of which could always be easily obtained by interpreting the different oscillatory movements into nods of approbation and dissent. The figures of the Apollo Didymæus, on the Syrian coins above-mentioned, are placed sitting upon the point of the cone, where the more rude and primitive symbol of the logging rock is found poised ; and we are told, in a passage before cited, that the oracle of this god near Miletus existed before the emigration of the Ionian colonies; that is, more than eleven hundred years before the Christian æra : wherefore we are persuaded that it was originally nothing more than one of these βαιτυλια or symbolical groups; which the luxury of wealth and refinement of art gradually changed into a most magnificent temple and most elegant statue.

198. There were anciently other sacred piles of stones, equally or perhaps more frequent all over the North, called by the Greeks *ΛΟΦΟΙ 'ΕΡΜΑΙΟΙ* or *hillocks of Mercury ;*[1] of whom they were probably the original symbols. They were placed by the sides, or in the points of intersection, of roads ; where every traveller that passed, threw a stone upon them in honor of Mercury, the guardian of all ways or general conductor ;[2] and there can be no doubt that many of the ancient crosses observable in such situations were erected upon them ; their pyramidal form affording a commodious base, and the substituting a new object being the most obvious and usual remedy for such kinds of superstition. The figures of this god sitting upon fragments of rock or piles of stone, one of which has been already cited, are probably more elegant and refined modes of signifying the same ideas.

199. The old Pelasgian Mercury of the Athenians consisted, as before observed, of a human head placed upon an inverted Obelisk with a phallus ; of which several are extant ; as also of a

---

[1] ——— ὑπερ πολιος, ὁθι 'Ερμαιος λοφος εστιν. Odyss. Π. 471. This line, however, together with those adjoining 468 75, though ancient, is proved to be an interpolation of much later date than the rest of the poem, by the word 'Ερμαιος formed from the contracted 'Ερμας for 'Ερμειας, unknown to the Homeric tongue.

[2] Anthol. lib. iv. Epigr. 12. Phurnut. de nat. Deor.

female draped figure terminating below in the same square form. These seem to be of the Venus Architis, or primitive Venus; of whom there was a statue in wood at Delos, supposed to be the work of Dædalus;[1] and another in a temple upon Mount Libanus, of which Macrobius's description exactly corresponds with the figures now extant; of which one is given in plate lviii. of vol. i. of the Select Specimens. " Her appearance," he says, " was melancholy, her head covered, and her face sustained by her left hand, which was concealed under her garment."[2] Some of these figures have the mystic title *ΑΣΠΑΣΙΑ* upon them, signifying perhaps the welcome or gratulation to the returning spring : for they evidently represent nature in winter, still sustained by the inverted obelisk, the emanation of the sun pointed downwards ; but having all her powers enveloped in gloom and sadness. Some of these figures were probably, like the Paphian Venus, androgynous ; whence arose the Hermaphrodite ; afterwards represented under more elegant forms, accounted for as usual by poetical fables. Occasionally the attribute seems to be signified by the cap and wings of Mercury.

200. The symbol of the ram was, it seems, explained in the Eleusinian mysteries ;[3] and the nature and history of the Pelasgian Mercury in those of Samothrace ;[4] the device on whose coins, is his emblem either of the ram or the cock ;[5] and where he was distinguished by the mystic title Casmilus or Cadmilus ;[6] of which, probably,

---

[1] Και Δηλιοις Αφροδιτης εστιν ου μεγα ξοανον (τεχνη Δαιδαλου) κατεισι δε αντι ποδων ες τετραγωνον σχημα. Paus. in Bœot. c. xi. s. 2.

[2] Capite obnupto, specie tristi, faciem manu læva intra amictum sustinens. Sat. i. c. 21.

[3] Pausan. lib. ii. c. 3.

[4] Herodot. lib. ii. c. 51.

[5] Mus. Hunter. tab. xlvi. fig. 21. et nummul. argent. ined. apud R. P. Knight, Londini.

[6] Μυουνται δε εν τη Σαμοθρακη τοις Καβειροις, ὡν Μνασεας φησι και τα ονοματα. Τεσσαρες δε εισι τον αριθμον, Αξιερος, Αξιοκερσα, Αξιοκερσος. Αξιερος μεν ουν εστιν ἡ Δημητηρ· Αξιοκερσα δε ἡ Περσεφονη· Αξιοκερσος δε ὁ ῾Αδης. ὁ δε προστιθεμενος τεταρτος Κασμιλος ὁ ῾Ερμης εστιν, ὡς ἱστορει Διονυσιδωρος. Schol. in Apoll. Rhod. lib. 1. v. 917.

Οἱ δε προστιθεασι και τεταρτον Καδμιλον. εστι δ' οὑτος ὁ ῾Ερμης. ibid.

the Latin word Camillus, and the Greek name of the fabulous hero Cadmus are equally abbreviations:[1] for the stories of this hero being married to Harmony, the daughter of Mars and Venus; and of both him and his wife being turned into serpents, are clearly allegorical ; and it is more probable that the colony which occupied Thebes, were called Cadmeians from the title of their deity than from the name of their chief.

201. The Ægyptian Mercury carried a branch of palm in his hand, which his priests also wore in their Sandals,[2] probably as a badge of their consecration to immortality : for this tree is mentioned in the Orphic poems as proverbial for longevity ; and was the only one known to the ancients, which never changed its leaves ; all other evergreens shedding them, though not regularly nor all at once.[3] It has also the property of florishing in the most parched and dry situations ; where no other large trees will grow ; and therefore might naturally have been adopted as a vegetable symbol of the sun; whence it frequently accompanies the horse on the coins of Carthage ;[4] and in the Corinthian Sacristy in the temple at Delphi was a bronze palm-tree with frogs and water-snakes round its root, signifying the sun fed by humidity.[5] The pillars in many ancient Ægyptian temples, represent palm-trees with their branches lopped off; and it is probable that the palm-trees in the temple of Solomon were pillars of the same form ;[6] that prince having admitted many prophane symbols among the ornaments of his sacred edifice. The palm-tree at Delos, sacred to

---

[1] Lycophron. v. 162. Καδμιλος ὁ Ἑρμης Βοιωτικως. schol. in eund. et κατα συγκοπην Καδμον. ib. in v. 219.

[2] Apuleii Metam. lib. ii. p. 39. et lib. xi. p. 241 et 246.

[3] Ὁ δε φοινιξ ουθεν αποβαλλων αφ' αὑτου των φυομενων, βεβαιως αειφυλλος εστι, και τουτο δη το κρατος αυτου μαλιστα της νικης τῳ ισχυρῳ συνοικειουσι. Plutarch. Sympos. lib. viii. probl. 4.

[4] See Gesner. tab. lxxxiv. fig. 40 and 42.

[5] Την εξ ὑγρων ηνιξατο τροφην του ἡλιου και γενεσιν και αναθυμιασιν ὁ δημιουργος. Plutarch. de metro non utente Pyth. dialog.

[6] See Pococke's Travels, vol. i. p. 217.

Apollo and Diana, is mentioned in the Odyssey; [1] and it seems probable that the games and other exercises performed in honor of those deities, in which the palm, the laurel, and other symbolical plants were the distinctions of victory, were originally mystic representations of the attributes and modes of action of the divine nature. Such the dances unquestionably were: for when performed in honor of the gods, they consisted chiefly of imitative exhibitions of the symbolical figures under which they were represented by the artists.[2] Simple mimicry seems also to have formed a part of the very ancient games celebrated by the Ionians at Delos; [3] from which, probably, came dramatic poetry; the old comedy principally consisting of imitations, not only of individual men, but of the animals employed as symbols of the Deity.[4] Of this kind are the comedies of the birds, the frogs, the wasps, &c. ; the choral parts of which were recited by persons who were disguised in imitation of those different animals, and who mimicked their notes while chanting or singing the parts.[5] From a passage of Æschylus, preserved by Strabo, it appears that similar imitations were practised in the mystic ceremonies,[6] which may have been a reason for their gradual disuse upon all common occasions.

202. The symbolical meaning of the olive, the fir, and the apples, the honorary rewards in the Olympic, Isthmian, and Pythian games, has been already noticed; and the parsley, which

---

[1] Z. 162.

[2] Ἡ γαρ ορχησις εκ τε κινησεων και σχεσεων συνεστηκεν———φορας μεν ουν τας κινησεις ονομαζουσι, σχηματα δε σχεσεις και διαθεσεις, εις ἁς φερομεναι τελευτωσιν αἱ κινησεις, ὁταν Απολλωνος, η Πυνος, η τινος Βακχης, σχημα διαθεντες επι του σωματος γραφικως τοις ειδεσιν επιμενωσιν. Plutarch. Sympos. lib. ix. probl. 15.

[3] Παντων δ' ανθρωπων φωνας και κρεμβαλιαστυν
Μιμεισθαι ισασιν· φαιη δε κεν αυτος εκαστος
Φθεγγεσθαι. Homer. Hymn. in Apoll. 162.

[4] See Aristoph. Ἱππ. 520, &c.

[5] Ejusd. Βατραχ. 209.

[6] ψαλμος δ' αλαλαζει,
ταυροφθογγοι δ' ὑπομηκωνται κοθεν
εξ αφανους φοβεριοι μιμοι·
τυμπανῳ δ' ηχω,
ὡσθ' ὑπογειου βροντης, φερεται βαρυταρβης.
Æschyl. Edon. apud Strab. lib. x. p. 719.

formed the crown of the Roman victors, was equally a mystic plant ; it being represented on coins in the same manner as the fig-leaf, and with the same signification,[1] probably on account of a peculiar influence, which it is still supposed to have upon the female constitution. This connexion of the games with the mystic worship was probably one cause of the momentous importance attached to success in them ; which is frequently spoken of by persons of the highest rank, as the most splendid object of human ambition ;[2] and we accordingly find the proud city of Syracuse bribing a citizen of Caulonia to renounce his own country and proclaim himself of theirs, that they might have the glory of a prize which he had obtained.[3] When Exænetus of Agrigentum won the race in the ninety-second Olympiad, he was escorted into his native city by three hundred chariots ;[4] and Theagenes the Thasian, the Achilles of his age, who long possessed unrivalled superiority in all exercises of bodily strength and agility, so as to have been crowned fourteen hundred times, was canonised as a hero or demigod, had statues erected to him in various parts of Greece, and received divine worship; which he further proved himself worthy of, by miraculous favors obtained at his altars. Euthymus too, who was equally eminent as a boxer, having won a great number of prizes, and contended once even against Theagenes with doubtful success, was rewarded with equal or even greater honors : for he was deified by command of the oracle even before his death ;[5] being thus elevated to a rank, which fear has often prostituted to power ; but which unawed respect gave to merit in this instance only : and it is peculiarly degrading to popular favor and flattery that in this instance it should have been given not to the labors of a statesman or the wisdom of a legislator, but to the dexterity of a boxer.

203. This custom of canonising or deifying men seems to have

---

[1] Σελινον. το γυναικειον. Hesych.

[2] Sophocl. Electr. Platon. Polit. lib. v. p. 419.

[3] Pausan. lib. vi. c. 3.

[4] Diodor. Sic. lib. xiii. c. 82.

[5] Plin. lib. vii. c. 47.

arisen from that general source of ancient rites and opinions, the system of emanations ; according to which all were supposed to partake of the divine essence, but not in an equal degree : whence, while a few simple rites, faintly expressive of religious veneration, were performed in honor of all the dead,[1] a direct and explicit worship was paid to the shades of certain individuals renowned for either great virtues or great vices, which, if equally energetic, equally dazzle and overawe the gaping multitude.[2] Every thing being derived, according to this system, from the deity, the commanding talents and splendid qualities of particular persons were naturally supposed to proceed from particular emanations ; whence such persons were, even while living, honored with divine titles expressive of those particular attributes of the Deity, with which they seemed to be peculiarly favored.[3] Such titles were, however, in many instances given soon after birth ; children being named after the divine personifications, as a sort of consecration to their protection. The founder of the Persian monarchy was called by a name, which in their language signified the sun ;[4] and there is no doubt that many of the ancient kings of Ægypt had names of the same kind ;[5] which have helped to confound history with allegory ; though the Ægyptians, prior to their subjection to the

---

[1] Odyss. Λ. Lucian. περι πενθ'. s. 9.

[2] Θαλης, Πυθαγορας, Πλατων, οἱ Στωικοι Δαιμονας ὑπαρχειν ουσιας ψυχικας· ειναι δε και Ἡρωας τας κεχωρισμενας ψυχας των σωματων, και αγαθους μεν, τας αγαθας· κακους δε, τας φαυλας. Plutarch. de Placit. Philos. lib. i. c. 8.

—————— οἱ γαρ Ἡρωες κακουν,
'Ως φασ᾽, ἑτοιμοι μαλλον, η ευεργετειν.
Menandr. ex Æqual. Fragm.

[3] ἐν ανδρων, ἐν θεων γενος· εκ
μιας δε πνεομεν
ματρος αμφοτεροι.
διειργει δε πασα κεκριμενα
δυναμις. Pindar. Nem. 5. v. 1.

[4] Και τιθεται το ονομα αυτου (Κυρου) απο του ἡλιου. Ctes. Persic.
Κυρον γαρ καλειν Περσας τον ἡλιον. Plutarch. in Artax.
Τον γαρ ἡλιον Περσαι Κυρον λεγουσι. Hesych.

[5] See Jablonsk. Panth. Ægypt.

Macedonians, never worshipped them, nor any heroes or canonised mortals whatsoever.[1]

204. " During the Pagan state of the Irish," says a learned antiquary of that country, " every child at his birth received a name generally from some imaginary divinity ; under whose protection it was supposed to be : but this name was seldom retained longer than the state of infancy ; from which period it was generally changed for others arising from some perfection or imperfection of the body ; the disposition or quality of the mind ; achievements in war or the chace ; the place of birth, residence, &c."[2] When these descriptive titles exactly accorded with those previously imposed, and derived from the personified attributes of the Deity, both were naturally confounded ; and the limited excellences of man thus occasionally placed in the same rank with the boundless perfections of God. The same custom still prevails among the Hindoos, who when a child is ten days old give him the name of one of their deities ; to whose favor they think by this mean to recommend him ;[3] whence the same medley of historical tradition and physical allegory fills up their popular creed, as filled that of the Greeks and other nations. The ancient theism of the North seems also to have been corrupted by the conqueror Odin assuming the title of the supreme God, and giving those of other subordinate attributes to his children and captains ;[4] which are, however, all occasionally applied to him :[5] for the Scandina-

---

[1] Νομιζουσι δ' ων Αιγυπτιοι ουδ' ηρωσιν ουδεν. Herodot. lib. ii. s. 50. See also s. 142 and 3.

[2] Collectan. Hibern. No. xi. p. 259.

[3] Sonnerat Voyage aux Indes. T. 1. p. 84.

[4] Mallet Introd. à l'Hist. de Danemarc.

[5] *Odinus* ego nunc nominor ;
Yggus modo nominabar ;
Vocabar *Thundus* ante id,
Vacus et *Skilfingus*,
Vafodus et *Hoopta-tyr*
Gautus et *Ialcus* inter Deos,
Ossier et *Suafner* ;
Quos puta factos esse
Omnes *ex uno me*.

Grunnismal liii. Edd. Sæmond. p. 61.

vians, like the Greeks, seem sometimes to have joined, and sometimes to have separated the personifications; so that they sometimes worshipped several gods, and sometimes only one god with several names.

205. Historical tradition has transmitted to us accounts of several ancient kings, who bore the Greek name of Jupiter ;[1] which signifying *Awe* or *Terror*, would naturally be assumed by tyrants, who wished to inspire such sentiments. The ancient Bacchus was said to have been the son of Jupiter by Ceres or Proserpine ;[2] that is, in plain language, the result of the ætherial Spirit operating upon the Earth, or its pervading Heat: but a real or fictitious hero, having been honored with his name in the Cadmeian colony of Thebes, was by degrees confounded with him in the popular mythology; and fabled to have been raised up by Jupiter to replace him after he had been slain by the Titans ;[3] as Attis and Adonis were by the boar, and Osiris by Typhon ; symbolical tales which have been already noticed. The mystic Deity was however duly distinguished as an object of public worship in the temples : where he was associated by the Greeks with Ceres and Proser-

---

[1] Παντας μεν ουν καταριθμησασθαι και προθυμηθεντι απορον, δποσοι θελουσι γενεσθαι και τραφηναι παρα σφισι Δια. Pausan. in Messen. c. xxxiii. s. 2.

[2] Φασι τον θεον (τον Διονυσον) εκ Διος και Δημητρος τεκνωθεντα, διασπασθηνα:. Diodor. Sic. lib. iii.

Αθηναιοι Διονυσον τον Διος και Κορης σεβουσιν· αλλον τουτον Διονυσον· και δ Ιακχος δ μυστικος τουτω τω Διονυσω, ουχι τω Θηβαιω, επαδεται. Arrian. lib. ii. An Attic writer during the independence of the Republic, would not have dared to say so much.

Μυθολογουσι δε τινες και έτερον Διονυσον γεγονεναι, πολυ τοις χρονοις προτερουντα τουτου. φασι γαρ εκ Διος και Περσεφονης Διονυσον γενεσθαι, τον υπο τινων Σεβαζιον ονομαζομενον· ού την τε γενεσιν και τας θυσιας και τιμας νυκτερινας και κρυφιας παρεισαγουσι δια την αισχυνην την εκ της συνουσιας επακολουθουσαν. Diodor. Sic. lib. iv. p. 148.

Σαββους γαρ και νυν ετι πολλοι τους Βακκους καλουσι, και ταυτην αφιασι την φωνην δταν οργιαζωσι τω θεω. Plutarch. Symp. lib. iv. qu. vi.

[3] Ηδη γαρ μενεαινε νεον Διονυσον αεξειν,
Ταυροφυες μιμημα παλαιγενεος Διονυσου,
Αινομορου Ζαγρηος εχων ποθον ύψιμεδων Ζευς,
'Ον τεκε Περσεφονεια δρακοντειη Διος ευνη. Dionysiac. lib. v. p. 173.

pine,[1] and by the Romans with Ceres and Libera, (who was their Proserpine,) the reason for which, as the Stoic interlocutor observes in Cicero's Dialogue on the Nature of the Gods, was explained in the Mysteries.[2]

206. The sons of Tyndarus were by the same means confounded with the ancient personifications of the diurnal and nocturnal sun, or of the morning and evening star ;[3] the symbols of whose attributes, the two oval or conic caps, were interpreted to signify their birth from Leda's egg, a fable ingrafted upon the old allegory subsequent to the Homeric times ; the four lines alluding to the deification of the brothers of Helen in the Odyssey being undoubtedly spurious, though extremely beautiful.[4] Perseus is probably an entirely fictitious and allegorical personage ; for there is no mention of him in either of the Homeric poems ; and his name is a title of the sun,[5] and his image the composite symbol of the gryphon humanised. Theseus appears likewise to be a personage who started into being between the respective ages of the two Homeric poems : there being no mention of him in the genuine parts of the Iliad, though the Athenian genealogy is minutely detailed ;[6] and he being only once slightly mentioned as the lover of Ariadne in the genuine parts of the Odyssey.[7] He seems, in reality, to be the Athenian personification of Hercules ; he having the same symbols of the club and lion's skin ; and similar actions and adventures being attributed to him, many of which are mani-

---

[1] Και πλησιον ναος εστι Δημητρος· αγαλματα δε αυτη τε και ἡ παις, και δαδα εχων Ιακχος. Pausan. in Attic.

Η που γ' αν ετι την Πραξιτελους Δημητρα, και Κορην, και τον Ιακχον τον μυστικον, θεους ὑπολαμβανομεν. Clem. Alex. in Protrep.

[2] Lib. iii. s. 21.

[3] Και τους Τυνδαριδας δε φασι την των Διοσκουρων δοξαν ὑπελθειν παλιν (lege παλαι) νομιζομενων ειναι θεων. Sext. Empir. lib. ix. s. 37.

[4] Od. Λ. 300—4 λελογχασ' ισα betrays the interpolator, the adjective having been written with the digamma.

[5] Περσευς ὁ ἡλιος. Schol. in Lycophr. v. 18.

[6] B. 546—50. Several of these lines seem to have been interpolated in compliment to the Athenians.   [7] Λ. 321.

festly allegorical; such as his conflict with the Minotaur, with the Centaurs, and with the Amazons.

207. This confusion of personages, arising from a confusion of names, was facilitated in its progress by the belief that the universal generative principle, or its subordinate emanations, might act in such a manner as that a female of the human species might be impregnated without the co-operation of a male;[1] and as this notion was extremely useful and convenient in concealing the frailties of women, quieting the jealousies of husbands, protecting the honor of families, and guarding with religious awe the power of bold usurpers, it was naturally cherished and promoted with much favor and industry. Men supposed to be produced in this supernatural way, would of course advance into life with strong confidence and high expectations; which generally realise their own views, when supported by even common courage and ability. Such were the founders of almost all the families distinguished in mythology; whose names being, like all other ancient names, descriptive titles, they were equally applicable to the personified attributes of the Deity: whence both became blended together; and historical so mixed with allegorical fable, that it is impossible in many instances to distinguish or separate them. The actions of kings and conquerors were attributed to personages purely symbolical; and the qualities of these bestowed in return upon frail and perishable mortals. Even the double or ambiguous sex was attributed to deified heroes; Cecrops being fabled to have been both man and woman;[2] and the rough Hercules and furious Achilles represented with the features and habits of the softer sex, to conceal the mystic meaning of which the fables of Omphalè and Iolè, and the daughters of Lycomedes, were invented; of which there is not a trace in the Homeric poems.

---

[1] Ουθεν οιομαι δεινον, ει μη πλησιαζων ο θεος, ωσπερ ανθρωπος, αλλα ετεραις τισιν αφαις δι' ετερων και ψαυσεσι τρεπει, και υποπιμπλησι θειοτερας γονης το θνητον. Plutarch. Symposiac. lib. viii. probl. 1.

[2] Justin. lib. ii. c. 6. Suidas in Κεκροχ. Euseb. et Hieron. in Chronic. Plutarch. de sera numin. vindicta. Eustath. in Dionys. Diodor. Sic. l. i. c. 28.

208. When the Greeks made expeditions into distant countries, either for plunder, trade, or conquest; and there found deified heroes with titles corresponding either in sound or sense to their own, they without further inquiry concluded them to be the same; and adopted all the legendary tales which they found with them : whence their own mythology, both religious and historical, was gradually spread out into an unwieldy mass of incoherent fictions and traditions, that no powers of ingenuity or extent of learning could analyse or comprehend. The heroes of the Iliad were, at a very early period, so much the objects of public admiration, partly through the greatness of the war, the only one carried on jointly by all the States of Greece prior to the Macedonian usurp- ation, and partly through the refulgent splendor of the mighty ge- nius by which it had been celebrated; that the proudest princes were ambitious of deducing their genealogies from them, and the most powerful nations vain of any traces of connexion with them. Many such claims and pretensions were of course fabricated, which were as easily asserted as denied ; and as men have a natural par- tiality for affirmatives, and nearly as strong a predilection for that which exercises their credulity, as for that which gratifies their vanity, we may conclude that the assertors generally prevailed. Their tales were also rendered plausible, in many instances, by the various traditions then circulated concerning the subsequent for- tunes and adventures of those heroes; some of whom were said to have been cast away in their return ; and others expelled by usurpers, who had taken advantage of their long absence; so that a wandering life supported by piracy and plunder became the fate of many.[1] Inferences were likewise drawn from the slenderest traces of verbal analogies, and the general similarity of religious rites; which, as they co-operated in proving what men were pre- disposed to believe, were admitted without suspicion or critical examination.

209. But what contributed most of all towards peopling the coasts and islands both of the Mediterranean and adjoining ocean,

---

[1] Strabon. lib. iii. p. 150.

with illustrious fugitives of that memorable period, was the practice of ancient navigators in giving the names of their gods and heroes to the lands which they discovered, in the same manner as the moderns do those of their saints and martyrs: for in those early ages every name thus given became the subject of a fable, because the name continued when those who gave it were forgotten. In modern times every navigator keeps a journal; which, if it contains any new or important information, is printed and made public; so that, when a succeeding navigator finds any traces of European language or manners in a remote country, he knows from whence they came: but, had there been no narratives left by the first modern discoverers, and subsequent adventurers had found the name of St. Francis or St. Anthony with some faint traces of Christianity in any of the islands of the Pacific Ocean, they might have concluded, or at least conjectured, that those saints had actually been there: whence the first convent of monks, that arose in a colony, would soon make out a complete history of their arrival and abode there; the hardships which they endured, the miracles which they wrought, and the relics which they left for the edification of the faithful and the emolument of their teachers.

210. As the heroes of the Iliad were as familiar to the Greek navigators, as the saints of the Calendar were to the Spanish and Portuguese, and treated by them with the same sort of respect and veneration; there can be little doubt that they left the same sort of memorials of them, wherever they made discoveries or piratical settlements; which memorials, being afterwards found among barbarous nations by succeeding navigators, when the discoverers were forgotten and the settlers vanished; they concluded that those heroes had actually been there: and as the works of the Greek poets, by the general diffusion of the Greek language after the Macedonian conquest, became universally known and admired, those nations themselves eagerly co-operated in the deception by ingrafting the Greek fables upon their own, and greedily catching at any links of affinity which might connect them with a people, from whom all that was excellent in art, literature, and society, seemed to be derived.

211. Hence, in almost every country bordering upon the Mediterranean Sea, and even in some upon the Atlantic Ocean, traces were to be found of the navigations and adventures of Ulysses, Menelaus, Æneas, or some other wandering chieftain of that age; by which means such darkness and confusion have been spread over their history, that an ingenious writer, not usually given to doubt, has lately questioned their existence; not recollecting that he might upon the same grounds have questioned the existence of the Apostles, and thus undermined the very fabric which he professed to support: for by quoting, as of equal authority, all the histories which have been written concerning them in various parts of Christendom during seventeen hundred years, he would have produced a medley of inconsistent facts, which, taken collectively, would have startled even his own well-disciplined faith.[1] Yet this is what he calls a fair mode of analysing ancient prophane history; and, indeed, it is much fairer than that which he has practised: for not content with quoting Homer and Tzètzes, as of equal authority, he has entirely rejected the testimony of Thucydides in his account of the ancient population of Greece; and received in its stead that of Cedrenus, Syncellus, and the other monkish writers of the lower ages, who compiled the Paschal and Nuremberg Chronicles. It is rather hard upon our countrymen Chaucer and Lydgate to be excluded; as the latter would have furnished an account of the good king Priam's founding a chauntry in Troy to sing requiems for the soul of his pious son Hector, with many other curious particulars equally unknown to the antiquaries of Athens

---

[1] Metrodorus of Lampsacus anciently turned both the Homeric poems into Allegory; and the Christian divines of the third and fourth centuries did the same by the historical books of the New Testament; as their predecessors the eclectic Jews had before done by those of the Old.

Metrodorus and his followers, however, never denied nor even questioned the general fact of the siege of Troy, (as they have been mis-stated to have done) any more than Tatian and Origen did the incarnation of their Redeemer, or Aristeas and Philo the passage of the Red Sea.

Tasso in his later days declared the whole of his Jerusalem Delivered to be an allegory; but without, however, questioning the historical truth of the crusades.

and Alexandria, though'full as authentic as those which he has collected with so much labor from the Byzantine luminaries of the thirteenth and fourteenth centuries.'

212. A conclusion directly contrary to that of this ingenious gentleman was drawn by several learned writers of antiquity, from the confusion in which the traditions of early times were involved : instead of turning history into mythology, they turned mythology into history ; and inferred that, because some of the objects of public worship had been mortal men, they had all been equally so; for which purpose, they rejected the authority of the mysteries ; where the various gradations of gods, dæmons, and heroes, with all the metaphysical distinctions of emanated, personified, and canonised beings, were taught ;² and instead of them, brought out the old allegorical genealogies in a new dress, under pretence of their having been transcribed from authentic historical monuments of extreme antiquity found in some remote country.

213. Euhemerus, a Messenian employed under Cassander king of Macedonia, seems to have been the first who attempted this kind of fraud. Having been sent into the Eastern Ocean with some commission, he pretended to have found engraven upon a column in an ancient temple in the island of Panchæa, a genealogical account of a family, that had once reigned there ; in which were comprised the principal deities then worshipped by the Greeks. ³ The theory, which he formed from this pretended dis-

---

¹ See Bryant on Ancient Mythology.

² Περι μεν ουν των μυστικων, εν οἱς τας μεγιστας εμφασεις και διαφασεις λαβειν εστι της περι δαιμονων αληθειας, ευστομα μοι κεισθω, καθ' Ἡροδοτον. Plutarch. de Orac. Defect. p 417.

³ Euseb. Præp. Evang. lib. ii. c. 2.

—Μεγαλας μεν τῳ αθεῳ λεῳ κλισιαδας ανοιγοντας, και εξανθρωπιζοντι τα θεια, λαμπραν δε τοις Ευημερου του Μεσσηνιου φενακισμοις παρρησιαν διδοντας, ὁς αυτος αντιγραφα συνθεις απιστου και ανυπαρκτου μυθολογιας, πασαν αθεοτητα κατασκεδαννυσι της οικουμενης, τους νομιζομενους θεους παντας ὁμαλω, διαγραφων εις ονοματα στρατηγων και μουναρχων και βασιλεων· ὡς δη παλαι γεγονοτων, εν δε Παγχαιᾳ γραμμασι χρυσοις αναγεγραμμενων, εις ουιε βαρβαρος ουδεις, ουτε Ἑλλην, αλλα μονος Ευημερος, ὡς εοικε, πλευσας εις τους μηδαμοθι γης γεγονοτας, μηδε οντας Παγχαιους και Τριφυλιους, εντετυχηκει. Plutarch. de Is. et Osir.

covery, was soon after attempted to be more fully established by a Phœnician history, said to have been compiled many centuries before by one Sanchoniathon from the records of Thoth and Ammon; but never brought to light until Philo of Byblos published it in Greek with a prooem of his own; in which he asserted that the mysteries had been contrived merely to disguise the tales of his pretended Phœnician history,[1] notwithstanding that a great part of these tales are evidently nothing more than the old mystic allegories copied with little variation from the theogonies of the Greek poets, in which they had before been corrupted and obscured.

214. A fragment of this work having been preserved by Eusebius, many learned persons among the moderns have quoted it with implicit confidence, as a valuable and authentic record of very ancient history; while others have as confidently rejected it, as a bungling fraud imposed upon the public by Philo of Byblos, in order to support a system, or procure money from the founders of the Alexandrian Library; who paid such extravagant prices for old books, or for (what served equally well to furnish their shelves) new books with old titles. Among the ancients there seems to have been but one opinion concerning it: for, except Porphyry, no heathen writer has deigned to mention it; so contemptible a performance, as the fragment extant proves it to have been, seeming to them unworthy of being rescued from oblivion even by an epithet of scorn or sentence of reprobation. The early Christian writers, however, took it under their protection, because it favored that system, which by degrading the old, facilitated the progress of the new religion: but in whatever else these writers may have excelled, they certainly had no claim to excellence in either moral sincerity or critical sagacity; and none less than Eusebius; who, though his authority has lately been preferred to that of Thucydides and Xenophon, was so differently thought of by ecclesiastical writers of the immediately subsequent

---

[1] Αλλ' οἱ μεν νεωτατοι των ἱερολογων, τα μεν γεγονοτα πραγματα εξ αρχης απεπεμψαντο, αλληγοριας και μυθους επινοησαντες, και τοις κοσμικοις παθημασι συγγενειαν πλασαμενοι, μυστηρια κατεστησαν· και πολυν αυτοις επηγον τυφον, ὡς μη ῥαδιως τινα συνοραν τα κατ' αληθειαν γενομενα. Philon. Bybl. apud Euseb. Præp. Evang. lib. i. c. 9.

ages, that he is one of those, by whose example they justified the practice of holy lying,[1] or asserting that which they *knew* to be false in support of that which they *believed* to be true.

215. Among the numberless forgeries of greater moment which this practice poured upon the world, is one in favor of this system, written in the form of a letter from Alexander the Great to his mother, informing her that an Ægyptian priest named Leo had secretly told him that all the gods were deified mortals. Both the style and matter of it are below criticism ; it being in every respect one of the most bungling counterfeits ever issued from that great manufactory of falsehoods, which was carried on under the avowed patronage of the leading members of the Church, during the second, third, and fourth centuries.[2] Jablonski only wasted his erudition in exposing it ;[3] though Warburton, whose multifarious reading never gave him any of the tact or taste of a scholar, has employed all his acuteness and all his virulence in its defence.[4]

216. The facility and rapidity, with which deifications were multiplied under the Macedonian and Roman empires, gave considerable credit to the system of Euhemerus ; and brought proportionate disgrace on religion in general. The many worthless tyrants, whom their own preposterous pride or the abject servility of their subjects exalted into gods, would naturally be pleased to hear that the universally recognised objects of public worship had no better title to the homage and devotion of mankind than they themselves had ; and when an universal despot could enjoy the honors of a god, at the same time that consciousness of his crimes prevented him from daring to enter a mystic temple, it is natural that he should prefer that system of religion, which decorated him

---

[1] Pro libro adv. Jovinian.

[2] Hieronym. ibid. Chrysostom. de Sacerdot.

[3] Prolegom. s. 16. It is alluded to in the Apology of Athenagoras, and therefore of the second century.

[4] Div. Leg. vol. i. p. 213.

M

178

with its highest honors, to that which excluded him from its only solemn rites.[1]

217. This system had also another great advantage : for as all persons acquainted with the mystic doctrines were strictly bound to secresy, they could not of course engage in any controversy on the subject ; otherwise they might have appealed to the testimony of the poets themselves, the great corrupters and disguisers of their religion ; who, nevertheless, upon all great and solemn occasions, such as public adjurations and invocations, resort to its first principles, and introduce no fabulous or historical personages : not that they understood the mystic doctrines, or meant to reveal them ; but because they followed the ordinary practice of the earliest times ; which in matters of such solemn importance was too firmly established to be altered. When Agamemnon calls upon the gods to attest and confirm his treaty with Priam, he gives a complete abstract of the old elementary system, upon which the mystic was founded ; naming first *the awful and venerable Father of all ; then the Sun, who superintends and regulates the Universe, and lastly the subordinate diffusions of the great active Spirit, that pervade the waters, the earth, and the regions under the earth.*[2] The invocation of the Athenian women, who are introduced by Aristophanes celebrating the secret rites of Ceres and Proserpine, is to the same effect, only adapted to the more complicated and philosophical refinements of the mystic worship. First they call upon *Jupiter, or the supreme all-ruling Spirit ; then upon the golden-lyred Apollo, or the Sun, the harmoniser and regulator of the world, the centre and instrument of his power ; then upon Almighty Pallas, or the pure emanation of his wisdom ; then upon Diana or nature, the many-named daughter of Latona or night ; then upon Neptune, or the emanation of the pervading Spirit, that animates the waters ; and lastly upon the Nymphs or subordinate generative ministers of both sea and land.*[3] Other invocations to the same purport are to be found in many of the choral odes both tragic and comic ; though the order, in which the personifications are introduced is often varied, to prevent the mystic allusions from being

---

[1] See Sueton. in Ner.   [2] Il. Γ. 276, &c.   [3] Θεσμοφ. 315, &c.

too easily discernible. The principles of theology appear to have been kept equally pure from the superstructures of mythology in the forms of judicial adjuration; Draco having enacted that all solemn depositions should be under the sanction of Jupiter, Neptune, and Minerva;[1] whilst in later times Ceres was joined to the two former instead of Minerva.

218. The great Pantheic temples exhibited a similar progression or graduation of personified attributes and emanations in the statues and symbols which decorated them. Many of these existed in various parts of the Macedonian and Roman empires; but none are now so well known as that of Hierapolis, or the *holy city* in Syria, concerning which we have a particular treatise falsely attri buted to Lucian. It was called the temple of the Syrian goddess Astartè; who was precisely the same as the Cybelè, or universal mother, of the Phrygians; whose attributes have been already explained, and may be found more regularly detailed in a speech of Mopsus in the Argonautics of Apollonius Rhodius.[3] " She was," as Appian observes, " by some called Juno, by others Venus, and by others held to be Nature, or the cause which produced the beginnings and seeds of things from Humidity;"[4] so that she comprehended in one personification both these goddesses; who were accordingly sometimes blended in one symbolical figure by the very ancient Greek artists.[5]

219. Her statue at Hierapolis was variously composed; so as to signify many attributes like those of the Ephesian Diana, Berecynthian Mother, and others of the kind.[6] It was placed in

---

[1] Schol. Ven. in Il. O. 36.   [2] Demosthen. επι Τιμοκρατ. apud eund.

[3] Lib. i. 1098.

[4] Οἱ μεν Αφροδιτην, οἱ δε Ἡραν, οἱ δε τας αρχας και σπερματα πασιν εξ ὑγρων παρα-σχουσαν αιτιαν και φυσιν νομιζουσιν. de Bello Parth. Plutarch describes her in the same words, in Crasso, p. 271.

[5] Ξοανον αρχαιον καλουσι (Λακωνες) Αφροδιτης Ἡρας. Pausan. lib. iii. p. 240. Την Ἡραν εκεινοι (Τυρρηνοι) Κυπραν καλουσι. Strabon. lib. v. p. 369.

[6] Εχει δε τι Αθηναιης, και Αφροδιτης και Σεληναιης, και Ῥεης, και Αρτεμιδος, και Νε-μεσιος, και Μοιρεων. Lucian. de D. S.

the interior part of the temple, accessible only to priests of the higher order; and near it was the statue of the corresponding male personification, called by the Greek writers Jupiter; which was borne by bulls, as that of the goddess was by lions,[1] to signify that the active power or ætherial spirit is sustained by its own strength alone; while the passive or terrestrial requires the aid of previous destruction. The minotaur and sphinx, before explained, are only more compendious ways of representing these composite symbols.

220. Between them was a third figure with a golden dove on its head, which the Syrians did not choose to explain, or call by any name; but which some supposed to be Bacchus, others Deucalion, and others Semiramis.[2] It must, therefore, have been an androgynous figure; and most probably signified the first-begotten Love, or plastic emanation, which proceeded from both and was consubstantial with both; whence he was called by the Persians, who seem to have adopted him from the Syrians, Mithras, signifying the Mediator.[3] The doubt expressed concerning the sex, proves that the body of the figure was covered, as well as the features effeminate; and it is peculiarly remarkable that such a figure as this with a golden dove on its head should have been taken for Deucalion; of whom corresponding ideas must of course have been entertained: whence we are led to suspect that the fabulous his-

---

[1] —— αμφω έξονται· αλλα την μεν Ἡρην λεοντες φορεουσιν, ὁ δε ταυροισιν εφεξεται. Lucian. de D. S.

Λεοντες μιν φορεουσι, και τυμπανον εχει, και επι τη κεφαλη πυργοφορεει, ὁκοιην Ῥεην Λυδοι ποιεουσι. Lucian. de Syr. Dea. s. 15.

Και δητα το μεν του Διος αγαλμα, ες Δια παντα ὁρη, και κεφαλην και εἱματα και ἑδρην· και μιν ουδε εθελων αλλως εικασεις. Lucian. de Syr. Dea. s. 31.

It was therefore the same figure as that on the Phœnician medal with the bull's head on the chair; and which is repeated with slight variations on the silver coins of Alexander the Great, Seleucus I. Antiochus IV. &c.

[2] —— ουδε τι ουνομα ιδιον αυτω εθεντο, αλλ' ουδε γενεσιος αυτου περι, και ειδεος λεγουσι. και μιν οἱ μεν ες Διονυσον· αλλοι δε ες Δευκαλεωνα· οἱ δε ες Σεμιραμιν αγουσι. Ibid. s. 16.

[3] Μεσον δ' αμφοιν τον Μιθρην ειναι· διο και Μιθρην Περσαι τον μεσιτην ονομαζουσι. Plutarch. de Is. et Osir. p. 369.

tories of this personage are not derived from any vague traditions of the universal deluge ; but from some symbolical composition of the plastic spirit upon the waters, which was signified so many various ways in the emblematical language of ancient art. The infant Perseus floating in an ark or box with his mother, is probably from a composition of the same kind ; Isis and Horus being represented enclosed in this manner on the mystic or Isiac hands ; and the Ægyptians, as before observed, representing the Sun in a boat instead of a chariot ; from which boat being carried in procession upon men's shoulders, as it often appears in their sculptures, and being ornamented with symbols of Ammon taken from the ram, probably arose the fable of the Argonautic expedition ; of which there is not a trace in the genuine parts of either of the Homeric poems.[2] The Colchians indeed were supposed to be a colony of Ægyptians,[3] and it is possible that there might be so much truth in the story, as that a party of Greek pirates carried off a golden figure of the symbol of their god : but had it been an expedition of any splendor or importance, it certainly would have been noticed in the repeated mention that is made of the heroes said to have been concerned in it.

221. The supreme Triade, thus represented at Hierapolis, assumed different forms and names in different mystic temples. In that of Samothrace it appeared in three celebrated statues of Scopas, called Venus, Pothos, and Phaëthon,[4] or Nature, Attraction, and Light ;[5] and at Upsal in Sweden, by three figures equally symbolical, called Odin, Freia, and Thor ; the first of which comprehended the attributes of Jupiter and Mars, the second those of Juno and Venus, and the third those of Hercules and Bacchus, together with the thunder of Jupiter : for Thor, as mediator be-

---

[1] La Chausse Mus. Rom. vol. ii. pl. 11 and 13.

[2] The four lines in Odyss. M. 69-72. are manifestly interpolated.

[3] Herodot. lib. ii. c. 104.   [4] Plin. lib. xxxiv. c. 4.

[5] Ποθος, desire. Φαεθων is an Homeric title of the Sun, signifying splendid or luminous; but afterwards personified by the mythologists into a son of Apollo.

tween heaven and earth, had the general command of the terrestrial atmosphere.[1] Among the Chinese sects, which have retained or adopted the symbolical worship, a triple personification of one godhead is comprehended in the goddess Pussa, whom they represent sitting upon the lotus, called, in that country, Lien, and with many arms, carrying different symbols, to signify the various operations of universal nature. A similar union of attributes was expressed in the Scandinavian goddess Isa or Disa ; who in one of her personifications appeared riding upon a ram accompanied with music, to signify, like Pan, the principle of universal harmony ; and, in another, upon a goat, with a quiver of arrows at her back, and ears of corn in her hand, to signify her dominion over generation, vegetation, and destruction.[2] Even in the remote islands of the Pacific Ocean, which appear to have been peopled from the Malay shores, the supreme deities are God the Father, God the Son, and the Bird or Spirit ; subordinate to whom are an endless tribe of local deities and genii attending to every individual.[3]

222. The Ægyptians are said to have signified their divine Triade by a simple triangle ;[4] which sometimes appears upon Greek monuments :[5] but the most ancient form of this more concise and comprehensive symbol, appears to be that of the three lines, or three human legs springing from a central disk or circle, which has been called a Trinacria, and supposed to allude to the island of Sicily ; but which is of Asiatic origin ; its earliest appearance being upon the very ancient coins of Aspendus in Pamphylia ; sometimes alone in the square incuse ; and sometimes upon the

---

Mallet Hist. de Danemarc. Introd. c. vii. p. 115. Thor bore the club of Hercules ; but like Bacchus he was the God of the seasons, and his chariot was drawn by goats. Ibid. et Oda Thrymi Edd. xxi. Ol. Rudbeck. tab. x. fig. 28.

[2] Ol. Rudbeck. Atlant. vol. ii. p. 209 and 10.

[3] Missionaries First Voyage, p. 343.

[4] —— εικαστεον ουν, την μεν προς ορθας, αρρενι, την δε βασιν, θηλεια, την δε ὑποτεινουσαν, αμφοιν εγγονῳ· και τον μεν Οσιριν, ὡς αρχην, την δε Ισιν ὡς ὑποδεχην, τον ε Ωρον, ὡς αποτελεσμα. Plut. de Is. et. Osir. p. 373.

[5] Particularly on the coins of the Colonies of Magna Græcia.

body of the eagle or back of the lion.[1] The tripod, however, was more generally employed for this purpose ; and is found composed in an endless variety of ways, according to the various attributes meant to be specifically expressed. On the coins of Menecratia in Phrygia it is represented between two asterisks, with a serpent wreathed round a battle-axe inserted into it, as an accessary symbol signifying preservation and destruction.[2] In the ceremonial of worship, the number *three* was employed with mystic solemnity ;[3] and in the emblematical hands above alluded to, which seem to have been borne upon the point of a staff or sceptre in the Isiac processions, the thumb and two fore-fingers are held up to signify the three primary and general personifications, while the peculiar attributes of each are indicated by the various accessary symbols.

223. A bird was probably chosen for the emblem of the third person to signify incubation, by which was figuratively expressed the fructification of inert matter, caused by the vital spirit moving upon the waters. When represented under a human form, and without the emblem, it has generally wings, as in the figures of Mithras ; and, in some instances, the priapic cap or Ægyptian mitre upon its head, with the hook or attractor in one hand, and the winnow or separator in the other.[4] The dove would naturally be selected in the East in preference to every other species of bird, on account of its domestic familiarity with man ; it usually lodging under the same roof with him, and being employed as his messenger from one remote place to another. Birds of this kind were also remarkable for the care of their offspring, and for a sort of conjugal attachment and fidelity to each other ; as likewise for the peculiar fervency of their sexual desires ; whence they were sacred

---

[1] See Mus. Hunter. tab. vii. No. 15.

A similar old coin with the symbol on the back of a lion is in the cabinet of Mr. Knight.

[2] Brass coin in the cabinet of Mr. Knight.

[3] Προς τας ἁγιστειας των θεων χρωμεθα τῳ ἀριθμῳ τουτῳ. Aristot. de Cœl. lib. i. c. i.

[4] See Phœnician coins of Melita.

to Venus, and emblems of love.[1]   On the same account they were
said by the poets to carry ambrosia from the ocean to Jupiter :[2]
for, being the symbols of love or attraction, they were the symbols
of that power, which bore the finer exhalations, the immortal and
celestial infusions called ambrosia, with which water the prolific
element of the earth had been impregnated, back to their original
source, that they might be again absorbed in the great abyss of the
divine essence.   Birds, however, of two distinct kinds appear in
the attitude of incubation on the heads of the Ægyptian Isis ; and
in a beautiful figure in brass belonging to Mr. Payne Knight, a
bird appears in the same posture on the head of a Græcian deity ;
which by the style of work must be much anterior to the adoption
of any thing Ægyptian into the religion of Greece.   It was found
in Epirus with other articles, where the ΣΤΝΝΑΟΣ, or female personification of the supreme God, Jupiter of Dodona, was Dione ;
who appears to have been the Juno-Venus, or composite personage
above mentioned.   In this figure she seems to have been represented with the diadem and sceptre of the former, the dove of the
latter, and the golden disk of Ceres ; which three last symbols
were also those of the Ægyptian Isis.   The dove, being thus common to the principal goddess both of Dodona and Ægypt, may
account for the confused story told by Herodotus, of two pigeons,
or priestesses called pigeons, going from Thebes in Ægypt, and
founding the oracles of Dodona and Libya.[3]   Like others of the
kind, it was contrived to veil the mystic meaning of symbolical
figures, and evade further questions.   The beak of the bird, however, in the figure in question, is too much bent for any of the
dove kind ; and is more like that of a cuckoo ; which was the
symbol on the sceptre of the Argive Juno in ivory and gold by

---

[1] Ælian. de Animal. lib. iii. c. xliv. and v. and lib. iv. c. ii.

[2] Odyss. M. 69-72. Athenæ. Deipnos. lib. xi. p. 491. The lines of the
Odyssey are, as before observed, interpolated : but nevertheless they are
sufficiently ancient to serve the purpose, for which they are here quoted.
Allegories so refined were unknown in the Homeric times, at least to the
Greeks.

[3] Lib. ii. c. 54. &c.

Polycletus, which held a pomegranate in the other hand ;[1] but what it meant is vain to conjecture. Another bird, much celebrated by the Greek poets as a magical charm or philtre, under the name of Íunx,[2] appears by the description of Aristotle [3] to be the larger spotted woodpecker; which, however, we have never observed in any monuments of ancient art; nor do we know of any natural properties belonging to it that could have authorised its use. It seems to be the Picus of the Italians, which was sacred to Mars.[4]

224. After the supreme Triade, which occupied the adytus of the temple at Hierapolis, came the personifications of their various attributes and emanations ; which are called after the names of the corresponding Græcian deities ; and among which was an ancient statue of Apollo clothed and bearded, contrary to the usual mode of representing him.[5] In the vestibule were two phalli of enormous magnitude ;[6] upon one of which a person resided during seven days twice in each year to communicate with the gods,[7] and pray for the prosperity of Syria ; and in the court were kept the sacred or symbolical animals ; such as bulls, horses, lions, bears, eagles, &c.[8] In an adjoining pond were the sacred fish, some of which were tame and of great size ; and about the temple were an

---

[1] Pausan. lib. ii. c. 17.

[2] Pindar. Pyth. iv. 380. Nem. iv. Theocrit. Pharmac.

[3] Hist. Anim. lib. ii. c. 12.

[4] Εκ της Σαβινης οἱ Πικεντινοι, δρυοκολαπτου την ὁδον ἡγησαμενου τοις αρχηγεταις, αφ' οὑ και τουνομα· Πικον γαρ τον ορνιν τουτον ονομαζουσι, και νομιζουσιν Αρεος ἱερον. Strab. lib. v.

[5] Κεαται ξοανον Απολλωνος, ουκ οἱον εωθεε ποιεεσθαι. οἱ μεν γαρ αλλοι παντες Απολλωνα νεον τε ἡγηνται και πρωθηβην ποιεουσι· μουνοι δε οὑτοι Απολλωνος γενειητεω ξοανον δεικνυουσι.
Εν δε και αλλο τῳ σφετερῳ Απολλωνι καινουργεουσι· μουνοι Απολλωνα εἱμασι κοσμεουσι. Lucian. de D. S.
Similar figures of Apollo are upon some of the very early coins of Syracuse and Rhegium.

[6] According to the present reading, 300 ells high ; probably 30.

[7] Οἱ μεν πολλοι νομιζουσι, ὁτι ὑψου τοισι θεοισι ὁμιλεει, και αγαθα πασῃ Συριῃ αιτεει. Lucian. de Deâ Syr.

[8] Εν δε τῃ αυλῃ αφετοι νεμονται βοες μεγαλοι, και ἱπποι και αετοι, και αρκτοι, και λεοντες· και ανθρωπους ουδαμᾳ σινονται, αλλα παντες ἱροι τε εισι και χειροηθεις. Ibid.

immense number of statues of heroes, priests, kings, and other deified persons, who had either been benefactors to it, or, from their general celebrity, been thought worthy to be ranked with them. Among the former were many of the Macedonian princes, and among the latter several of the heroes and heroines of the Iliad, such as Achilles, Hector, Helen, Hecuba, Andromachè, &c.[1]

225. The most common mode of signifying deification in a portrait was representing the figure naked, or with the simple chlamys or mantle given to the statues of the gods. The head, too, was sometimes radiated ; or the bust placed upon some sacred and appropriate symbol; such as the cornucopiæ,[2] the flower of the lotus,[3] or the inverted obelisk; which last mode was by far the most frequent; the greatest part of the busts now extant of eminent Græcian statesmen, poets, and philosophers, having been thus represented; though many of them are of persons who were never canonised by any public decree: for, in the loose and indeterminate system of ancient faith, every individual could consecrate in his own family the object of his admiration, gratitude, or esteem, and address him with whatever rites of devotion he thought proper, provided he did nothing contrary to the peace and order of society, or in open violation of the established forms of worship. This consecration, however, was not properly deification, but what the Roman Catholic Church still practises under the title of canonisation ; the object of it having been considered, according to the modern acceptation of the words, rather as a saint than a god ; wherefore a deified or canonised Roman emperor was not called *Deus,* but *Divus;* a title which the early Christians equally bestowed on the canonised champions of their faith.

226. Among the rites and customs of the temple at Hierapolis, that of the priests castrating themselves, and assuming the manners and attire of women, is one of the most unaccountable. The le-

---

[1] This temple having been in an alluvial country near the Euphrates, it is probable that most of the marble statues which adorned it still exist under the accumulated soil.

[2] Of which there are many instances in gems.

[3] See the beautiful marble bust called Clytia in the British Museum.

gendary tale of Combabus adduced by the author of the treatise
ascribed to Lucian, certainly does not give a true explanation of it;
but was probably invented, like others of the kind, to conceal rather
than develope: for the same custom prevailed in Phrygia among
the priests of Cybelè and Attis, who had no such story to account
for it. Perhaps it might have arisen from a notion of making themselves emblems of the Deity by acquiring an androgynous appearance; and perhaps, as Phurnutus conjectures, from some allegorical fiction, such as those of the castration of Heaven by Time, of
Time by Jupiter,[1] &c. It is possible, likewise, that they might have
thought a deprivation of virility an incentive to that spiritual enthusiasm, to which women were observed to be more liable than
men; and to which all sensual indulgence, particularly that of the
sexes, was held to be peculiarly adverse: whence strict abstinence
from the pleasures of both the bed and table was required preparatory to the performance of several religious rites, though all abstinence was contrary to the general festive character of the Greek
worship. The Pythian priestesses in particular fasted very rigidly
before they mounted the tripod, from which their predictions
were uttered; and both they and the Sibyls were always virgins;
such alone being qualified for the sacred office of transmitting divine inspiration. The ancient German prophetesses, too, who exercised such unlimited control over a people that would submit to
no human authority, were equally virgins consecrated to the Deity,
like the Roman Vestals; or chosen from the rest of the species by
some manifest signs of his predilection.[2] Perpetual virginity was
also the attribute of many of the ancient goddesses; and, what may
seem extraordinary, of some who had proved themselves prolific.
Minerva, though pre-eminently distinguished by the title of the
virgin,[3] is said to have had children by the Sun, called Corybantes;
who appear to have been a kind of priests of that god, canonised
for their knowledge; and, therefore, fabled to have been his children
by Divine Wisdom.[4] Diana, who was equally famed for her vir-

---

[1] De Nat. Deor. c. vi. p. 147.   [2] See Tacit. de M. G.

[3] Παρθενων, ναος ην εν τη ακροπολει, Παρθενου Αθηνας.   Schol. in Demosth. Orat.
in Androt.

[4] Strabon. lib. x. p. 723.

ginal purity, has the title of mother in an ancient inscription ;[1] and Juno is said to have renewed her virginity every year, by bathing in a certain fountain in the Peloponnesus, the reason of which was explained in the Argive mysteries ;[2] in which the initiated were probably informed that this was an ancient figurative mode of signifying the fertilising quality of those waters, which renewed and reintegrated annually the productive powers of the earth. This figurative or mystic renovation of virginity seems to be signified in the Orphic hymns by the epithet *ΠΟΛΥΠΑΡΘΕΝΟΣ* ;[3] which, though applied to a male personification, may equally signify the complete restoration of the procreative organs of the universe after each periodical effort of nature.

227. Upon this principle, the placing figures upon some kinds of fish appears to have been an ancient mode of consecration and apotheosis, to veil which under the usual covering of fable, the tales of Arion, Taras, &c. were probably invented. Fish were the natural emblems of the productive power of the waters ; they being more prolific than any other class of animals, or even vegetables, that we know. The species consecrated to the Syrian goddess seems to have been the Scarus, celebrated for its tameness[4] and lubricity ; in which last it held the same rank among fish, as the goat did among quadrupeds.[5] Sacred eels were kept in the fountain of Arethusa :[6] but the dolphin was the common symbol of the Greeks, as the thunny was of the Phœnicians; both being gregarious fish, and remarkable for intelligence and sagacity ;[7] and therefore probably signifying other attributes combined with the generative. The thunny is also the symbol upon all the very ancient gold coins struck by the Greeks, in which it almost invariably serves as the base or substratum for some other symbolical figure to rest

---

[1] Gruter. Thesaur. xli. 5.

[2] Ενταυθα την ʻΗραν φασιν Αργειοι κατα ετος λουμενην παρθενον γινεσθαι· ουτος μεν δη σφισιν εκ τελετης, ἡν αγουσι τῃ ʻΗρᾳ, λογος των απορητων εστιν. Pausan. lib. ii. c. xxxviii.

[3] Hymn. li.   [4] Xenophon. Anab.

[5] Ælian. de Animal. lib. i. c. ii.   [6] Plutarch. de Solert. Anim. p. 976.

[7] Ælian. de Animal. lib. i. c. xviii.   Plutarch. de Solert. Animal. p. 979.

upon;[1] water being the general means, by which all the other powers of nature act.

228. The remarkable concurrence of the allegories, symbols, and titles of ancient mythology in favor of the mystic system of emanations, is alone sufficient to prove the falsity of the hypotheses founded upon Euhemerus's narrative; and the accurate and extensive researches of modern travellers into the ancient religions and traditions of the East, prove that the narrative itself was entirely fiction; no trace of such an island as Panchæa, or of any of the historical records or memorials which he pretended to have met with there, being now to be found. On the contrary, the extreme antiquity and universal reception of the system of emanations, over all those vast countries which lie between the Arctic and Pacific oceans, has been fully and clearly demonstrated. According to the Hindoos, with whose modification of it we are best acquainted, the supreme ineffable God, called Brame, or the *great one*, first produced Brama the creator, who is represented with four heads corresponding with the four elements; and from whom proceeded Vishnoo the preserver and Shiven the destroyer; who is also the regenerator: for, according to the Indian philosophy, nothing is destroyed or annihilated, but only transmuted; so that the destruction of one thing is still the generation of another. Hence Shiven, while he rides upon an eagle, the symbol of the destroying attribute, has the lingam, the more explicit symbol of generation, always consecrated in his temples. These three deities were still only one in essence; and were anciently worshipped collectively under the title of Trimourti; though the followers of the two latter now constitute two opposite and hostile sects; which, nevertheless, join on some occasions in the worship of the universal Triade.[2]

---

[1] Six are in the cabinet of Mr. Knight, in which it is respectively placed under the triton of Corcyra, the lion of Cyzicus, the goat of Ægæ, the ram of Clazomenæ, the bull of Samos, and the gryphon of Teios. For the form and size of these coins see Mus. Hunt. tab. 66. fig. 1. They are probably the Homeric talents stamped, and may be considered as the first money.

[2] Maurice's Indian Antiquities, vol. iv. ad fin.

229. This triform division of the personified attributes or modes of action of one first cause, seems to have been the first departure from simple theism, and the foundation of religious mythology in every part of the earth. To trace its origin to patriarchal traditions, or seek for it in the philosophy of any particular people, will only lead to frivolous conjecture, or to fraud and forgery; which have been abundantly employed upon this subject : nor has repeated detection and exposure either damped the ardor or abashed the effrontery of those, who still find them convenient to support their theories and opinions.[1] Its real source is in the human mind itself; whose feeble and inadequate attempts to form an idea of one universal first cause would naturally end in generalising and classing the particular ideas derived from the senses, and thus forming distinct, though indefinite notions of certain attributes or modes of action; of which the generic divisions are universally three ; such as goodness, wisdom, and power; creation, preservation, and destruction ; potential, instrumental, and efficient, &c. &c. Hence almost every nation of the world, that has deviated from the rude simplicity of primitive Theism, has had its Trinity in Unity ; which, when not limited and ascertained by divine revelation, branched out, by the natural subdivision of collective and indefinite ideas, into the endless and intricate personifications of particular subordinate attributes, which have afforded such abundant materials for the elegant fictions both of poetry and art.

230. The similitude of these allegorical and symbolical fictions with each other, in every part of the world, is no proof of their having been derived, any more than the primitive notions which they signify, from any one particular people ; for as the organs of sense and the principles of intellect are the same in all mankind, they would all naturally form similar ideas from similar objects ; and employ similar signs to express them, so long as natural and not conventional signs were used. Wolves, lions, and panthers, are equally beasts of prey in all countries ; and would naturally be em-

---

[1] See Sibylline verses, oracles, &c. forged by the Alexandrian Jews and Platonic Christians, but quoted as authentic by Mr. Bryant, on Ancient Mythology; and Mr. Maurice's Indian Antiq. vol. iv.

ployed as symbols of destruction, wherever they were known : nor
would the bull and cow be less obvious emblems of creative force
and nutrition ; when it was found that the one might be employed
in tilling the earth, and the other in constantly supplying the most
salubrious and nutritious of food. The characteristic qualities of
the egg, the serpent, the goat, &c. are no less obvious ; and as
observation would naturally become more extensive, as intellect
became more active, new symbols would everywhere be adopted,
and new combinations of them be invented in proportion as they
were wanted.

231. The only certain proof of plagiary or borrowing is where
the animal or vegetable productions of one climate are employed as
symbols by the inhabitants of another; as the lion is in Tibet; and
as the lotus and hooded snake were in Ægypt; which make it
probable that the religious symbols of both those countries came
originally from the Hindoos. As commercial communications,
however, became more free and intimate, particular symbols might
have been adopted from one people by another without any common origin or even connexion of general principles ; though,
between Ægypt and Hindostan the general similarity is too great
in points remote from common usage, to have been spontaneous
or accidental. One of the most remarkable is the hereditary division into casts derived from the metempsychosis ; which was a
fundamental article of faith with both; as also with the ancient
Gauls, Britons, and many other nations. The Hindoo casts rank
according to the number of transmigrations which the soul is supposed to have undergone, and its consequent proximity to, or
distance from re-absorption into the divine essence, or intellectual
abyss, from which it sprang : and in no instance in the history of
man, has the craft of imposture, or the insolence of usurpation,
placed one class of human beings so far above another, as the
sacred Bramins, whose souls are approaching to a re-union with
their source, are above the wretched outcasts, who are without
any rank in the hierarchy ; and are therefore supposed to have all
the long, humiliating, and painful transmigrations yet before them.
Should the most respectable and opulent of these degraded mortals
happen to touch the poorest, and, in other respects, most worthless

person of exalted religious rank, the offence, in some of the Hindoo governments, would be punished with death : even to let his shadow reach him, is to defile and insult him ; and as the respective distinctions are in both hereditary, the soul being supposed to descend into one class for punishment and ascend into the other for reward, the misery of degradation is without hope even in posterity ; the wretched parents having nothing to bequeath to their unfortunate offspring that is not tainted with everlasting infamy and humiliation. Loss of cast is therefore the most dreadful punishment that a Hindoo can suffer ; as it affects both his body and his soul, extends beyond the grave, and reduces both him and his posterity for ever to a situation below that of a brute.

232. Had this powerful engine of influence been employed in favor of pure morality and efficient virtue, the Hindoos might have been the most virtuous and happy of the human race ; but the ambition of a hierarchy has, as usual, employed it to serve its own particular interests, instead of those of the community in general : whence to taste of the flesh of a cow, or be placed with certain ceremonies upon the back of a bull, though unwillingly and by constraint, are crimes by which the most virtuous of men is irrevocably subjected to it, while the worst excesses of cruelty, fraud, perjury, and peculation leave no stains nor pollutions whatsoever. The future rewards, also, held out by their religion, are not to any social or practical virtues, but to severe penances, operose ceremonies, and above all to profuse donations to the priesthood. The Bramins have even gone so far as to sell future happiness by retail ; and to publish a tariff of the different prices, at which certain periods of residence in their paradise, or regions of bliss, are to be obtained between the different transmigrations of the soul.[1] The Hindoos are of course a faithless and fraudulent, though in general a mild and submissive race : for the same system which represses active virtue, represses aspiring hope; and by fixing each individual immovably in his station, renders him almost as much a machine as the implement which he employs. Hence, like the ancient Ægyptians, they have been eminently successful in all works of art, that require only methodical labor and manual dexterity, but have

[1] Maurice's Indian Antiquities, vol. v.

never produced any thing in painting, sculpture or architecture that discovers the smallest trace or symptom of those powers of the mind, which we call taste and genius ; and of which the most early and imperfect works of the Greeks always show some dawning. Should the pious labors of our missionaries succeed in diffusing among them a more pure and more moral, but less uniform and less energetic system of religion, they may improve and exalt the characters of individual men ; but they will for ever destroy the repose and tranquillity of the mass. The lights of European literature and philosophy will break in with the lights of the gospel ; the spirit of controversy will accompany the spirit of devotion ; and it will soon be found that men, who have learned to think themselves equal in the sight of God, will assert their equality in the estimation of men. It requires therefore no spirit of prophecy, nor even any extraordinary degree of political sagacity, to fix the date of the fall of European domination in the east from the prevalence of European religion.

233. From the specimens that have appeared in European languages, the poetry of the Hindoos seems to be in the same style as their art ; and to consist of gigantic, gloomy, and operose fictions, destitute of all those graces which distinguish the religious and poetical fables of the Greeks. Nevertheless the structure of their mythology is full as favorable to both ; being equally abundant and more systematic in its emanations and personifications. After the supreme Triade, they suppose an immense host of inferior spirits to have been produced ; part of whom afterwards rebelling under their chiefs Moisasoor and Rhaabon, the material world was prepared for their prison and place of purgation ; in which they were to pass through eighty-nine transmigrations prior to their restoration. During this time they were exposed to the machinations of their former leaders ; who endeavour to make them violate the laws of the Omnipotent, and thus relapse into hopeless perdition, or lose their cast, and have all the tedious and painful transmigrations already past to go through again ; to prevent which, their more dutiful brethren, the emanations that remained faithful to the Omnipotent, were allowed to comfort, cherish, and assist them in their passage ; and that all might have

N

equal opportunities of redeeming themselves, the divine personages of the great Triade had at different times become incarnate in different forms, and in different countries, to the inhabitants of which they had given different laws and instructions suitable to their respective climates and circumstances ; so that each religion may be good without being exclusively so; the goodness of the deity naturally allowing many roads to the same end.

234. These incarnations, which form the principal subjects of sculpture in all the temples of India, Tibet, Tartary, and China, are above all others calculated to call forth the ideal perfections of the art, by expanding and exalting the imagination of the artist, and exciting his ambition to surpass the simple imitation of ordinary forms in order to produce a model of excellence worthy to be the corporeal habitation of the Deity : but this, no nation of the East, nor indeed of the Earth, except the Greeks and those who copied them, ever attempted. Let the precious wrecks and fragments, therefore, of the art and genius of that wonderful people be collected with care and preserved with reverence, as examples of what man is capable of under peculiar circumstances ; which, as they have never occurred but once, may never occur again !

END.

ALPHABETICAL INDEX

OF THE PRINCIPAL MATTERS,

With Numerals referring to the Sections.

———

P. S. The Author takes this opportunity of correcting an error, into which he and others of the Committee of Publication were led by a most respectable and lamented Member, in attributing the Formation of the Petworth Collection of Marbles to the Duke of Somerset aided by Mr. Brettingham; whereas the country owes it entirely to the taste and magnificence of the late and present Earls of Egremont. See Explanation of pl. lxxii. and lxxiii. of the first Volume of " Select Specimens, &c."

For EU product safety concerns, contact us at Calle de José Abascal, 56–1°, 28003 Madrid, Spain or eugpsr@cambridge.org.